My House in Damascus

Diana Darke has specialised in the Middle East for over thirty years, living and working in a range of Arab countries as an Arabic translator and consultant for both public and private sectors. She is well known as an authority on Syria, contributing to the *Guardian*, the *Financial Times* and the BBC's *From Our Own Correspondent*, and is the author of Bradt guides to Eastern Turkey and Syria.

With her house in use as a refuge for displaced friends since September 2012, her links with Syria are deep and ongoing. She has been back five times since the revolution began and remains actively committed to helping Syrians achieve a better future.

www.dianadarke.com

My House in Damascus

An Inside View of the Syrian Revolution

Diana Darke

First published in Great Britain in 2014 by Haus Publishing Limited

HAUS PUBLISHING LTD.
70 Cadogan Place, London SW1X 9AH
www.hauspublishing.com

print ISBN 978-1-908323-64-4
ebook ISBN 978-1-908323-65-1

Typeset in Minion by MacGuru Ltd
info@macguru.org.uk

Printed in Great Britain by the CPI Group (UK) Ltd, Croydon, CRO 4YY

A CIP catalogue for this book is available from the British Library

Dedication

My mother died while I was writing this book. Part of it was even written sitting at my childhood desk in her flat, gazing out over the cherry trees that shielded her from the street. She was 89 and had been ready for some time. 'If I die tomorrow,' she used to say, 'I can say I had a wonderful life.' Sometimes she would say it several times an hour – she had the beginnings of dementia.

Hers was a 'good' death. I was there with her at the end and she knew me. I saw the bright light behind her eyes: she knew where she was going, and I see death differently now.

But how do people cope with a 'bad' death? Syria is tearing itself apart as I write: young people, children, whose lives have barely started, are dying. How do their families survive the trauma of their deaths, with no preparation, no warning, no chance to say all the things left unsaid? How will the parents of Hamza al-Khatib live now, after the body of their mutilated 13-year-old son was returned to them? How do they come to terms with what he endured at the end of his short life, in detention with the Syrian security forces for a month, followed by the final two days of mind-distorting torture that killed him? Bruised, battered, electrocuted, castrated – and to what end?

I dedicate this book to my mother and to Hamza al-Khatib – two opposites in death.

Contents

Preface   xiii

1. Worlds of Conflict and Harmony   1
2. Unescorted   13
3. Escorted   25
4. Nobody's Poodle   44
5. Into the Unknown   58
6. The Dead Auntie   68
7. Insurance Against Fate?   78
8. Revelations   85
9. Friends and Brides   100
10. The Donkey Between Two Carrots   109
11. The Law and Educational Corruption   126
12. Completion and the Caretaker   137
13. No Return   147
14. Monasteries and Desperation   159
15. Thugs and Tamerlane   180
16. The Triumph of *Asabiyya*   191
17. Future Imperfect and Perfect   213

Acknowledgements   235
Glossary   237
Cast of Characters   247
A Note on the Choice of Charity   253

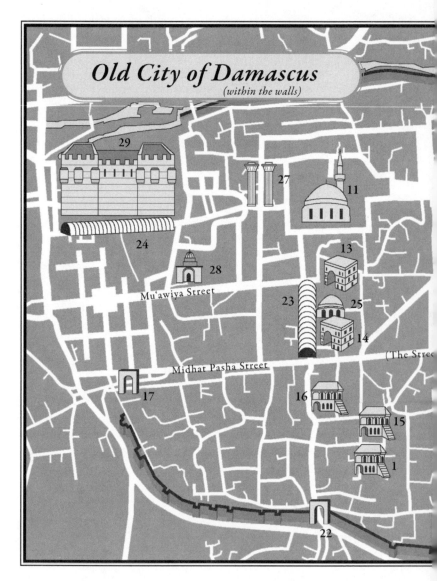

Old City of Damascus
(within the walls)

Mu'awiya Street

Midhat Pasha Street

(The Stree

1. Bait Baroudi
2. Greek Melkite Cathedral
3. Ananias Chapel
4. Franciscan Monastery
5. Jesuit Church
6. Church of the Maronites
7. Miryamiya Church
   (Greek Orthodox)
8. Church of St George
   (Syrian Orthodox)
9. Syrian Catholic Church
10. Bakri Hammam
11. Umayyad Mosque
12. Maktab Anbar
13. Azem Palace
14. Khan As'ad Pasha Al-Azem

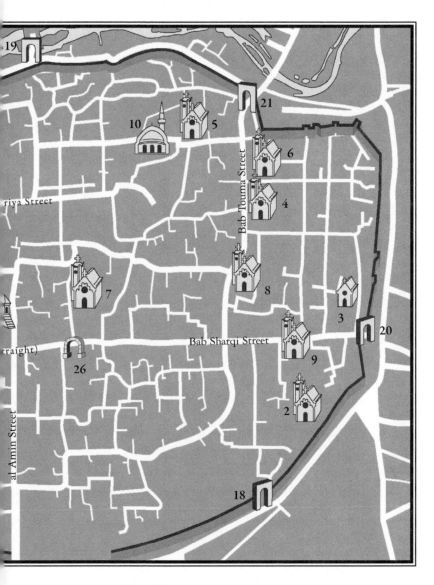

15. Bait Nizam
16. Bait Siba'i
17. Bab al Jabiye
18. Bab Kissan
19. Bab as Salam
20. Bab Sharqi
21. Bab Touma
22. Bab as Saghir

23. Bzouriya souk
    (spice market)
24. Souk al Hamidiya
25. Hammam Nur Ad-Din
26. Roman arch
27. Temple of Jupiter
28. Maristan Nur Ad-Din
29. Citadel

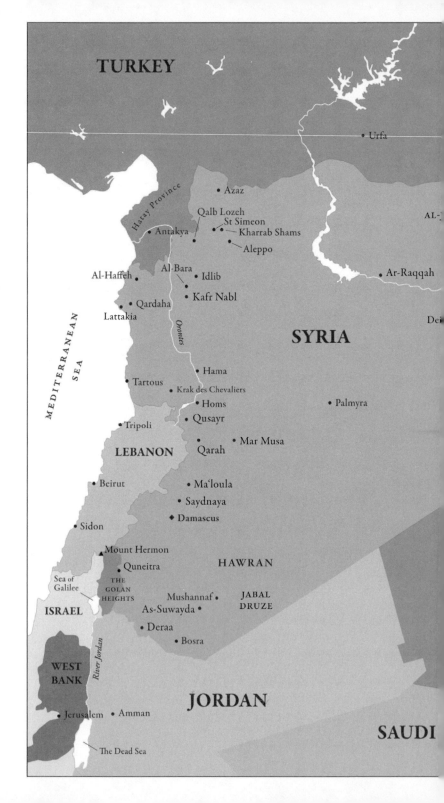

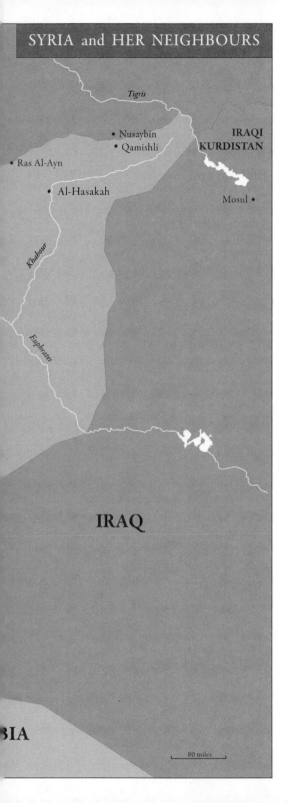

SYRIA and HER NEIGHBOURS

Tigris

• Nusaybin
• Qamishli

IRAQI
KURDISTAN

• Ras Al-Ayn

• Al-Hasakah

Mosul •

Khabour

Euphrates

IRAQ

BIA

80 miles

Preface

Our waking world is no better than dreaming,
compared to the life after death.

Prophet Muhammad

'It will end one day. But it will not be quick,' say my Syrian friends. As I write, the Syrian regime is entangled in the web of a popular revolution inspired by the example of fellow Arabs in Tunisia, Egypt, Libya, Bahrain and Yemen. The seeds of what is happening in Syria now were sown long ago, and I have watched them germinate. Seasoned experts both inside and outside the country insisted right up until mid-March 2011 that it would not happen in Syria. I did not believe them. I had observed and experienced first-hand why people were so frustrated and angry, and why this frustration had led to revolution.

Ever since my first visit to Syria in 1978 I have always felt at home there. Each Arab country drew me differently, but it was in Syria that I found, and continue to find, everything I like best about the Arab world: friendly but dignified people, an attachment to traditional family values, deep loyalties and friendships – all set within a multi-coloured tapestry of biblical, classical and medieval sites in landscapes of astonishing beauty.

Years later, commissioned to write the Bradt *Syria* guide, the country's spell was as strong as ever. 'I don't know why,' I said to my travelling companion, 'but I feel Damascus is somewhere I could spend time in.'

'How on earth would you do that?' she asked.

'I have no idea,' was my honest reply.

This story has been in my head for some years now, and many people have urged me to write it. At first I did not really understand why. What was so interesting about someone buying a house in Syria? To me, it had become normal, and my regular stays in Syria routine. But gradually I came to see that the ongoing violence made it all the more important to show a side of Syria beyond the hysteria of media reportage and behind the clinical analysis. I wanted to explore the depths of its social and spiritual cohesion and to examine how its rich diversity might help it face the future beyond the revolution. Why was it so complex and why was the country so misunderstood?

Our western prejudices run deep. After 35 years of specialisation, I thought I knew the Middle East quite well. But I was on the outside, looking in. Now, thanks to my ownership of Bait Baroudi, I have been on the inside looking out – my perspective has changed.

How did it all begin? In pursuit of a dream, that much I knew, a dream to buy and restore a courtyard house. But dreams rarely lead where you expect.

⁂

Who are you?
I am Time who subdues all things and is ever running.
And why do you have wings on your feet?
Because I fly with the wind.
And why does your hair hang over your face?
So that he who meets me can take me by the forelock.
And why, in Heaven's name, is the back of your head bald?
Because none whom I have once raced past on my winged feet will now, though he wishes it sore, take hold of me from behind.

Poseidippos, Greek poet, on *Kairos*, 'the opportune moment'

1

Worlds of Conflict and Harmony

The pleasure of food and drink lasts an hour, of sleep a day, of women a month, but of a building, a lifetime.

Arab proverb

The Syrian Revolution began with a series of peaceful demonstrations. The very first took place in Damascus outside the Umayyad Mosque on Tuesday, 15 March 2011. Clutching my passport, I ran from my house to find it.

That mosque, the spiritual heart of the Old City, was sacred to the Arameans as the Temple of Haddad, to the Romans as the Temple of Jupiter and to the Christians as the Cathedral of John the Baptist. It is, like every mosque in Syria, not just a place you go to pray, but also a timeless space for living, a home from home, somewhere to meet people, have a picnic, enjoy a nap. Children play on the soft carpets inside, or chase each other round the flag-stoned courtyard. Forever busy with local families and shopkeepers from the adjacent souks, it still somehow serves as a refuge, a place of calm and serenity. Generations mingle together there. No one is excluded, visitors of all races, nationalities and religions are welcomed.

The Arab Spring had begun in mid-December 2010, with both Tunisia's and Egypt's regimes falling to spontaneous popular uprisings within weeks of each other in early 2011. Jordan, Algeria, Yemen, Libya, Bahrain and even Oman had seen demonstrations against their governments. All eyes were now on Syria. Listed 127th out of 178 on the World Corruption Index (alongside Lebanon, but performing better than Libya, Yemen, Iran and Russia), it had the classic revolution formula, as perceived by the analysts: a heavily youth-dominated population, unemployment officially at 10 per cent but probably closer to 25 per cent in the under-25 age group, a rich elite and a massively poor underclass. Surely Syria would not be immune?

That first demonstration was over so quickly, I could not get there in time. A peaceful march of just a dozen or so young men, chanting slogans of reform and freedom, it was an experiment that gauged the regime's reaction, and they dispersed spontaneously before the police arrived. A week earlier, in the quarter of al-Hariqa just yards from the Umayyad Mosque, an elderly shopkeeper had been beaten up by police, prompting an angry riot by fellow shopkeepers. So nervous was the regime about provoking unrest that the Interior Minister had come down in person to discuss their grievances. Friends laughed and told me how all police officers had then received instructions not to upset people, and for a short and glorious interlude, traffic police waved drivers on at red lights instead of fining them. 'The *mukhabarat* (secret police) keep calling at my shop every hour to check everything is ok,' one friend sneered, tossing his head angrily. 'They are very nervous. I am glad. At last they have something to keep them busy.'

Three days later, in Deraa, in the south of the country near the Jordanian border, the instructions were ignored, and the authorities over-reacted to anti-regime graffiti scribbled on school walls by teenagers. The parents, marching in protest at their children's detention, were shot at by regime security forces. Some were killed. The president, Bashar al-Assad, went to Deraa himself to try to smooth things over. He even sent an official delegation to offer condolences to the families and sacked the Deraa governor, but it was too late. Syria's revolution had begun, and by late March regime tanks rolled into Deraa, imagining they could crush the protests with a show of force. As the protests escalated, so did the violence of their response. Their calculation – or gross miscalculation – was always the same. The course of this revolution was set.

Syria is no stranger to revolutions. Under the French Mandate, when Syria's artificial borders had first been drawn up by the vagaries of British and French foreign policy after World War One, Syrians rose up against their French masters in the Great Revolt of 1925. The French response, like Bashar's, was unequivocal. They unleashed an artillery bombardment that flattened a whole quarter of the Old City of Damascus – a quarter now known simply as *al-Hariqa*, 'the Conflagration'. The French did not stop there. They killed thousands, strung up corpses and held public executions in the central Marja Square to serve as a warning to the rebels. They fuelled sectarian divisions in a 'divide and rule' policy whilst their propaganda made them out to be the noble guarantors of peace. It worked. After two years of fighting, the rebellion was crushed and the French went on to control Syria for another 20 years, until independence was finally achieved in 1946.

Bashar followed the French example, calling the peaceful protesters 'sectarian extremists' and 'foreign terrorists' who wanted to destroy the Syrian motherland. 'They needed to be taught a firm lesson,' ran the regime narrative on Syrian state TV, otherwise all hell would break loose, a fanatical Islamist government would take over and Syria's precious minorities would be wiped out. Assad with his powerful security apparatus and tightly controlled armed forces declared himself the only possible saviour of Syria's future. Was it possible that Bashar, like the French, might succeed?

How different it had all been when the first Muslim armies entered Damascus in 635. After a six-month siege, they had negotiated terms with the Christian inhabitants, even agreeing to share their place of worship at the heart of the city. For the next 70 years the Cathedral of St John doubled as mosque to the Muslim residents, with both religions using the same entrance on the south side. The pious inscription in Greek above the door, now blocked-up and heavily disguised by an electricity sub-station, reads: 'Thy Kingdom, O Christ, is an everlasting Kingdom, and Thy Dominion endureth throughout all generations.'

As the Muslim population grew, more space was needed, so the new rulers negotiated again with the Christians, giving them sites for four smaller churches in return, including the current Greek Orthodox Patriarchate. The two religions learnt to live together and still today there are some 20 mosques and 13 churches within the walled Old City. On Sunday mornings church bells ring out together with the call to prayer in that effortless blend of cultures which has long been Syria's hallmark, predating the Assad regime by centuries.

I have been back to Syria five times since those first demonstrations and watched as a seemingly unstoppable civil war has engulfed the country. The last time I sat in the courtyard of the Umayyad Mosque in summer 2012 the atmosphere was unchanged, timeless as ever, the soft evening light glowing on the marble flagstones. There was no fear on peoples' faces. Maybe whatever tension they felt was dispelled as soon as they crossed the mosque's threshold. But how will it be now that Damascus has witnessed a chemical attack, large-scale massacres, bombings by warplanes and helicopter gunships, now that the death toll is spiralling beyond the comprehensible? Clashes between regime forces and rebels across the city suburbs in the north, south, east and west are displacing thousands from their homes, and driving thousands more to flee across the borders into neighbouring Turkey, Jordan, Lebanon and Iraq. Can the Old City be spared?

⁂

Seven years earlier, on a research trip to Syria, the story began unexpectedly when I found an open door. It must have been fate, or serendipity, as the concept of fixed visiting hours, I was warned, did not apply to these magnificent Ottoman palaces tucked away in the winding alleyways of Old Damascus. They sounded so unlikely: forgotten relics of a bygone age, decaying quietly within the ancient Roman walls.

So here I lingered on the threshold of a palace. Retreating from the prying eyes of the street in a zigzag pattern, the entry-corridor keeps the world of the courtyard sacred and serene. Then, in a sudden moment of transition, it leads from the unlit passageway into the dazzling sunlight of the courtyard, into another world. It was my first such moment.

Blinking rapidly to adjust to the brightness, my senses were overwhelmed. The warmth of the February sun was welcome after the chilly shade of the street. Winter in Damascus is colder than you might imagine – it even snows from time to time. I felt embraced, enfolded by the warm space, and knew instinctively that the whole purpose of the courtyard house was to protect, to shield the people inside from the world outside, and to give them a space of total tranquillity. Where to look first? The sheer beauty of the old stones, their soft hues of golden limestone, the deep pinkish red of the local marble, the fierce contrast with the harsh black volcanic basalt that ran in alternating bands round the courtyard walls. It took me by surprise. The elaborate stone patterns continued in the courtyard floor, gently polished by the wear of centuries. In the centre was a pale marble fountain, *bahra* in Arabic, literally 'little sea'. The sound of the clear water splashing from the bronze dragon-heads drew me irresistibly to its octagonal rim. Beneath the surface, a pair of care-free terrapins glided in the sparkling pool. All round the edge of the courtyard were orange trees, vines, bougainvillea and delicate climbers like jasmine, their intense colours and scents mingling intoxicatingly on the breeze. It was a kind of paradise. The architects of such a space can only have had heavenly visions in mind. 'Surely the God-fearing shall be among gardens and fountains,' says the Quran (51:15). Transfixed by the fountain, I do not know how long I stood there. Something in my face must have mirrored these emotions. Maybe my expression conveyed disorientation.

'Do you need help?'

Re-entering the earthly world, I saw a young Syrian approaching from the other side of the fountain. His face was friendly and open. I could have just declined, whereupon he would certainly have withdrawn and let me be. Syrians are too dignified to hassle, but they will offer help if they think you need it. The course of life can change in just such a moment, in taking an opportunity or letting it pass, a *kairos* moment. For whatever reason, I answered: 'Yes ... thank you. Do you know anything about this place?'

He looked pleased, and introduced himself as Bassim, an architect working on restoration projects in the Old City. I was astonished. What restoration projects? Where? He smiled and explained what work he had done on the house I had just entered, the Bait Siba'i, or the House of the Siba'i family, dating from the 17th and 18th centuries. It had been one of the earliest restoration projects in the city, and at one point it had served as the German Consulate. He described how this first courtyard, closest to the street, was the *salamlik*, the Ottoman term for the men's reception area, where male guests were entertained. Keeping this area ready at all times to receive unannounced male visitors meant that family life could go on as normal in the rest of the house.

He led me into a further courtyard, reached by another dog-leg corridor. This, he clarified, was the *haramlik*, where the women and children lived and where no male visitors ever penetrated unless they were direct family members. Of course, I immediately recognised the word from *harem*, with all its connotations, but Bassim explained that it simply meant the inviolate area.

Off the *haramlik* was yet another courtyard, smaller this time and more modest, where the servants of the household lived and where the kitchens were housed. It was called the *khadamlik*. I knew the terms from earlier visits to the Topkapi Palace in Istanbul, but here, with the smaller scale of the palace, it seemed to me that each courtyard had a strict hierarchy, and curiously, the biggest and most elaborate of them, the one where the most decorative effort was concentrated, was the *haramlik*. Wealthy families, Bassim explained, would have had palaces such as this, consisting of a trio of courtyards, totally blocked off from outside eyes, with just one entrance from the street, always into the male area.

His English was good, so I did not volunteer that I spoke Arabic. Pointing out some of the architectural features, he explained about the *iwan*, the huge covered alcove that always faced north onto the courtyard, designed as the coolest spot to sit in summer, since the sun would never shine directly into it. This was where the family would sit, in the shade, on cushions round the edge, the breeze from the courtyard and the coolness from the fountain wafting over them. I could visualise them as he spoke, in their coloured robes and bare feet, like romanticised paintings I had seen of such courtyards, part of the Orientalist tradition. One such painting I recalled from the Tate was *The Courtyard of the Coptic Patriarch's House in Cairo*, by John Frederick Lewis, dated 1864, in which the head of the household sat while his womenfolk and servants engaged in domestic chores, surrounded by camels, goats, ducks and pigeons in a careless and chaotic harmony round the central pool. Clearly there was nothing specifically Muslim about this lifestyle – it was simply the way all wealthier people had lived, irrespective of their religion.

Bassim noted the level of my interest, and became more expansive. He explained that the rooms on either side of the *iwan* were the main indoor reception areas with ceilings six metres high, perfectly adapted to the climate. Windows on two levels, looking onto the *iwan* itself, provided natural air-conditioning in hot summers, catching any breezes during the day and trapping any cooler air at night. Each room was a self-contained unit, its door leading directly onto the courtyard, and there was no access between the rooms, so that many sections of the same family could live in privacy. On the ground floor there were about eight rooms, and in Ottoman times, Bassim elaborated, three generations of one family would have shared this space, maybe some 20 to 30 people in all. Little did I know how soon, during the coming revolution, things would revert to such a system from necessity and how my own future house would play its part.

Having finished the tour of the ground floor, he led me up a flight of steps and I was amazed at how the temperature of the rooms on the first floor was a good five degrees Centigrade warmer. In winter, he said, the family would move upstairs to benefit from the warmth, as the sun beating on the flat mud-brick roofs meant that they reached an ambient temperature much more quickly than the downstairs rooms. The upstairs rooms were also smaller, with lower ceilings. These simple but harmonious design techniques struck me as wonderfully pragmatic – yet functionality at no point gave way to dullness. On the contrary, here was something I had not come across before – functionality combined with an exceptional degree of beauty and style.

What I did not know then was that these courtyard houses were the culmination, through centuries of trial and error since they were first conceived in ancient Mesopotamia around 2,500 BC, of a design that neared perfection. Their microclimates and internal thermal environments have recently been scientifically measured and found to provide a variety of rooms and spaces designed to be lived in during different seasons and at different times of day – the ultimate eco-house.

Bassim had put a small kettle on a kerosene stove, and while it was boiling, he scampered agilely downstairs and returned a few moments later with a handful of shiny greenery plucked from the courtyard trees. 'Naranj leaves,' he said, putting them in the kettle, 'they give a special flavour.'

We sipped at the fragrant tea from our tiny elegantly-shaped glasses, and even though he didn't ask, I felt the need to explain myself. 'The reason I'm so interested in these houses,' I began, 'is because I'm researching a new guide to Syria, for a British publisher.' He seemed to find this entirely normal, and led me into a small neighbouring room fitted out with a trio of computers and extensive maps on the walls. One was a gigantic map of the Old City in intricate detail, appearing to show every single building within the Roman walls. The writing was all in Arabic.

'This is where the other restoration projects are,' he said, and put his finger on several blackened blobs on the map. I expressed surprise at how organised this all seemed to be, and he told me about the *Mudiriyyat Dimashq al-Qadima,* the Directorate of Old Damascus. It was a kind of Historic Buildings Council, he said, whose job it was to specialise in looking after the old buildings of the city, *intra muros,* 'within the walls', as the academics called it. He must have read my thoughts, as he then said: 'You realise that you can buy property here if you are interested. The government does not have the money to save all these houses. There are so many of them, neglected, abandoned, falling down, but what can we do? Our budget only allows us to save about 300 maximum. The rest will be lost.'

I felt my heart racing. 'But surely,' I said, convinced I had misunderstood, 'you don't mean that I, as a foreigner, can just come along and buy a chunk of a UNESCO World Heritage site?' How insane of me even to think such a thing.

'Why yes, of course,' said Bassim straightforwardly, 'it is possible. Why not?'

'Because it must be *mamnou.*' It was the first Arabic word I had used up until that point in our conversation, but Bassim appeared not to notice. The power of the word *mamnou* in the Arabic language is considerable. Its three Arabic root consonants, as well as meaning to forbid or prohibit in a secular context, also mean to declare something impossible or out of the question. It has a finality to it that goes way beyond anything conveyed by the English 'forbidden'. Surely everything to do with foreigners getting involved in Syria had to be *mamnou*.

For years, ever since I had first driven out here in my old Citroen *Deux Chevaux*, way back in 1978, everyone had told me how paranoid and xenophobic the Syrian regime was, convinced all foreigners were spies or journalists with evil intent. 'Beware of anyone in a uniform' and 'It is a police state', and 'Steer well clear of officialdom', all the diplomats had told me. Based for six months at MECAS, the language school run by the British government in Lebanon where I was completing my Arabic studies, I had made many trips east over the mountains, at weekends and during the holidays. Lebanon was in the thick of its own civil war, so mostly out of bounds. I had always followed their advice, just driving through Syrian cities to reach the various tourist destinations that interested me – the ruins of Roman Palmyra in the desert, the Crusader castles in the mountains, St Simeon's Basilica and the Byzantine Dead Cities in the hills – in the days when you were almost guaranteed to be the only person there. I never went near a government office and my contact with men in uniform was limited to border officials. I had rarely stopped in Damascus all those years ago – just a few times, to visit the Umayyad Mosque and to buy a black silk Bedouin gown with red embroidery and a bronze water ewer in the adjacent Souk al-Hamadiya – I have them still. I had no idea in those days that people actually lived in the Old City. I imagined it was all souks and mosques.

But Bassim assured me it was not *mamnou*. It was all above board and normal. 'After all', he said, 'a Frenchman has just done it.'

It was February 2005. Exactly two weeks earlier, on Valentine's Day, Rafiq al-Hariri, Lebanon's Prime Minister, a Sunni Muslim, had been blown up in his motor cavalcade along with 22 others on the Beirut corniche. Across the world, fingers were immediately pointed at Syria. The international community was in no doubt about where the blame lay. It rarely is. Syria of course denied any involvement. What could be in it for them? But no one was listening. Israel's propaganda machine switched into gear and Syria's name was dragged though the mud. I realised it was probably the perfect time to invest in property.

✢

Seven years later, in the full blaze of Syria's revolution, I walked along the Street Called Straight to St Ananias' Church in the Christian Quarter of the Old City. This, the city's ancient main thoroughfare, was the same street along which the Roman citizen Saul, struck blind on his 'road to Damascus', had been led to what is now called the Chapel of Ananias. Saul's mission had been to round up the Christians, the troublesome new sect who were proving to be a headache for the Roman governor, but after being cured by the Christian Ananias, he became instead Christianity's greatest evangelist. Inside the stillness of the subterranean chapel, at the Roman ground level, five metres lower than today's, I opened the Visitor's Book:

> God please we ask you to protect us and let our people live with peace and take action against our president Bashar al-Assad. 19/3/2012.

Such was the mood of total despair that I had shared on arrival, on 10 April 2012, the day of Kofi Annan's ceasefire. I found all my friends, a mix of Muslims and Christians from a range of professions, deeply pessimistic about the future, given the way the uprising had evolved to this point. Politically they are neither activists nor regime supporters. They are the silent majority caught in the middle. Their futures have been taken away from them. Most are now unemployed, and all have suffered terrible winters of exceptional cold, with gas and fuel shortages, rising prices and up to twelve hours of electricity cuts a day. All felt powerless to affect the outcome. They were convinced things were going to get worse, and that Syria, caught between the two extremes of a ruling elite fighting for its life and a poorly organised opposition increasingly taking up arms, would descend inexorably into the abyss of full-blown civil war. Could anything be done to avert such a course?

A ray of hope appeared. Weirdly, unexpectedly, something changed in Damascus. By late afternoon on Friday, 13 April, the entire mood of the city had lifted. Instead of the high tension of recent weeks there was an almost tangible lightening of spirit. We all felt it. More and more people started to come out onto the streets, to walk about freely in family groups – in recent months people had begun to stay inside on Fridays for their own safety. We ventured out to Rabweh, to the restaurants along the river on the old Beirut road.

We had all been waiting for the bomb explosions. In the run-up to previous deadlines there had always been a bomb or two, blamed by the regime on the rebels and by the rebels on the regime. I had heard the first two myself the previous November, just after the dawn call to prayer, from my own bed. In the morning the news had carried footage from the regime's TV station claiming there had been an explosion at the ruling Ba'ath Party Headquarters, but when we went to look there was nothing to be seen. Sound bombs became a common scare tactic, or bombs without a detonator, like the one the regime sent through the walls of the Saydnaya Monastery to frighten the nuns. When nothing exploded this time in Damascus or Aleppo, we all hoped there might be a sea change. Where were all these armed groups, the *jihadi*s and Al-Qaeda elements the media so loved to talk about? At that stage my friends all dismissed their existence in any serious numbers. 'Even if there are a few, trying to take advantage, we will never accept them. We are not extremists, it is not in our nature. Just because some have beards, it doesn't mean they are Al-Qaeda.' It had been true, back in April 2012, before the black-bannered brigades started to enter Syria, filling the vacuum and taking advantage of international inertia and the disarray of the opposition.

Civil disobedience began in Damascus with people not paying utility bills: 'Why should we pay for services we do not have?' Jokes were doing the rounds about checkpoints between the capital and Deir Ez-Zour in the east, where Syria's oilfields are. At the first checkpoint, the soldiers would ask: 'Are you with the regime or against it?' The traveller would answer 'With' and get beaten because it turned out to be a Free Syrian Army rebel checkpoint. At the next one, when asked the same question he would answer 'Against' and get beaten because it was a regime checkpoint. Most now flew on Syrian Air between the cities to avoid the dangers of the open road.

On that Friday in St Ananias's Chapel, where, some 2,000 years ago, the future St Paul was cured of his blindness and converted, it seemed that maybe another miracle had taken place. Maybe the regime had finally understood it would never be able to make a comeback. My ties to Syria and its people were now so strong that I wanted desperately to believe it could all still be saved.

But it was just a pause, tragically brief, and the opportunity was squandered. The regime broke off from its killing spree, looked up to take stock of the world's reaction, realised there was no unified voice, and continued in its single-minded aim – to crush the opposition. It was on the way to self-destruction. Addicted to power, oblivious to all pleas to change course, in denial about the size and nature of the problem, it would almost certainly have to reach its own personal rock-bottom, like all addicts, before things could improve. Kofi Annan's resignation in August 2012 was a tragic acknowledgement of failure and of the impotence of the international community.

When Ramadan ended, on 23 August 2012, the last 100 UN monitors left and the UN mandate expired. The violence began to escalate immediately. Lakhdar Brahimi, another respected elder statesman, donned the mantle of the new UN and Arab League Special Envoy to Syria. Shuttling from capital to capital, he strove valiantly to achieve compliance from all sides to a ceasefire in October 2012 over the four-day Eid Al-Adha, Islam's biggest annual holiday. But it was 'mission impossible'. Each side blamed the other, each convinced they could still win. All restraints were gone and the pretence was over. Terrible times lay ahead.

How on earth had it got to this point and how had my dream led me to such involvement in a raging civil war? This is the true story behind the Syrian Revolution, the details that never reach the press. It is the story of Syria, its people, its society and secrets, told through the prism of an ancient building: my house.

2

Unescorted

*Sorrow we have to bear alone as best we can, it is not fair
to try to shift it on others, be they men or women.*

Axel Munthe

On my first 2005 research trip to Syria, the Ministry of Tourism fell
short. In spite of four months' advance notice by post and by email, it
had still not produced the necessary permissions for the use of a com-
plimentary car by the time I arrived. Welcome to Syria, land of snail-
paced bureaucracy. The run-down ministry building was a microcosm
of the sort of organised chaos to which I later grew accustomed, even
to like. But during this encounter, all I could see was the chaos. The
hierarchy of people's room sizes was very important, and the furniture
in these rooms even more important, as reflections of status.

Walid Maqta, the new PR director whose room boasted two black
leather settees, was a tall handsome man who looked severely over-
worked. Of course, he would have had at least two other jobs as well
as this one – all government employees did. They were proud of their
work, considering themselves at the top of their fields, but their salaries were too low to live off. His phones were always ringing – there
were three fixed handsets on his huge desk, and his mobile was permanently glued to his ear. There was a steady stream of people coming

and going from his office, clutching papers for signature and making other minor requests. How he sustained this level of constant multi-tasking was beyond me, but squashed in with all his other supplicants and favour-seekers, my only thought was for myself.

'When will my permission come through?' I asked, struggling not to show too much annoyance and impatience. 'Can't you just give it to me now? I contacted you months ago.'

'No', said the chain-smoking Walid, he was very sorry, but he could not authorise anything himself, not until the permission came through from the Minister personally. I knew it was not his fault. Bloated and underfunded, all ministries in Syria are highly central-ised, controlling organisations. Without access to the top, the wait could be long.

'It will be *bukra*, tomorrow, *in sha Allah*, or the next day for sure,' said Walid. I knew the '*bukra*' mentality. Everything would happen tomorrow, but as we all know, tomorrow never comes. There was no point in getting angry. It would have changed nothing and just made me seem ridiculous in their eyes. I could not stoop to bribery in such a public arena – I was not sufficiently practised in the art – so my best bet was to get on with it and rent my own car for the first chunk of my self-organised itinerary, a loop round the south of the country, to Quneitra, Bosra and the Jabal Druze. That would give them four more days to sort out their permissions.

My patience had already been sorely tried by the absurd bureau-cratic process of obtaining the permit that was required to visit Quneitra. Even finding the government building to issue the permit had been depressingly difficult. The Syrian government actually wants people to visit Quneitra, a town 50 kilometres southwest of Damascus, flattened by Israeli tanks in a highly sensitive border zone, but you would not know it from the procedures involved – except that it is free of charge. Had it not been for my research I would prob-ably not have bothered. Most visitors were likely to be VIPs who had minions to get the permit for them.

After two abortive attempts, my third taxi driver stumbled upon the building – more by accident than design – not far from the dis-creet National Security Headquarters in Rawdah where an explosion seven years later was to assassinate four of Bashar's top security chiefs.

The clue, the taxi driver informed me with a knowing look, was the armed military kiosk outside – that was a sure sign it was a government office involved in security issues. He should know – I was told around half of the taxi drivers are *mukhabarat*, secret police, some even proving it with their state security ID card, hoping for an extra tip. Apart from the kiosk, there was nothing on the outside that suggested it was anything other than a large, run-down private residence, the same as all the others in the street. We were not allowed to park anywhere near it, even though there was a space directly opposite – that, we were told, was *mamnou*. Even then car bombs were clearly thought to be a threat.

Lest we forget, the Syrian government still considers itself in a permanent state of war with 'the Zionist entity', as it always calls Israel, and it was on that pretext that it introduced its 1963 Emergency Law, giving the police and security services absolute power to arrest and detain anyone indefinitely without trial. Thousands of dissidents languish in Syrian prisons as a result, often subjected to grotesque torture. 'Death is easier than Syrian prison,' said activists who survived it. 'Inside prison you wish for death a million times.' Fear of prison and detention was often cited as the reason why Syria's rate of petty crime was so low. My own future guidebook was to describe it as 'one of the safest countries in the world', a place 'where no foreigner had even been the target of violence.' It had been true before the revolution, but by 2014 several foreign nationals including Britons had been killed whilst fighting against the regime or whilst reporting against it.

I was not allowed to enter the scruffy building, but was gestured to sit and wait outside on a sawn-off tree stump that had thoughtfully been placed on the pavement while an armed soldier took my passport to conduct the formalities inside. Twenty minutes later, he reappeared and handed it back to me together with a separate chitty covered in a few Arabic handwritten scribbles. This process, I was later to discover, was one of Syria's more minor bureaucratic procedures, compared to the joys of extending a visa at the Ministry of Immigration, one of whose 15 stages involved going out into the gutter to buy a stamp off a man at his barrow. It had to be complicated to ensure that there were ample opportunities for both employment and bribery.

In one of the many ironies of the Syrian crisis, there had been plans at the time the revolution broke out to introduce 'e-government', an attempt to reduce face-to-face contact between civil servants and the public, and thereby reduce the opportunities to offer bribes for a speedy passage through the interminable bureaucracy.

At the car hire office I performed the ritual circumambulation of a beaten up once-silver Toyota with its bald tyres and malfunctioning seatbelt, pointing out the scratches to the car rental employee. 'Not the little ones,' he said waving his hand dismissively, 'only the big ones we will write in the report.' I crawled out of Damascus, asking the way repeatedly at each roundabout. Even if there had been signposts, Quneitra, the only part of the Golan Heights still under Syrian control, would not have merited one. This city and the entire Golan was lost to Israel in the disastrous 1967 Six Day War. Before giving Quneitra back in a UN-brokered disengagement agreement in 1974, the Israelis razed the place to the ground in an act of gratuitous violence worthy of the Mongol Tamerlane. Since then it has been kept exactly as it was, a showcase of what Israel can do when its wrath is incurred. Hafez al-Assad, father of the current President Bashar and creator of the Assad regime and Syria as it is today, took the decision not to rebuild Quneitra. The original intention had been to do so, but then he thought it would be a more powerful statement to the outside world if it were left destroyed, as an example of what the Israelis were capable of. How ironic that towns all across Syria would, in the course of the uprising against him and his regime, be similarly flattened, this time by his own armed forces.

The road becomes quite narrow once clear of the Damascus suburbs, heading south into countryside that is still heavily farmed. This region, known as the Hawran, has been Syria's breadbasket since Roman times, widely cultivated for its wheat. Avoiding the potholes required concentration, but whenever feasible I glanced west towards the mountain range of the Golan, and the snow-crowned peak of Mount Hermon, which at 2,814 metres is Syria's highest mountain. Known locally as Jabal Ash-Shaikh, the 'Mountain of the Wise Old Man', because of the white beard it wears for over six months of the year, I had heard that there were significant remains of a temple complex on its summit, though I knew the chances of it being accessible in my lifetime were close to zero. The mountains have all the gentle, graceful curves of Biblical Antiquity. Israeli archaeologists have for years been engaged in trying to prove the Golan was part of Biblical Israel back in the Iron Age, to substantiate their right to be there, while Arab scholars claim the Amorites, Arabs of Semitic origin, had lived there since the 3rd millennium BC.

Today's reality is that Israel controls over two thirds of the Golan Heights, depriving Syria of its access to mountain villages, gorges and spectacular classical sites like Baniyas, 'City of Pan'. Agriculturally its volcanic soil is the richest in the entire region, famed for its orchards and apple farms, and when you look across the border from the Syrian side, the contrast is striking. The countryside around Majdal Shams, the largest town on the Golan, is green, well-irrigated and well-organised with luxuriant farms and fields, compared to Syria's neglected villages. The tourism income from the Golan could have been considerable for Syria, but Israel now takes those revenues for itself: it has turned the Heights into a year-round weekend getaway, offering summer escapes from the heat, and winter escapes to its own ski resort.

Even beyond the tourism, Israel would never give up the Golan for two other reasons – wine and water. Its snow-melt feeds Israel's largest reservoir, Lake Tiberias, the biblical Sea of Galilee. Also, from the highest points Damascus itself is in direct view, and Syria, in response to Israeli-initiated firing, launched bomb attacks from the Golan down onto northern Israel from 1948 until 1967, as part of their ongoing border war. In retaliation Israel lost no time in establishing Jewish settlements on the Heights, over 40 of them now, on hillsides of volcanic basaltic soil which is akin to that of the vineyards of Bordeaux and Tuscany. The settlers now produce award-winning kosher wine: red, white and sparkling, marketed internationally under names like Hermon and Golan, cementing their de facto ownership in the minds of people across the globe. The Golan (or the Jolan, as the Syrians pronounce it, with their soft French-style 'j') is in political stalemate, rarely in the media and largely forgotten by the international community – so much so that Israel has felt confident enough to start exploiting the region for oil and gas, and has built a 'security barrier' to protect itself against the dangers of a spill-over from Syria's civil war.

'We feel we have won the lottery in the Golan,' a former Israeli diplomat Dr Alon Liel boasted during a January 2013 lecture at London's School of Oriental and African Studies (SOAS). 'When Obama comes next month and tells us we must return the Golan to Syria, we will say to him, "But who shall we return it to – Bashar or the rebels?" There is no Syria, there is no one to give it to! It is ours now.'

Much good may it do, but international law is on Syria's side in the case of the Golan. Israeli withdrawal from Syrian sovereign territory was demanded by Resolution 242 of the UN Security Council issued in 1967. Yet although US-brokered negotiations came close to agreement in 2000 under Bill Clinton and Ehud Barak, Hafez al-Assad refused to give up Syria's land on the northeast shoreline of the Sea of Galilee, insisting on retaining the 1967 border, while Ehud Barak demanded a reversion to the pre-1948 border. Talks broke down over this stretch of strategic territory, which is little more than 100 metres wide. To date Syria is the only neighbour of Israel that has not arrived at some sort of peace agreement, the last of the so-called 'Resistance Front' states. The barren waterless areas of the Sinai Peninsula and the Gaza Strip have been returned to Egypt and Palestine respectively, but the West Bank, still occupied, has major underground aquifers. Syria's defiant denial of the reality on the ground also shows in its own maps, which continue to mark the Golan as Syrian territory.

What a sad scenario. Most of the Syrians still living under Israeli occupation in the Golan are Druze, a monotheistic mountain people, neither Muslim nor Christian, who form one of Syria's many minorities: just 3 per cent of the population. Considering their small numbers, the Druze have often played a surprisingly large part in Syria's history, 'the dangerous minority' as one former president called them. Proud and fierce fighters, they were the first, under their bold leader Sultan Pasha al-Atrash, to rise up against the French in the 1925 Syrian uprising, and were so feared and respected that they were given their own autonomous area on the Jabal Druze, an area still overwhelmingly inhabited by them. 'My enemies are like a serpent,' said one prime minister of the 1950s, 'the head is the Jabal Druze, the stomach Homs and the tail Aleppo. If I crush the head, the serpent will die.' He was subsequently assassinated – by a Druze.

In the current uprising the Druze were at first surprisingly quiet, unsure what to do, in spite of Walid Jumblatt, the aging leader of Lebanon's Druze, urging them to support the opposition against the Assad regime. Would they listen and would it make any difference? I would find out soon enough.

Druze history is shrouded in secrecy. Their religion was founded by an Iranian mystic and a Turkish preacher, and the village elders wear a distinctive tall, white headdress and baggy black trousers to show their state of enlightenment. The young dress in Western style and are known as *al-juhaal*, 'the ignorant'. Both sexes are usually very good-looking – many presenters and newsreaders on Syrian TV are Druze. Here in the Golan their opportunities are far more limited – only 400 have been allowed to return to Syria. In the days before mobile phones and Skype, the hill above Majdal Shams was known as the 'Shouting Hill', where relations would use megaphones across the valley to communicate with their families on the other side. It was the only contact permitted. Most of the 400,000 Syrians displaced in 1967 were Druze, for whom intermarriage is not allowed. From time to time Druze brides are permitted to cross the valley to marry Druze grooms, with barbed wire the backdrop to their wedding photos. Some 18,000 Syrians still live on the Golan under Israeli occupation, most of them Druze. The overwhelming majority of them have refused to give up their Syrian citizenship, but the 20,000 Israeli settlers with whom they have to share the territory are out-breeding them, thanks to what they see as their religious duty to multiply and produce more settlers.

Approaching Quneitra there are a few roadblocks, where plain-clothes policemen, the dreaded *mukhabarat*, looking grim and brutal in their black leather jackets, step out to check your passport and scrappy permit. I had been told that Syria has over a million *mukhabarat* – even charities have to have a member on their boards – spread over at least 17 agencies, and that their powers are extensive, but I felt no fear. After all, I was doing nothing wrong. And as a foreigner, I imagined I was not subject to the dreaded Emergency Law of 1963 that allowed arrests for no specified reason, the law that guaranteed a quiescent population for so long.

The secret police are rarely communicative, and if they found it unusual that a foreign woman was driving alone to see Quneitra in a hire car, they did not say so. Months of driving in Lebanon during the Civil War in the late 1970s had taught me how to behave at these checkpoints – I'd make the briefest eye contact, then wait with total patience for however long it took, eyes lowered in complete submission and obedience. Once, heading up the Bekaa Valley in my battered Citroen, I accidentally passed a checkpoint without noticing, and was shot at. But youth and ignorance are wonderful things. I simply learnt to be more observant.

At the final Quneitra roadblock an armed, young soldier got in the car with me as an escort, to direct me round the flattened town, as was his duty. He was probably posted there on his military service, compulsory for all young men over the age of 18. He kept silent, and I knew that discussing politics of any sort was taboo, so I confined my occasional remarks to simple questions: 'What is this building?' 'Which way do I go now?' He appeared mildly surprised that I spoke Arabic, but then seemed to assume I was Lebanese. He was polite, but stoical and distant, no doubt following orders.

Among the trees and flattened concrete debris, a few buildings remained recognisable: the black basalt hospital, heavily pockmarked with gunfire, an early Mamluk mosque with a red stone minaret and an Orthodox church, its bell tower still standing. UN personnel posts were all around, manned by cheerful soldiers from Canada, Poland, Japan and Austria in their blue berets – perhaps another snapshot into Syria's future. In the centre of the destruction, one new place stood out, and I asked the soldier what it was. 'Restaurant,' he answered. I headed towards it and parked in its enormous empty car park.

'Is it working?' I asked.

'Of course,' he replied. Evidently built in the days when it was hoped many visitors would come to survey this desolate scene of destruction, the restaurant was an enormous two-storey place, built in a rather kitsch style, with a large garden and playground attached. I walked through the neglected garden, looking at the faded red plastic train engines, decaying yellow see-saws and lethal slides with their steps missing and jagged edges. Inside, an open fire was blazing in the hearth and a friendly waiter approached. Simple fare was on offer, so I had lunch; I was their sole customer that day and who knows for how many others.

Dropping off my glum soldier and driving on from Quneitra, I headed southeast towards Bosra. The landscape all around became increasingly strewn with black stones, the famous basalt that had been spewed out thousands of years earlier by the volcanoes of the Hawran. The basalt was designed to last, and all ancient buildings in the region – churches, caravanserais, temples, basilicas, castles – were built of this sombre stone, and all were still extant. The map marked dozens of sites in this area with the usual black dot triangles. There were so many, but they were never mentioned in any source I could find. Years later, before the war broke out, I explored them thoroughly with Syrian friends over the course of many weekends. Their names, Sha'ara, Al-Mismiyeh, At'taf, Qirata, are never seen in print, but the remarkable thing about them, apart from their intrinsic interest as unusually intact Roman remains, is their setting amongst modern villages whose inhabitants were a peaceful mix of Muslims and Christians. The murdered 13-year-old Hamza al-Khatib, icon of the revolution, had come from just such a village, and one year into the war a Syrian friend from Deraa told me they were still models of peaceful co-existence, with no sectarian incidents of the type the media so loves to report.

On this first research trip though, I could focus only on the main places, like Bosra, a UNESCO World Heritage site with its intact Roman theatre hidden inside a 13th century Ayyubid citadel; or Shahba, a whole city of basalt complete with mosaic floors, home town of Philip the Arab, Emperor of Rome; or Qanawat, a Roman temple complex adapted to become a pair of Byzantine basilicas; or like the Greek Orthodox church of Saint George, Syria's earliest church still in use, the unlikely burial place of England's patron saint. All were extraordinary, all were crafted from black basalt, all in eclectic blends of architectural styles.

While wondering how on earth people had managed to carve this incredibly hard, unforgiving rock, I thought back to the events of the previous day, to my chance meeting with Bassim in Bait Siba'i. It already seemed so long ago, another world entirely.

I recalled how, from the street, the palace entrance had been just a door, like any other door in the Old City. Everyone seemed to live *incognito* – the expression 'behind closed doors' took on a whole new meaning in Damascus. Princes and Paupers lived side by side. Down a narrow street, along a shadowy alley, the approach from the outside was always the same, as if it were a maze. But behind each door might lie a tiny humble dwelling or a sumptuous palace.

All I knew was that there were separate segments shown on the map – the Muslim quarter with its mix of Sunni and Shi'a areas, the Christian quarter and the Jewish quarter – but was it really that simple, religious groupings self-segregating? In a city that has been continuously inhabited for over five thousand years, claiming to be one of the oldest continuously inhabited cities in the world, could this segregation just have been a random process or did it in some way reflect the society that had produced it? What unfathomable layers of history must be hidden here, waiting to be unravelled? Buried deep under these buildings would be remains of all Damascus's earlier civilisations, but buried they would remain, since nothing can be excavated today in such a populous city. I knew from my research that the Old City's location had never changed, unlike Cairo, where the centre would move around according to its ruler. Waves of history have washed over Damascus, each leaving some mark, with conquerors from Egypt, Asia Minor, Assyria, Babylon, Persia, Greece, Rome and Arabia. But through some mysterious alchemy, it had learnt the secret of how to accommodate and even be enhanced by all these disparate elements.

I must have been gripped by some sort of insanity to think I might ever be able to buy a house in such a place. I had no money and my future was uncertain. Even this hire car was going to leave a financial hole I could not fill from my own coffers. Perversely, those certain obstacles seemed to me a lot less daunting than the even more certain pitfalls of Syrian law and property ownership. I was no stranger to the labyrinthine ways of Arab bureaucracy. I had lived already in several Arab countries as a translator, interpreter and diplomatic wife and had no illusions about the way things worked in this part of the world. Bribery, corruption, the cheating of foreigners – no one in their right mind would consider buying a house here.

Meanwhile, back in Bosra I met a pair of young Syrians, the only other people visiting the site, while strolling round the basalt Roman baths. They told me how they were setting up a business to export traditional herbal medicines from Syria to the West, and my heart warmed to see such youthful enterprise and energy. 'These things were invented here,' they explained enthusiastically, 'our ancestors knew how to cure themselves of many illnesses, and now we have rediscovered our roots.'

They were right: in Damascus I recalled examining the exhibits in the Maristan Nur Ad-Din, a 12th century medical school and research centre, now the Museum of Arab Science and Medicine, with its display cabinets full of herbs, cataloguing their properties: garlic for hypertension, valerian for nervous illnesses, parsley as a diuretic and so on. I was particularly struck by how 'nervous illnesses' were treated with calming teas and a simple diet, with patients sitting in beautiful plant-rich courtyards listening to the sound of fountains and gentle lutes – the soothing influences of nature, water and music. In Europe we called them 'mental illnesses', imprisoning and abusing patients until the 20th century. The traumas that would soon come to Bosra, when indiscriminate regime shelling resulted in extensive damage to the town and the site, would require such tenderness and understanding in their treatment. I hoped the young entrepreneurs would use their skills well.

Driving up into the villages of the Jabal Druze massif, there were still patches of snow on the ground. The roads were empty and remote, and signposts were few and far between. Sometimes it felt like a forgotten corner of the earth, with long distances of bleak mountain landscapes between the settlements. In one, named Mushannaf, I stumbled across a Roman temple, its façade facing onto a stagnant pool in the centre of the village. A herd of goats was foraging for scraps outside, and inside its *cella*, the holy of holies, a beaming matronly woman in colourful robes and a headdress stood out against the black stone. She was stirring a huge cauldron of bubbling soapy water and in the temple forecourt her washing line was draped with the village laundry. She invited me in for tea, and I accepted, sitting on a pink plastic stool among the white drying sheets, gazing up at the elaborately carved façade of the temple with its rosette motifs and Corinthian capitals, and listening to her happy chatter.

Is she still happy now, high in her temple, with her menfolk diminished and her sons leaving? Today an uneasy calm hangs over this province of As-Suwayda in the south; the Druze have tried to remain neutral, on the edges of the conflict. Neutrality has become increasingly difficult to sustain as the war grinds on, especially once the regime began summoning extra reserve units from Druze and Christian areas, threatening to execute their families if they refused. Some Druze in the Golan have even sought Israeli citizenship, desperate to avoid making a choice between the regime and the rebels, and in a further layer of complexity, Israel, with its superior and well-equipped hospitals, has been quietly treating Syrian victims of chemical warfare and other emergency cases which Syria cannot handle. Friends and relations carry the injured to the security fence on the Golan, from where they are collected, treated, then discreetly returned.

Bassim the architect later told me he had been born in the Jabal Druze, but had left when he had turned 16 for lack of employment opportunities. He had made his way to Damascus, like most young men from this poverty-stricken backwater. His father, a village elder, told him after the revolution broke out: 'We all support the revolution here and have solidarity with the refugees, but we fear the spectre of civil war. We have no weapons, but if the revolution were against foreign aggressors we would be the first to battle.' Little did they know, sitting high in their mountain stronghold, how foreigners would soon enter the battle and how it would become a fight to the death.

3

Escorted

*I have spread my dreams under your feet; Tread
softly because you tread on my dreams.*

WB Yeats

Returning to Damascus from my research tour of the south, I was
immersed in my own battle with hordes of Iranian pilgrims in the
southern suburbs. Midan, a poor district 10 kilometres south of the
Old City, later to become a 'hot-spot' of the revolution, was clogged, as
ever, by large numbers of them wandering blindly all over the streets.
The women were fully veiled from head to toe in black chadors and
didn't concern themselves with traffic.

The object of their pilgrimage, a shrine housed in a garish, modern
Iranian-funded mosque, is one of several sacred to Shi'ites in and
around Damascus. It is dedicated to Sayyida Zaynab, granddaughter
of the Prophet Muhammad and sister of Hussein, whose death at the
Battle of Karbala in 680 AD marked a major stage in Islam's big rift
between Sunni and Shi'a over political succession. Hussein's head is
believed to be buried in a side hall of the Umayyad Mosque, making it
another site of Shi'ite pilgrimage. The schism arose between those who
believed that the Prophet Muhammad's successor should be elected
by consensus, who became known as Sunnis, followers of the 'custom'

or *sunna,* and between those who believed his successor should be the closest relation of the Prophet, starting with the Prophet's son-in-law Ali, who became known as the Shi'ites, 'those who split off', from *Shi'a* meaning the 'faction'. The split took 300 years to emerge fully.

Further confusing matters, the Caliph Mu'awiya, from the Sunni side, promptly broke with tradition by appointing his son to rule after him, thereby creating the Umayyad dynasty with Damascus as its capital. The overwhelming majority of Syria's population today is still Sunni Muslim, while only around 12 per cent are loosely Shi'a (further divided into the Alawi, Twelvers and Isma'ili traditions). It is an important divide, easily as important as that between Protestants and Catholics in Christianity, and the pretext for just as many wars – maybe more.

In 2010 the Assad regime took the relationship with Iran to new heights by lifting the visa requirement for Iranian tourists, thereby opening the floodgates to hundreds of thousands of extra visitors. Mutual commercial benefit spurred the relationship on, and in partnership with the Syrian government Iran began financing a variety of developments around Shi'ite shrines, both in Damascus and around the rest of the country. Ministry of Tourism figures show an 84 per cent rise between 2009 and 2010, with close to a million Iranians arriving in Syria. In an interview, the Director of the Iranian Hajj and Visiting Organisation in Syria, Sayyed Akhawan, was quoted as saying that Syria had a special place in the hearts of Iranians: 'The majority of Iranians like to visit the holy mosques and shrines and they feel that Syria is their second country ... In 2010 every week 72 charter and ordinary airplanes flew from Iran into Damascus International, compared to 42 planes a week in 2009. Ten thousand buses of Iranian pilgrims came to Syria in 2010, compared to 6,000 buses in 2009, when visas were still required.'

Before the Iranian invasion Sayyida Zaynab was a small village, but now there are over 2,000 motels for Shi'ite visitors. Religious tourism to Syria was also encouraged from the Iranian end, with the government even providing heavily discounted flights between Tehran and Damascus for pilgrims, from the usual $380 return to just $60 for a return, on top of all sorts of other financial inducements. They were still coming in droves in 2011 and 2012, long after the European tourists started cancelling. My contact Bassam Barsik, Director of

Marketing and Promotion at the Ministry of Tourism, was pinning all his hopes on them as the only remaining buoyant sector: 'Religious tourism is not affected by the crisis,' he told me, 'because it is a spiritual issue. They come even when times are hard, to gain *baraka* [religious blessing].' Further expansion had been in the pipeline with airlines planning to provide extra seats and beds, before the civil war became so bad that even the Shi'ite pilgrims stopped coming.

The suburb of Midan negotiated, I arrived at the fine old offices of the Ministry of Tourism beside the National Museum – the offices that sadly caught fire in a random accident before the civil war. Double-parked illegally like everyone else, I ran inside for courtesy's sake to tell the staff I was now heading north. I wanted to press on that evening straight to Hama, 210 kilometres north of Damascus, famous throughout Antiquity for its magnificent moaning waterwheels. I had been promised free accommodation, arranged myself. Hotel managers actually reply to emails, unlike ministry officials. I also wanted to walk freely in the streets of Hama after dark, to see first-hand if the mood there really was as conservative, traditional and hostile to Westerners as I had read. My first visit there in the late 1970s had, after all, been before the 1982 Muslim Brotherhood uprising against the Assad regime, and its now equally famous massacre.

'Where have you been?' Walid threw his hands up in relief. 'Your car is ready and the driver and guide have been waiting for you for the last two days.' His room was as chaotic as ever, but sitting opposite him, with an expression of supreme calm on his face in the midst of the general hubbub, was the man I was later to name 'Ramzi the Philosopher'.

I could not conceal my bewilderment. 'What do you mean? I do not want a driver and guide. I only want a car. I have my itinerary planned out, and I know where I want to go.'

'Yes,' said Walid, 'but a guide will be able to help you, to tell you more about the places, about the history and the culture.'

'But I have read about the places and the history and the culture, and I will be writing the book in my own style.'

'But you have to take a guide,' Walid insisted, 'it is not a choice. It is the necessity. To go without a guide is *mamnou*.'

Syria is a police state. I was asking a favour of its government

27

apparatus, so they made the rules. A guide would make sure I did not go to places I was not supposed to, did not talk to people I was not supposed to.

Trapped between my own financial constraints and this imposed restriction on my freedom, I looked at Ramzi sitting on the leather couch, trying to work out what sort of travelling companion he might be. He sat, patiently waiting for instructions, unperturbed by my dilemma. Realizing the futility of my position, I bowed to the inevitable and accepted their offer.

The usually inert bureaucracy can move with great speed once the top man has given the go-ahead, and within moments, no signatures or contracts required, Ramzi and I were heading outside to find the Ministry car and driver among all the other illegally parked cars. We drove in convoy for a few blocks to hand back my Toyota. As soon as the hire office had satisfied itself on the matter of the scratches, we sped out of Damascus on the main road north towards Hama.

Ramzi seemed to have my measure from the start. He said very little and waited until speech was necessary. He was a big man, over six foot, and moved in a way that was a curious mix of slow deliberation and carefree nonchalance. He and Redwan the driver sat in the front, exchanging the odd sentence. I sat in the back, doing more itinerary planning and looking out of the window, keeping a deliberate distance. Once Damascus was well behind us, I outlined to Ramzi my perhaps rather ambitious itinerary for the trip. He appeared quite content and made no attempt to dissuade me or to suggest an alternative.

It was the first time in a very long while that I had seen Syria north of Damascus. Looking at the mountains, I allowed my mind to drift back to the last time I had been travelling along this main road towards Aleppo. It had been in 1978; I was en route to Turkey and in a state of high excitement. Whitehall had taken the decision to evacuate all students from Shemlan, the Lebanese village where the British government ran its state-sponsored school for Arabic. The school had first closed in 1975 when the Lebanese Civil War broke out, had then reopened in 1977 when things appeared to improve, had stayed open for just over a year, and then closed again hurriedly, shutting its doors forever.

I was among that final batch, the last of the MECAS students, and had decided to drive back to England where the school was to reopen after six weeks. For me it was an unexpected bonus – a chance to explore Turkey on full evacuation expenses. The rest of the students, already weary with the Middle East and its conflicts, were only too delighted to jump on the ferry from Beirut to Marseilles, eager to return to the comforts of civilisation.

Even before that evacuation, I had driven this road north on a number of occasions, often taking with me any other students who fancied exploring. The Civil War meant that travel in most of Lebanon was either *mamnou* or heavily restricted, so most of the time we headed either to Syria or Jordan. Setting off with a tent, bedding and cooking gear in the boot, and the space under the back seat stashed with provisions, we left the war in Lebanon behind. It was not my war, so I was not afraid.

Camping in the green hills of Syria's Ansariye range was magical. We would drive up small tracks until we were well away from all forms of habitation, then look for a suitably sheltered spot with a few trees for company. By the morning, the only disturbance was the occasional donkey wandering over to investigate. Many of the villages in those mountains were Christian, and still are; each has a church that pops into view as you round the corner. Syria's Christians, estimated at 10 per cent of the population, are largely concentrated in the big cities of Damascus, Aleppo and Homs, but many are also scattered in the mountains and villages of what is called the Wadi Al-Nasara, the Valley of Christians, as well as in the Qalamoun Mountains of the Anti-Lebanon range and in the northeast around Al-Hasakah. The women there wear a traditional headscarf just as in any Muslim village, so only the churches give away the villages' identity.

Self-sufficient and cocooned in my car I had not needed their hospitality. In the morning, I would stroke the donkeys and skip round the fields, seeking out Mazarine Blues and Clouded Yellows, specimens for my butterfly collection back in England. These were times of innocence.

My own environmental awareness, I reflected, had been in its infancy in those days, but in Syria such a concept was non-existent. The Ministry of the Environment was not set up until 2006 and, even then, had no clear idea what to do. Ministries in Syria have some good individuals but as organisations they cannot plan or evaluate, and they most certainly do not coordinate with each other. There had for years been a Ministry of Irrigation, but its approach was far from environmental. Land existed in order to be used, or rather exploited – that was the Ministry's default setting. There was no sentimentality about nature and wilderness, just as there is none about animals in the Arab world. The countryside is there to provide food, as are animals, not to be nurtured and fussed over.

Reconciling Syria as it is today with our vision of the old 'Fertile Crescent' has always been a challenge. Lack of water and land for grazing livestock forced thousands of poverty-stricken farmers to leave northeast Syria and settle round Deraa in the southwest. Their grievances made them a tinderbox for the flames of revolution, and it was no accident that the first serious anti-regime demonstrations began there, leading to those first deaths. True, in pockets such as the Orontes Valley, the rich red soil and fecund vegetation may conjure up some archetypal Fertile Crescent memories, but over two thirds of Syria's population today now lives in cities and this population is increasingly losing its connection with the land and the environment. The 'Beirutisation' of Damascus was well under way by 2011, with exclusive fashion shops starting to appear, like *Villa Moda* on the Street Called Straight where $25,000 Swiss watches, $4,000 mobile phones and $6,000 designer jeans were on sale to the city's gilded youth whose rich daddies were in bed with the regime. The divisions between rich and poor, and between city and countryside remain very important in driving the course of the revolution. Bashar neglected the country dwellers, preferring to hobnob with the city elites. It was a mistake that his father Hafez would never have made. Today, many rebel fighters are recruited from poor, rural areas where unemployment and illiteracy rates are high and they can, therefore, often be perceived as a *Lumpenproletariat* by the city dwellers who then, as in the case of Aleppo, give them a cold reception when they arrive offering 'liberation'. Whole areas of rural Syria have been under rebel control for months or even years, run by their own local councils and elders; the regime forces don't bother to try and hold them, but focus their attentions instead on holding the cities.

Historically, the country has been agriculturally self-sufficient, with nearly half of its land considered arable. Most fertile of all is the Orontes Valley and its low-lying *ghaab* ('depression'). Here the Orontes River runs recalcitrantly south-north unlike all the other rivers in the region, earning it its Arabic name, *al-'Asi* ('the Rebel'). Today its name is even more apt, as it flows through contested territory, acting as a fault-line between mainly Sunni rebel villages on the east bank and regime-supporting 'Alawi villages on the west bank.

Labour, too, has been self-sufficient historically, and all the workers in the fields on both sides of the river – digging potatoes or picking cotton – are Syrian men, women and children, whole families have toiled together across generations, unlike the situation in the Arabian Gulf, where imported labourers from the Subcontinent do the lion's share of manual work. Syrians have learnt that the state is not worth depending on. The Ministry of Social Affairs and Labour, well known as a front for the security services, has the smallest budget of any ministry and had no computers until 2003. Its main function has been to create inertia and make life difficult for NGOs. Syrians depend instead on each other, making the extended family a very strong and tightly-knit network. This self-sufficiency is a godsend – without it the country would be starving by now, thanks to US and EU-imposed import sanctions.

Yet while Syria may feel itself culturally superior to the Gulf states that are heavily dependent on foreign skills, it is in desperate need of proper policies on environmental issues. Without them, what hope will there be for the future? Especially vulnerable to climate change and drought, Syria is already listed as one of ten countries 'at extreme risk' of future water shortage. Foreign studies have recorded over 2,500 animal species and over 3,700 plant species within Syria, but none are protected. Syria lags a good 15 years behind its neighbour Turkey on environmental issues, with just two nature reserves compared to Turkey's 57, neither of which allows public access without cumbersome bureaucratic processes.

I once heard a depressing story about Jaboul, 35 kilometres southeast of Aleppo, where an enterprising group of young Syrians concerned for their country's future wildlife found sponsorship some years ago from the Swiss to convert an Ottoman caravanserai into an eco-lodge. Located on the edge of what is widely recognised as the

Middle East's largest wetland for migrating birds, the caravanserai, originally built to gather salt, was to be converted into a boutique hotel for bird-watchers, with escorted trips on solar-powered boats by qualified rangers.

The Governor of Aleppo dragged his feet in giving the necessary permissions, and the Swiss, tired of being told it would be granted *bukra, bukra, in sha Allah*, pulled out, their sense of time-keeping deeply offended. Maybe they were not sufficiently *au fait* with the system. The young group despaired, not only because of the lack of money, but also because of the local attitudes. Hunters see the birds as 'bounty from God' and feel they have every right to shoot as many as possible, for sport and for food. 'The birds come in, but they do not always go out,' Khalid, one of the young enthusiasts told me woefully. 'If we try to put in a police post to control the shooting, the police will just take bribes from the hunters who will shoot them anyway. The education and vision is lacking.'

The ruling Ba'ath Party, in power since the early 1960s, has long stifled initiative, creating *wasta* instead, a system of corrupt patronage where only the well-connected can break through the bureaucratic barriers. Undaunted by the odds against success, Khalid produced, along with seven Syrian experts, the country's first ever guidebook to Syrian birds, and was trying, when the uprising broke out, to distribute copies to schools and universities. Maybe the bird population will be a rare beneficiary of the revolution as men find other targets to shoot at. The hide so carefully built by Jaboul's pioneer project, the Conservation of Biodiversity through Eco-Tourism, is now a rebel hideout. Maybe Khalid's vision will be revived in the future by the next generation, since Khalid himself has, thanks to the revolution, now been forced to close down his tour operator company, pay off his staff and move to Jordan in order to find work in someone else's company to feed his family. He was one of the lucky ones who left Syria in the early days, while work abroad could still be found.

Meanwhile, my own vision – to buy and restore a courtyard house – was undiminished, but I was not yet sure whether to confide in Ramzi about my idea. Perhaps he had been appointed by the authorities to keep an eye on me as a suspicious foreigner. Who knows what I might be secretly doing?

In Hama, without telling Ramzi, I had walked out alone on the streets of the city after dinner as I had planned. No one had given me a second glance. In the morning he told me the hotel where we were staying had been built on the flattened rubble of the aftermath of the Hama uprising, accounting for the hillock which gave it such a good view. He escorted me at a leisurely pace across the Orontes River, explaining how there were waterwheel doctors who could diagnose any waterwheel ailments by listening to their moanings. He led me along the same alleys I had walked along nearly 30 years earlier, into the renovated areas of Hama's Old City. He pointed out the stone walls that had been rebuilt after 1982. In the Azem Palace, now, as then, a museum, we chatted with a group of young European researchers who were working on the restoration of the wooden panel work upstairs. It had been badly charred, they explained, by the bombardments of 1982, taking several direct hits, and the funding for repairs had taken years to organise. Ramzi spoke openly, answering my questions as fully as he could. He did not appear to have had instructions not to talk about it. On the contrary, he seemed pleased someone was taking an interest.

We were not to know that when my guidebook was published in London a year later it would fail the censor in Syria for talking of the 10,000–25,000 lives brutally lost. 'You can mention the uprising,' said my contact at the Information Ministry, 'but you cannot call it brutal and you cannot mention the casualty figures. They killed them gently, remember.' He smiled awkwardly. We were also not to know that seven years later, further massacres would be committed in Hama. Violence is the default setting of the Assad regime.

At Apamea, Syria's largest classical site, it was the same. We strolled along the full length of its Grand Colonnade, and Ramzi explained how the 400 columns we could see now were just a third of what had lined the avenue when Antony and Cleopatra had visited. He ignored the local villagers who kept arriving on mopeds, surreptitiously pulling out Roman coins and artefacts from their pockets. 'These things are all fakes,' he said, casually waving his hand to dismiss the touts. 'Pay no attention.' Again, we were not to know that the Roman mosaics we had admired in Apamea's museum, a converted caravanserai below the site, would be taken by looters, that armed gangs with bulldozers would carry out illegal 'excavations' and that future touts might be selling the real thing.

It was at al-Bara that I first began to realise that my fears about Ramzi were unfounded. Peopled in past centuries by Christian farmers, al-Bara was the largest of the so-called 'Dead Cities': Byzantine ghost towns of which Syria boasts over 700, built of the local limestone. Today these ruins sprawl over the mountains of Idlib Governorate, the scene of so many massacres and battles between the regime and the local opposition. The nearby town of Kafr Nabl, one of the centres of resistance sometimes called 'the conscience of the revolution', became famous for the defiant humour of its protest banners, slogans like: 'Our Dead are calling for the fall of the regime', signed by the cemeteries, and 'Dear defectors, the Syrian Revolution is in Syria, not in Turkey.'

Village elders have ruled communities like these for months now, arbitrating in local disputes, free of regime interference. They have no weapons, so are not actively fighting, but they support the rebels in other ways, offering them refuge and medical help. They are mainly farmers, living off their olive groves and tobacco crops. Northwest of Aleppo many villages are Druze, on good terms with neighbouring Sunni villages, and their village elders are determined to keep it that way: 'The regime wishes to divide the Syrian people, but we will not fall into the trap.' They can still tell jokes, like the one about the man who comes home with a live chicken for dinner. His wife tells him they don't have a knife to kill it or gas to cook it. The chicken clucks 'Long live Bashar!'

In Byzantine times these villages would have been entirely Christian, their churches important precursors to the Romanesque and Gothic cathedrals of Europe. The 5th century church of Qalb Lozeh, with its elaborately carved entrance arch flanked by square twin towers, is a miniature version of French cathedrals like Chartres and Rouen, the style evidently taken back by the 12th century Frankish crusaders. Sir Christopher Wren, after carrying out extensive research, even declared that the style should have been called not Gothic but 'Saracen' to acknowledge its Middle Eastern origins.

The earlier Christian residents who worshipped in churches like Qalb Lozeh grew wealthy on their wine and olive harvests. Then their trade routes shifted, destroyed by 7th century wars between the Byzantines and the Arabs, leaving them without a market. In the space of one generation, they were forced to move to the coast, crossing the mountains and finding new outlets for their produce. War's commercial fallout had changed the local population's fortunes in unforeseen ways, and not for the last time. The Ministry of Tourism, in a flash of inspiration, decided to rename the Dead Cites in 2008, prophetically as it turns out, as 'The Forgotten Cities'. My own preference was for 'The Cities of the Dead', as valid now as it was then.

Al-Bara is the largest and most extensive of the Dead Cities, its ruins spread across an area of more than six square kilometres. In the heart of the rebellious Idlib province, it has been the frequent target of regime air raids during the revolution. The village today has about 15,000 inhabitants, but the original population in Byzantine times was estimated to have been 5,000, and among the heavily forested hills and valleys beside the modern town, the remains of five churches and three monasteries were identified by flamboyant 19th-century European travellers like the French Marquis de Vogüé. British adventurer Gertrude Bell also visited with her entourage in the early 1900s on horseback, as part of her reconnaissance of the Syrian countryside, spending two days here in a kind of mystical trance. In her book *The Desert and the Sown* she writes:

> It is like the dream city which children create for themselves to dwell in between bedtime and sleeping, building palace after palace down the shining ways of the imagination, and no words can give the charm of it, nor the magic of the Syrian spring.

Her dreams, alas, were not to last, and she committed suicide some 20 years later in Baghdad, alone, disheartened and disillusioned. As a child I too had fantasised about beautiful palaces in faraway lands. I hoped my dreams would not end like hers.

As we wandered, poking around in the undergrowth in search of hidden buildings, we stumbled upon a large two-storey stone edifice that had a label, 'Deir Sobat, 6th C'. Behind me, Ramzi began reading aloud the Arabic translation of Gertrude Bell's reverie in his deep, considered voice. It was a fine moment, the more powerful for its unexpectedness. I said nothing, but after he had finished, we started looking more closely at this building, whose name, including the word *Deir*, suggested that it was a monastery. We tried to reconstruct its interior as we walked about the rooms, imagining balconies and the courtyards before us. It seemed to us unlikely to be a monastery. It was not isolated enough.

This, after all, was the era when the fashion in this region was for stylites, monks who spent their lives alone, perched on top of pillars, to escape the trivia of life on the ground. St Simeon Stylites the Elder had started the trend the century before, spending 36 years atop a pillar, trying to get away from people. Instead, people flocked to see him and ask for words of wisdom. He attempted to rise above it all, making his pillar higher and higher. It had begun just three metres high, then he raised it to six metres, then eleven metres and finally eighteen metres, complete with railings around the top to stop him falling off in his sleep. St Simeon's Basilica was, until the uprising began, the most visited site in the Dead Cities, just half an hour's drive northeast of Aleppo. The last time I had been there a Moroccan lady tourist was sporting a baseball cap emblazoned 'I love Bashar'.

The Bishop of Cyrrhus, a gentleman called Theodoret, witnessed Simeon's extraordinary practices with his own eyes and wrote an account of them, also detailing how Simeon's disciples would bring him food once a week on a ladder. In Hama's museum a 5th century mosaic, contemporary with Simeon, shows a faithful disciple passing him up a basket full of provisions from a precarious ladder set up against the pillar. This museum has now also been looted, so who knows whether the mosaic is still there? When Simeon died in 459, aged 69, the Byzantine emperor ordered his body to be carried off by an escort of 600 troops to Antioch, from where it was later transported to Constantinople.

Across the fields we came next upon the village wine press, built from the same beautiful golden stone as Deir Sobat. Maybe the wealthy landowner had owned the village vineyards. Despite being heavily choked with brambles and in ruins, there was still a legible inscription in Greek carved above a small opening at ground level, through which the harvested grapes would have been pushed: 'This nectar that you see – gift of Bacchus – is the fruit of the vines fed by warm sunshine.' It could have come straight off the label of some Californian Chardonnay. I said as much to Ramzi, and we talked about the Christians' very different attitude to alcohol. I asked him if he, as a Muslim, drank, and he said he did not, but not out of any religious belief in its evils. Indeed, as he explained and as I remembered from my own studies of the Quran when an Arabic undergraduate, the Muslim holy book at no point explicitly bans alcohol for Muslims. However it does say that like gambling (*maysir*), alcohol 'has advantages and disadvantages, but the disadvantages are greater.' The word used in the Quran is *khamr*, the classical Arabic word for wine, not *al-kuhoul*, the origin of our word alcohol. Public drunkenness is virtually unknown, not just in Syria, but across the Muslim world.

Beyond the wine press, crossing another field, Ramzi mentioned that we were walking through a graveyard. I had not noticed. It was an area of simple stones, at first glance just randomly scattered, but on closer inspection laid out in a particular pattern. He explained how in Muslim cemeteries the stones marked the head and the feet of the buried body. Close by was a huge stone pyramid tomb, part of the ruins of Byzantine Al-Bara, with an elaborate carved frieze of acanthus leaves. It contained five massive richly decorated sarcophagi, a family tomb for family members only. The contrast was striking, and Ramzi and I wondered why Christianity attached such importance to the burial place, while Islamic graves were marked in the most perfunctory of manners. Was Islam's outlook on life and death so very different?

'Islam is a practical religion,' I recalled my Arabic professor telling me, 'No ceremony is attached to death.' Ramzi agreed. 'The value system is not the same,' he told me, 'A life is judged by what is left behind of lasting value: a good son, a worthy book, charitable works.' It was true. In Islam wealth was only to be sanctioned if a wealthy man shared his wealth with the poor, something I had often noticed as a common motivator among Muslim businessmen. Again, it seemed to me that the Gulf Arabs had gone astray here. Even Ottoman sultans did not live in massive castles like European kings, but in more modest low-rise buildings behind high walls. A person's material wealth was not something to be flaunted – I thought again, with a twinge of longing, about the simple doors facing onto the streets and alleys of Old Damascus, that might lead into a palace or a hovel. Apart from *bait* there are other words in Arabic that can convey fancier dwellings, for example *dar*, which means 'residence', or *qasr*, which means 'palace', but they choose not to use them for a place that is a home. Those words are reserved for more formal official buildings, often with municipal functions. I found something very comforting about this value system, so simple and straightforward. Life was seen merely as a passage, a preparation for the next life, where the reward would be yours in heaven:

> Everyone shall taste death, and you shall be paid your full recompense on the Day of Judgement. He who is kept away from the Fire and is admitted to Paradise has indeed attained felicity. The life of this world is but illusory enjoyment.' (Quran 3:186)

The Quran stipulates that a body must be buried within 24 hours; washed, wrapped in a white shroud and put in a simple grave. No dressing up of the body in finery, no fancy coffin in limed oak or burnished walnut, no costly tombstone. Former Archbishop of Canterbury Rowan Williams, advocate of 'green funerals', would certainly approve. Extravagant banquets and lavish funerals are considered un-Islamic, false vanity and a waste of money that could be better deployed elsewhere. Grief is not prolonged, and the mourning period is often just three days. According to Islamic tradition, the Prophet Muhammad said, when his own son died: 'The eyes shed tears and the heart is grieved, but we will not say anything except that which pleases our Lord.'

Now, after thousands of funerals all over the country, burying the casualties of war, some Syrians have found themselves able not just to accept but to celebrate death rather than mourn it. Syrian state TV covered endless formal funerals of military personnel and police, calling them 'martyrs killed in the line of duty', while the funerals of activists were often highly provisional affairs constrained by the presence of security forces. The funeral of the Christian activist and filmmaker Bassel Shihade, killed with three others by a regime shelling in Homs, was filmed on YouTube. 'He was buried in a Muslim way, as they didn't know how to mourn him in a Christian way,' commented a Syrian Jesuit monk. 'It is a great symbol of the unity that young people like Bassel were calling for.' One young man blogged: 'Today I am prouder of my brother than ever. I even envy him. He was only 22 and killed in a protest. Even my mum is proud. When she heard the news she trilled loudly.' The dead are carried by male relations and friends as high as possible on the way to the grave. If they were killed protesting or fighting, they are often accompanied by chants of 'the revolution, freedom and the coming victory' and 'winning a place in Paradise.' Acceptance of death, no matter how it comes about, seems somehow to be easier for a Muslim than a Christian and I wanted to understand why.

Cremation is not permitted in Islam. It is regarded as *haram*, 'forbidden', in the religious sense, since the Quran prohibits the use of fire on Allah's creation. The belief is that we do not know for sure that the body feels nothing after the soul has left it, and the *Shar'ia*, the Islamic Law, with this in mind, stipulates that the body should be washed gently, not roughly, and in lukewarm, not hot or cold, water before burial. The extreme desperation of youths in the Islamic world who set themselves on fire in protest – like Bou Azizi in Tunisia whose self-immolation sparked the Arab Spring – should be understood against this background. There is nothing worse they could do to themselves – it is the ultimate despair.

We visited many of the Dead Cities, Ramzi and I, and had many such discussions. At Kharrab Shams, a wonderfully isolated ruin in rolling hills northwest of Aleppo, rarely visited and far away from any other habitation, we sat on column drums gazing up at the elegant 4th-century stone church, its graceful five-arched nave topped by ten windows in a near perfect state of preservation. An oak tree grew out from the centre of the stone altar to complete the picture of a bucolic idyll.

'A place like this,' said Ramzi reflectively, 'would offer a life of perfect contemplation. Who could not be happy in such a place? Look, we have everything anyone could ever want or need: the beauty of nature, the beauty of architecture. We could found a community here, bring it back to life, and be finished with all the tiring constraints of practical life. Here the spirit could be free, free to roam and soar, away from pettiness and *iz'aj*.' The Arabic word *iz'aj* conveys everything that is sent to try us, every form of annoyance and irritation. The root, *zain-'ain-jeem,* is used to conjure up all things that pester, molest, harass and upset; yes, freedom from *iz'aj* is indeed worth striving for.

It was at that moment, in that place, that I decided I could trust Ramzi with my vision, and, hesitatingly at first, I began to tell him about my scheme to buy and restore a courtyard house in Damascus' Old City. As I spoke, explaining about Bassim and Bait Siba'i and the huge map on the wall and the numbers of derelict, neglected houses that the government could not afford to save, I got more and more carried away. Suddenly I stopped, realising what it must have sounded like: the ravings of a fool, and what was more, a rich fool. What if Ramzi now saw me as a wealthy foreigner, with vast resources of cash, coming to exploit his country and profit from its distressing poverty?

I need not have worried. Ramzi's expression conveyed that he too found the idea immensely appealing: 'If you could do such a thing,' he said, 'you would be saving a part of Syria's national and cultural heritage. It would be a worthy and wonderful thing and we would be truly grateful to you always.'

From time to time, over the remainder of the research trip, we talked further about the idea. He thought he remembered seeing a private advertisement for the sale of a house in the Old City in one of the Arabic dailies, but he could not remember the price. There were of course, he explained, no estate agents as such. Any notion of a smart office with lovely photos of old houses in the window, billed as 'investment potential' or 'with scope for improvement' were to be put well out of mind. No such thing existed. Looking for property was a word-of-mouth thing. You asked around until you found someone who was selling, or who was thinking of selling or who knew someone who might be persuaded to sell. Clearly it was going to be a fairly hit or miss process. There was no way of getting an overview of what might be on the market, no means of knowing when everything had been seen, and no way of comparing prices except through sheer grind and diligence, trial and error, with no agents' particulars, no survey reports. The notion was becoming crazier by the moment, yet my zeal was undiminished.

There was another factor that affected house-buying, Ramzi told me. Since 2003 large numbers of Iraqis, displaced from their own country by the American-led invasion to topple Saddam Hussein – 2.5 million of them at the peak around 2006–7– had poured across the border into neighbouring Syria. Surrounded by countries in conflict, Syria has a long tradition of taking in refugees. As well as overcrowding in schools and the extra strain on Syria's infrastructure, there was also a knock-on effect on house prices, which were pushed artificially high by the increased demand. Now of course, it is Syrians who are pouring over the borders into Lebanon, Jordan and Turkey – the same number by early 2014 according to UNHCR figures, 2.5 million refugees, half of whom are children, are helplessly distorting labour markets and house prices in their neighbours' countries. Another 9.5 million are estimated by UN agencies to be displaced inside Syria, meaning that a staggering 50 per cent of the population has already been displaced, a number that is still rising.

The norm in Syrian society before the 2003 US-led invasion of Iraq had been for young men to move out into their own home when they married, but suddenly, because of the Iraqi refugee-generated spike in the market, many young men could no longer afford to marry. The result was that many men continued to live at home with their parents until well into their forties. Ramzi, it transpired, was one of them. Still unmarried at 45, a not unusual state of affairs in Syria, his case was further complicated by the fact that his father, a policeman, had died some years ago, and so he, as the eldest son, had become head of the household, with a duty to look after his mother and his sisters. Of these, only one was married and had left home to live with her husband. The other two were both teachers, financially independent, and both had taken a decision not to marry, preferring, Ramzi explained to me, to have the security, stability and freedom that went with living at home to the loss of freedom, extra work and servitude that acquiring a husband would inevitably entail. Neither of them, he said, had yet had an offer from a man they felt would make those sacrifices worthwhile. A further problem was the dearth of young men in gainful employment who could afford to marry. So his mother continued to cook for them and run the house, just as she had always done. She felt useful, they felt looked-after. It was a perfect arrangement and everyone seemed content with it.

The economic situation in the country was dire even then, well before the revolution. Sixty per cent of the population was under 25, and unemployment was well into double figures. Yet population growth in 2010 was already far too high at 2.45 per cent, six times higher than that of the European Union, building up huge problems for future youth unemployment. Almost a third of the population was thought to live below the poverty line, but autocratic regimes are good at keeping their populations under control, largely through fear. It was well known what happened to people who openly criticised the regime or the president; the fateful knock on the door in the middle of the night by the hated *mukhabarat*.

At least Ramzi and his family had avoided having to marry their first cousins, a tradition common across the Middle East as a means of keeping money and property within the family. In Syria it accounts for up to a third of all marriages, with the ensuing birth defects and mental health issues often denied and unacknowledged in rural areas. Statistics such as these are not unusual in the region. The figures for Egypt, Jordan, Tunisia, Algeria, Yemen and Morocco are not much better – often worse in fact.

We discussed many such issues, Ramzi and I, and over the course of this, our first of many trips round northern Syria, I experienced my first glimpses into the sheer overwhelming complexity of the country. Nothing was as it seemed. President Bashar al-Assad's wife Asma, I learnt, was actively campaigning countrywide against the genetic dangers of first-cousin marriage. At Palmyra I saw both the notorious Tadmur prison and the Al-Talila Nature Reserve, 35 kilometres beyond Palmyra on the road to Deir Ez-Zour. Visiting the former was out of the question, but the latter was within bounds.

Financed jointly by the Syrian Ministry of Agriculture, the Syrian Food and Agriculture Organisation and the Italian government, Al-Talila was the first nature reserve in Syria, opened in 1992, the state's embryonic attempt to reintroduce and breed the gazelle and oryx that had once been native to the Syrian *badia* or steppeland, but had been hunted to extinction. Excellent display panels hung inside attractive wooden chalets, explaining in Arabic, English and Italian the ethos and aims of the reserve. A solitary employee struggled to keep the cobwebs at bay, and the place was gradually falling into a sorry state of disrepair. No one came; visitors were deterred by the remote location and the bureaucracy of obtaining a permit. Money for maintenance had not been factored in to the original project.

Once the revolution broke out, the reserve and its wooden chalets, perceived as a legitimate 'regime' target, were attacked and looted by opposition rebels, who saw the animals as fair game. In the battle between starvation and conservation there is not much of a contest. Barbecued oryx and gazelle were eaten in the desert. The few remaining animals were taken for protection by the wardens to offices in Palmyra where they were kept in such terrible conditions that most died anyway.

As my exhaustive research tour neared its close, Redwan the driver was struck down by a bout of dysentery. Ramzi shrugged his shoulders and said he would drive instead. Never once had he criticised Redwan's often erratic driving or made any attempt to take over, but when he heaved his large frame into the driver's seat, I immediately felt at ease. He drove with exactly the same calm confidence as was mirrored in his behaviour.

By the end of the trip, I knew I had found in Ramzi a friend I could trust on any level. He for his part must have felt the same, for when I turned to say goodbye at the departure gate, he was crying.

4

Nobody's Poodle

Destiny caresses the few and molests the many.

Turkish proverb

Touching down on the tarmac at Damascus International Airport a month later I would be lying if I said I felt no anxiety. Derision and disbelief had been the overwhelming reactions in England when I explained why I was returning to Syria so soon. Only my mother understood it was an act of faith – faith in human nature, faith in a dream. Isolated and shunned by the West, receiving no US aid (unlike its neighbours Egypt and Jordan who were well rewarded for their separate peace deals with Israel), American and EU sanctions biting, its oil scheduled to run out by 2015 and the population predicted to double by 2050, the country was even then, in April 2005, in deep trouble.

But I was an optimist and had been doing my homework. Yes, undoubtedly Syria was an autocratic regime, but maybe the time was finally right for it to begin to emerge from its shadowy past, to step into the international arena and open up to the world. The young blue-eyed hope, President Bashar al-Assad, formerly head of the Syrian Computer Society, was highly computer literate and was gradually allowing internet cafes to open up. A good English-speaker who had done 18 months of his ophthalmology training in London, he would surely revolutionise Syria's future. He had come to power in 2000, groomed for the presidency, on the death of his canny and pragmatic father, Hafez al-Assad, the first person ever from the Alawi sect to rule Syria.

'To understand the psychology of the Assad regime,' Ramzi explained to me in the early days of the revolution, 'you have to understand the Alawi mentality, with its deep-seated persecution complex.' I wanted very much to understand. I listened as Ramzi told me how Alawis had been subjected to centuries of vilification as heretics by their Sunni Ottoman masters. I knew of course that Alawis form Syria's largest religious minority. No one knows for sure, but some estimates put their numbers far higher than the official 12 per cent, at closer to 20 per cent of the population. They are thought to be the descendants of the indigenous inhabitants of that region from the time of Alexander the Great. In the centuries that followed, the Alawis, remote in their mountain communities, clung to their own highly secretive, syncretistic pre-Islamic religion, which incorporates elements of Islam, Christianity and Zoroastrianism. To avoid persecution from orthodox Sunni Muslims they often practised *taqiyya*, literally 'dissimulation', where they concealed their Alawi identity – the perfect qualification, as Ramzi laughed, for membership of the secret services. I was surprised to learn from Ramzi that Alawis drink alcohol and celebrate Christmas, Easter and Epiphany, but that after hundreds of years of Shi'a Isma'ili influence, they had moved closer to Islam, worshipping a divine triad of Ali, Muhammad and Salman the Persian. I was even more surprised to learn that they do not use mosques, and do not observe the prayer times or Ramadan. When Bashar is filmed attending special prayers in mosques at religious festivals like the end of Ramadan, it is a carefully constructed photo opportunity designed to make him appear to be a 'normal' Muslim. 'If you watch him closely,' said Ramzi, 'he is not even sure of the right words and movements, but takes his cue from the religious leaders on either side.'

No wonder many consider Alawis barely Muslim. On one occasion, when I had entered an Alawi home, I had even assumed my hosts were Christian, from the pictures of the Virgin Mary on the walls and the wine that was served.

Ramzi told me how Hafez al-Assad had grown up resenting the privileged and arrogant land-owning families of the ruling class. 'Little did he know,' I said, 'how he and his own children would go on to become the ruling class and be just as hated.' One of eleven children, Hafez had been born into poverty, but through diligence and natural ability he became the first person from his village to win a place at secondary school. His own father, though poor, was a respected figure in the village, known for his early resistance to the French under the Mandate. His grandfather before him had resisted the Ottomans, refusing to pay taxes, and had been such a giant personality, physically large and strong to boot, that he was given the nickname *Al-Wahhish,* the 'Wild Beast', which became the family surname until Hafez's father later changed it to *Al-Assad,* meaning the Lion. Resistance, the *leitmotiv* of Hafez's foreign policy, must have been deeply embedded in the family DNA.

As Ramzi explained the story of Hafez's rise to power, I was repeatedly struck by the many ironies of Syrian history. Young Hafez, it turned out, had wanted to train as a doctor after school, but his father hadn't been able to afford the fees. How different things might have been if the only ladder for him to ascend had not been the Homs Military Academy. There, and in Russia, he trained as an Air Force pilot, winning many awards and distinctions along the way, and learning how to manipulate the ruling Arab Nationalist Ba'ath Party apparatus to further his own ends. Shrewd and ambitious, he rose to become head of the Air Force, filling posts around him with trusted Alawi colleagues and a smattering of Sunnis who looked to him for patronage. His methodology complied perfectly with the Ba'ath Party ideology; as early as 1966 a secret internal publication of the Syrian Regional Command of the Ba'ath Party read: 'O Comrades ... the nature of the independence struggle, and the fact that clear-cut class distinctions did not exist in our society, opened the possibility for a group of sons of farmers, labourers and people with small incomes to penetrate into the Military Academy in addition to members of important trading and bourgeois families, and later to become the revolutionary core of the Army.'

So here was another irony: even before 1970 the Syrian army was over 40 per cent Alawi, not because they had any idea of taking over the country, but simply because it was a safe profession free from Sunni persecution. Even their own Alawi shaikhs encouraged them to pursue an army career, and unlike the wealthier Sunnis, they did not have the money to buy their sons out of conscription. The foundations of the future Assad regime were taking shape, with its tightly woven fabric of military loyalists, a fabric that would not unravel. The Syrian army would follow orders obediently, unlike the Tunisian and Egyptian armies who rejected their political masters in their respective revolutions.

'I have prepared the country for you for the next twenty years,' Hafez told Bashar, shortly before his death. It was no idle boast, as those who predicted the swift collapse of Bashar's regime learnt to their cost. Hafez had been a visionary, and in his vision he saw Syria as a powerful new force, taking its rightful place as successor to the Ottoman province of 'Greater Syria', a region equating roughly to modern-day Lebanon, Jordan and Israel, and including parts of Turkey and Iraq. Hafez's vision included Syrians being able to swim once more in the Sea of Galilee, a memory he cherished, and in 2000, shortly before his death, he famously reminisced with Bill Clinton how, as a young man before the '67 War, he had admired the girls and enjoyed a barbecue on the shore. Today the shoreline has retreated even further out of reach, the lake level dropping as Israel over-pumps to make the desert bloom.

The Air Force became Hafez's power base, and he created within it a highly efficient security apparatus, specialising in uncompromising torture methods. 'The things they do to them there,' Bassim later told me, 'would make you sick just to hear about. They use electric shock and make them debase each other. They take them to behind the sun.' Not for nothing has the Air Force Intelligence branch always been so feared, and it became one of the first targets of the Free Syrian Army rebels.

Rising to the position of Defence Minister in 1966, Hafez took the presidency in a near bloodless military coup in 1970 and went on to rule Syria with a rod of iron for three decades, at the centre of a colossal personality cult, just like his fellow Ba'athist Saddam Hussein in Iraq, except that Hafez himself lived modestly and did not amass personal wealth. The two men detested each other all their lives.

Image-making is something of an industry in Syria. Wandering round on my research trips, I noticed the omnipresent posters of Bashar, huge pictures hung prominently round Damascus. Even inside the Old City there were special billboards with slogans that changed frequently, with a benevolent Bashar waving or smiling at his subjects, always in a suit, never in military uniform. One week they would read: *Souriyya Allah hamiha,* 'God is Syria's protector', particularly ironic given the regime's relationship with religion. The next week it would be: *Kullna ma'ak,* 'We are all with you', the 'we' referring to the Syrian people, the 'you' referring to Bashar, in an effort to cultivate an 'emperor' style of leadership typical of Arab autocratic regimes. In the revolution *Allah lillibada, Bashar lillqiyada,* 'God is for worship, Bashar is for leadership' became a common rhyming phrase scrawled on walls round the country by regime supporters keen to perpetuate the 'emperor' image.

Emperors have something in common with Ayatollahs, I thought to myself, remembering how Ramzi had told me about Ayatollah Khomeini and Hafez al-Assad's marriage of convenience, presenting a united front against the Sunni mainstream that had dominated the region for so long. After the 1979 Iranian Revolution in which the Shi'a identity was mobilised for the first time in many centuries, Ayatollah Khomeini obligingly issued a *fatwa* (religious edict) declaring the ruling Alawi sect in Syria to be within the fold of Islam. He even declared that it was related to Iran's own Twelver brand of Shi'ism. The Assad regime was duly grateful for this much needed legitimation at a time when it was under pressure from the growing strength of its Sunni Muslim Brotherhood opposition. The Syrian Constitution did after all state that the president had to be a Muslim.

The Iranian government obliged their Alawi partners again in 1982 by not condemning the Assad regime's violent crushing of the Hama Muslim Brotherhood uprising, just as they have refused now to condemn Bashar's equally violent crushing of the current revolution. For them it is just another battle against the supremacy of Sunni Islam, only this time, when it looked as if the regime might lose, they sent in their own militias and Hezbollah ('Party of God') fighters to help.

But for the Assad regime it is nothing to do with religion. It is all about retaining power; annihilation tactics had worked at Hama, so surely they would work again now. Many tactics were replayed and copied: the intense four-week bombardment of Hama in 1982 had been led by Rif'at, Hafez's younger brother, just as Maher, Bashar's younger brother, has been leading the savage 4th Armoured Division; Rif'at, now exiled and living in London's Mayfair, flattened the Old City of Hama with his pink-uniformed special forces, destroying centuries-old buildings, just as Maher has now flattened the Old City of Homs. Both Homs and Hama have great strategic importance as corridors to the coast, making them fiercely contested.

Hafez was unrepentant about the thousands killed in Hama. The Muslim Brotherhood had for years in the run-up to 1982 tried to unseat the regime through targeted political killings, including an assassination attempt on the president himself. 'The insurgents deserved to die a hundred times,' Hafez declared defiantly. The language of the Syrian media at the time echoed his sentiments, writing that the regime forces 'taught the murderers a lesson that snuffed out their breath.'

So Bashar's regime knows how to do violence – it comes naturally and they are well practised. What they struggle with is how to deal with peaceful protests, something for which Hafez's uncompromising rule could not provide a blueprint. No foreign journalists were allowed into the country during the first peaceful stages, to report independently on what was happening. Only the state narrative, broadcast on its own TV channels was allowed, labelling all demonstrators 'terrorists'. But once the protestors started taking up arms to defend themselves, the regime was back on familiar ground, calling them 'armed gangs'. Selected foreign journalists were miraculously granted visas and conducted to hotspots where they could film rebels with guns. Pictures of the government's 'terrorists' were transmitted round the global media. Bashar's regime also know how to do media control. It is the one area in which he outshines his father.

Hoping to glean some understanding of Hafez the man and how he is viewed in Syria today, I had included on my first research trip with Ramzi the Philosopher in February 2005, somewhat to his surprise, a visit to Hafez's tomb in the great leader's home village of Qardaha. Dictator's tombs can be very revealing. Turkey's Atatürk has an entire hill in central Ankara devoted to his mausoleum, an area over one square kilometre, guarded day and night by armed and uniformed soldiers; its immaculately manicured gardens feel like a sacred precinct, lined with monumental Hittite-style stone lions.

To reach Qardaha, nestling at the foot of the Ansariye Mountains, we drove up a specially-built four-lane approach road from the main Lattakia highway to the village. The wooded slopes on either side were liberally sprinkled with fine new villas facing the distant sea across the Mediterranean coastal plain, testimony to the prosperity of the Alawi heartlands, a far cry from their former lot as housemaids and labourers. I wondered even then if there might be a backlash in the future against this new pocket-lining class. The French, during their mandate over the country in the 1920s, had given them a brief taste of power by creating an Alawi enclave, a mini-state around Lattakia, courting them as allies in a divide-and-rule policy to play off the minorities against each other, just as they had done with the Christian Maronites in Lebanon.

As we entered the outskirts of the sprawling village, Ramzi told me that at the time of the funeral, all walls, doors, even tree-trunks lining the approach were painted black. 'Now the paint is all gone,' he explained, 'worn away, and look how the highway is neglected and full of weeds.' Here in Qardaha, Hafez's tomb was unsignposted and even Ramzi had to stop and ask the way. When we found the relatively small and simple precinct, there was no military presence, no security checks – just a handful of suited *mukhabarat* – and almost no visitors. Even in death, it seems, Hafez maintains his austerity.

When Bashar's time comes, another side alcove awaits him in the Qardaha family-mausoleum. The Bishop of Safita, a gentle man with his church inside the keep of a 13th century Templar castle, compared father and son: 'Bashar is a good man,' he told me in October 2012. 'That is why some even want Rif'at back, to be tougher in these tough times. They feel Bashar is too weak. We liked Bashar, we liked the way his wife was active and helped the poor. We never saw Hafez's wife, we never knew her.' It was true: Hafez was a known workaholic. His wife stayed at home, he stayed in the office.

For most, Bashar remains a puzzle. He is good at his *taqiyya*. Plucked untimely from his studies, he had greatness thrust upon him.

After studying medicine at Damascus University in 1988, he went on to Tehran for a four-year ophthalmology course – more Iranian links. Next, he was sent by the army to pursue a postgraduate degree in ophthalmology in London, where he arrived in 1992, training at the Western Eye Hospital. By chance I later met a senior British consultant who remembered him from those days. 'He used to come early to lectures', he recalled, 'then sit at the back and listen carefully. Sometimes, at the end, he would ask a well-considered question. He seemed very polite and wise for a young man.'

However, before he was able to complete his ophthalmology training, his elder brother Basil was killed in a car crash. Bashar had to be rushed back home. Grooming for the presidency had to begin fast, as Hafez was not in the best of health. Bashar was sent to the Homs Military Academy, graduating, according to the official records, as the best tank battalion commander of his class, though some scepticism may be in order – the same accolade was accorded his uncle, Rif'at, but it later emerged that the records had been doctored and he had in reality come 31st out of 37.

Pushed up quickly through the ranks, by 1999 Bashar was a colonel; just in time, as his father died months later. He assumed office in July 2000, was appointed leader of the Ba'ath Party and of the army like his father, and was then elected president with an unnatural 97.2 per cent of the vote, after the law was swiftly changed to lower the minimum age for presidents from 40 to 34, Bashar's age. No other candidates stood.

Bashar had never wanted this role for himself. Indeed, as Hafez's second son, it should never have fallen to him, but Basil's accident determined otherwise. Speeding up the airport road one night in 1994, trying out his latest Mercedes, Basil collided with a roundabout in heavy fog. His mother never appeared in public again. His fleet of racy cars had been famous.

Years later, I heard a radio interview with Basil's erstwhile English tutor, who had challenged him about his ownership of so many cars at the Syrian people's expense. Basil had looked surprised: 'But these are the people's cars', he had explained matter-of-factly. It was how not just Hafez's children but all members of the regime inner circle were known to treat the country – as their private fiefdom. In 2006 the

Azem Palace in Damascus, originally the governor's residence and meant to be a museum open to the public, was shut for four months during the tourist high season. The explanation, so a *mukhabarat* employee within the Ministry of Tourism told me, was that Bashar's father-in-law, Fawaz Akhras, wanted it tailored as a venue for his son's wedding reception, by having the entry access altered and the jasmine plants moved in order to improve the video-filming angles and the view. As for Basil, 'Everyone loved him,' Ramzi told me. 'He was handsome, and very popular with the women.' We saw his grave in a side alcove of the Qardaha mausoleum, maybe even attracting more visitors than his father. His picture, usually portraying him in dark glasses and military uniform, was surprisingly prevalent before the revolution out on street billboards, in public places, in people's offices and homes, usually as part of the stage-managed triple personality cult together with Hafez *pere* and Bashar *fils*, all in profile in a row, displaying their unmistakeable Alawi feature – the flat back of the head, perfect caricature material.

Increasingly though, in today's Syria, it has been Bashar alone who waves at you from the posters about town, before they were largely torn down by protesters, trampled and burnt. The favourite poster just before the revolution was of Bashar in jeans and a t-shirt kneeling down to plant a little pine tree, looking especially tender and caring. I knew it was regime propaganda, but even so, I allowed myself to feel reassured that my house-buying ambitions were not absurd, that all would be well in Syria.

🙞

Disgorging from the plane into the Damascus terminal building that April 2005, as I embarked on my first tentative steps towards house-buying in Syria, I again encountered the regime in action, just like everyone else. But even at that early stage, before all the rewards and punishments that lay ahead, I knew that this was not the real Syria. This was simply the official façade of Ba'athism, whose noble ideals had evaporated after gaining power.

That unfavourable initial impression with which all newcomers had to grapple, that sense of entering a police state, never got better with frequency of exposure, even though by 2011 the airport upgrade was finally completed, years behind schedule, just in time for the revolution. The filthy cracked lino on the floor was replaced and the plywood dividers gave way to proper walls, but the system was as it ever was, unforgiving to new arrivals, with no notices or guidance to help.

First there was the unseemly scrum to get to the tables and fill out the arrival forms, randomly printed on blue, yellow, pink or green cards. Most of the boxes seem irrelevant to non-Muslims, for example Father's name and Mother's name, in order to distinguish between all the Muhammads and Ahmads, but no matter, non-Syrians had to complete these forms before they could then join the queues at the passport control kiosks. Syrians in uniform, I had always been warned, undergo a personality change. Instead of being welcoming and dignified, they are cussed and curt. The queuing is haphazard, with notices above the kiosks saying 'Syrians', 'Other Arabs' and 'Foreigners', inviting people to line up accordingly; a system sometimes observed and sometimes not, for no discernible reason.

The contrast with the Syrian Embassy in London could hardly have been greater, its elegant Belgrave Square premises staffed with polite urbane diplomats trained to be helpful. They had ushered me into their thick pile-carpeted offices, offering tea and Syrian pastries while I waited for my English paperwork to be authenticated and legalised. The system could exude charm when required.

Damascus International Airport is very small, thanks to Syria's isolation in the international community. Only a handful of airlines use it, so usually there is only one flight being processed at any given time. As a result, by the time you emerge from queuing at passport control, your hold luggage is generally offloaded and you can even see it waiting for you in the baggage hall. One final passport check from the plainclothes policemen, one last security scan of your luggage, and you are free, free to enter Syria proper.

This was the system until 2008. The hubbub on emerging into the arrivals hall had always been the same, whatever the time of day or night; you would be assailed from all sides by taxi drivers making a grab for your bags, competing for your fare.

But suddenly it was strangely quiet, no taxi drivers or their beaten-up, yellow taxis anywhere. They were banned from the airport precincts, I was told. Instead, all unsuspecting newcomers not lucky enough to be met by a relation or a tour operator were channelled to the one and only tiny 'Julia Dumna' kiosk immediately outside the airport terminal building, absurdly named after the powerful Syrian wife of the Roman emperor Septimius Severus.

This, I was later told, was one of the many rackets run by one of the president's relations, his cousin Rami Makhlouf, who also controlled the mobile phone network Syriatel, along with 60 per cent of the country's business interests. Rami, still in his early forties, was known to be the most powerful economic figure in Syria, and very few foreign companies were able to do business inside the country without his consent. This kind of nepotism for regime favourites had increased noticeably since the early 2000s, I learnt, much to the anger of the larger Sunni business elite. So Rami was awarded the monopoly on the new airport taxi service and suddenly there was a fixed fare into the city centre, treble what it had been under the old system. Only after coughing up accordingly could you sit in your taxi, speeding down the airport road like Basil, on the half hour drive into the heart of Damascus.

Naturally, once the revolution began in March 2011, Rami Makhlouf was one of the first to be vilified in the banners of protesters. The EU subjected him to a travel ban and had his European assets frozen, a sanction that sounds good but assumes any were actually held in his name. The regime soon afterwards issued a statement saying Rami had decided to devote himself to 'charitable works' and withdraw from business life. As if to prove the point, the Julia Dumna taxi kiosk was well and truly boarded up from then on. Spoof Twitter accounts appeared in his name with tweets like 'We have a refinery in Tartous and it's totally safe, we can do a deal.'

Hopes of a new dawn had been so high when Bashar had first taken over the presidency. Political prisoners were released, media controls were eased and the retirement age of the army was lowered to neutralise a lot of his father's old guard. It was hailed as the 'Damascus Spring'. But after just two months the realities of what he had inherited hit home and the familiar security apparatus reappeared. It was as if he had tried to liberalise too quickly, bringing in reforms that

threatened to disrupt the wealthy elite and their entrenched interests. 'He is still governing under the ghost of his father,' said Ribal
al-Assad, son of the exiled Rif'at. 'Each person in Syria has an interest
in the secret service. He should have declared National Unity as soon
as he took over. He did things bit by bit, with internet cafes and so on.
But it was not enough. There was no real change.'

Superficially things seemed so much better than under his father,
but it was style, not substance. At what turned out to be Bosra's last
Arts Festival in the summer of 2010, Bashar and his beautiful British-
born wife Asma arrived unannounced, and the whole audience spontaneously leapt to their feet in delight, clapping enthusiastically. From
my seat just above them in the Roman theatre, I could see how they
interacted and bantered, totally relaxed with each other. They seemed
genuinely popular, and turning up unexpectedly became a special-
ity of theirs, at concerts, films, restaurants and wherever else, always
rapturously received. Syria's most famous cartoonist Ali Ferzat knew
Bashar personally and used to speak to him directly at the beginning of his presidency. Bashar even encouraged him to set up Syria's
first independent newspaper since the Ba'ath had taken power in
1963, called Al-Domari. It was published for two years then banned.
'By then,' Ali said, 'I was never able to reach Bashar, and when I did
finally get through, he told me to handle my own problems. When
you provoke a wasp into stinging you, he told me, you have to pull it
out yourself.' Ali was beaten up by Bashar's henchmen for drawing a
cartoon of Bashar carrying a stuffed suitcase and hitching a lift with
Gaddafi to escape. 'We are going to break your hands, so that you
can't draw again and dishonour your masters,' they told him. He fled
the country to live in exile.

'Democracy,' Bashar had said in an interview back in the pre-revolution days, 'will be a tool to a better life in Syria, but cannot be rushed
and will take time.' He would probably say the same again today.

Like most foreigners, seduced by the posters and the regime propaganda, I started out prepared to give Bashar the benefit of the doubt.
He had a winning smile and a dry sense of humour. His hobbies were
said to be cycling, photography and keeping up with the latest tech-
nology. I collected a whole series of souvenir fridge magnets showing
him engaged in harmless pastimes: one shows him sitting with Pope

John Paul II pointing out passages in the Quran during the 2001 papal visit to Syria; another shows him cycling in a tracksuit with his eldest son in the baby seat behind him – the 'Baba' figure again. Maybe they will become museum pieces. Bassim had a photo of Bashar's little daughter as his mobile phone screensaver: 'Isn't she beautiful?' he said to me, holding it out for me to see. She was. The image-making had worked.

Curious to find out more about Bashar, I was intrigued to discover he had known great suffering. Quite apart from the shock of his older brother's tragic car crash, which would have catapulted him into an emotional as well as a political maelstrom, there was also the tragic story of his younger brother Majd, who died from a 'chronic disease' aged 43. In the mid-1990s Majd was hospitalised in London, and Bashar, in between his studies, supervised his care and visited him frequently. I wondered if such suffering could have hardened him, making him able to inflict similar suffering now on others.

Of the remaining two sons, the youngest of all, Maher, was at one time considered for the succession after Basil's death, but was rejected as too emotionally unstable. Notoriously violent and unpredictable, Maher is said to enjoy the act of killing. Not for nothing do Syrians now call him the 'Butcher of Deraa'. In 1999 he was rumoured to have shot his brother-in-law, General Assef Shawkat, Head of Military Intelligence, in the stomach during a heated argument. The shot was not fatal, and they appeared to reconcile their differences, possibly in a need to close ranks, since they were both mentioned as suspects in the German policeman Mehlis' report on the assassination of Rafiq Al-Hariri.

In the current revolution Maher has been on the loose again, as head of the feared 4th Armoured Division. Rumours abound that he lost a leg in the July 2012 National Security Headquarters explosion that killed Assef Shawkat, or even that he died in Moscow from his wounds and has been flown back and secretly buried in Qardaha in the family mausoleum. The loyalty of the troops under his command is said to be guaranteed courtesy of their generous share of Syria's relatively modest oil revenues. Like Bashar, he married outside the Alawi clan, to a Sunni woman.

As for Bashar, despite his natural shyness and aversion to the limelight – he used to sweat horribly when giving televised speeches – he appears now to have learnt how to keep it all together, emotionally and politically, and has displayed considerable skill in his tricky balancing act. Making up for his regime's early mishandling of the peaceful demonstrations in Deraa and elsewhere, he has devised many subsequent clever strategies. Under the guise of a general amnesty in spring 2012 for example, he released many Al-Qaeda-affiliated prisoners, conniving to make his own prediction come true, that he was fighting 'sectarianism' and 'terrorism'. Through similar nifty footwork, he turned his chemical weapons attack on his fellow Syrians to his own advantage. By making his regime's cooperation indispensable for the successful implementation of the UN deal to remove the chemical weapons, he has prolonged his rule indefinitely. He controls the timetable and can simply blame the rebels for any delays. Plotting such elaborate double games, he has outmanoeuvred his critics, and still not fallen off his tightrope.

'I am not a puppet,' he declared defiantly, nearly two years into the revolution, 'and the West did not manufacture me in order that I leave to the West or any other country. I am Syrian, I am Syrian-made, and I must live and die in Syria.'

His choice of words was interesting and I even wondered if it was a conscious reference to the Top Goon series on YouTube, 'Diaries of a Little Dictator', where he was being caricatured as a puppet called Beeshu, unthinkable before the revolution.

Puppet or not, Bashar has continued his father's hard line on Israel, something which helps explain his resistance mentality, where he feels Syria has been at war and under attack from outsiders for years. It would clearly have been in the country's economic interest to bow to western pressure, but Syria, for all its corruption and repressive tendencies, has been nothing if not bold in its foreign policy. It has historically stood by the Palestinians, maintaining its principle that Israel must withdraw from all occupied territory, not just the Golan Heights, and for that, at least, it deserves some credit. Syria is nobody's poodle.

5

Into the Unknown

If you wish to squander your money, buy an old house and restore it.

Iraqi proverb

'My dear,' said the elderly lawyer sitting behind his huge desk, waving his hands about beneficently, 'in Syria everything is possible … and everything is impossible.'

'So that means it is possible?' My voice was unable to conceal its emotion. I was consulting a respected lawyer for his independent view.

'My dear, my advice would be, don't do it. It will be a nightmare, full of troubles you cannot imagine.'

His words sealed the matter – that was the moment I resolved to do it, there in his smart office with its filthy windows above a grubby shop near Marjeh Square where the French had strung up Syrian corpses. Whatever challenges might lie ahead, I preferred not to dwell on them. *'Ich habe nie über das Denken gedacht,'* ('I have never thought about thinking') said Goethe, and I knew exactly what he meant. I would take each step as it came, not worrying about the next. No doubt there would be some future price to pay – greater as it turned out, than any I could have imagined – beyond the obvious financial one.

So far I had encountered nothing but immense courtesy and respect, but it also seemed only wise to approach everything with a healthy degree of scepticism. In the quest for the courtyard house of my dreams I was, after all, a walking opportunity for exploitaton, ripe for the picking, and foreign and female to boot. I needed to protect myself.

Apart from Bassim and Ramzi, I did have one further source of help: Marwan. He was young, lithe, energetic, and a born Mr Fix-it. In the 19th century he would without a doubt have been an embassy factotum, knowing everyone's business and all the neighbourhood gossip. His most striking feature was his hair, thick and solid-looking. Years later, when he came to my mother's flat in London for supper, she kept stroking his hair, marvelling at how wonderful it felt. Marwan loved it too, loved the way she so unashamedly touched it just like his own mother would have done when he was a child. He owned a tiny souvenir and craft shop in the heart of Old Damascus. It was tucked in the shadow of the Umayyad Mosque's east wall where a monumental, Roman flight of steps, in one of the city's many casual blending of cultures, still led down to a streetful of shops heralded by the Nawfara Cafe, renowned for its traditional storyteller or *hakawati*.

I was instinctively wary of Marwan. How could he be loyal and trustworthy if he acted for so many people and had his fingers in so many pies? My introduction to him had come through Bassim, so that weighed in his favour. And furthermore, it turned out his uncle was a lawyer, exactly the kind of lawyer I needed, experienced in the vagaries of Syrian house purchases.

So in the course of the next two weeks I viewed about 30 properties, inside and out, arranging a hectic programme for myself, via my three contacts – Ramzi, Bassim and Marwan – determined to see whatever lay within my price range. I had given them all the same upper limit, based on the sum I was prepared to put up front – my entire life savings. I was not interested in entering into complex mortgage arrangements with any of the local private Lebanese banks which were newly on the scene following Bashar's wave of banking reforms. No, it would be an entirely cash-based project, with no dependence on any outside institution.

I was quite certain any such house had to be *intra muros*, 'within the walls'. UNESCO had designated the whole city a World Heritage Site in 1979, in recognition of the fact that many historically significant buildings existed in suburbs outside the walls too, in areas like As-Salihiya and Souk Sarouja. But these held far less appeal for me, surrounded as they were by noisy traffic and busy streets. Within the walls it was far quieter, and many lanes were too narrow to be passable to traffic, so bicycles and horse-drawn carts were the only means of transport. By summer 2013 even those were banned from the Old City, with cyclists given on the spot fines by zealous officials.

On my various viewings I was led off, twisting and turning through a confusing maze, this way and that, past markets and mosques, until I lost all sense of direction. The distances seemed enormous, yet I knew from the maps that the area of the Old City was barely more than three square kilometres. Crammed into this small space were so many alleyways, some of them dead ends, that I felt it was a bit like the human intestine, forced into a compact space, which, if you laid it out in a straight line could be up to an incredible 35 feet long. Surely these alleyways, if you made them into one long street, would be more like 50 kilometres long, and on some days it felt as if I had walked at least 15 kilometres within the walls. Just two main roads, the former *decumanus maximus*, the biblical Street Called Straight that ran east-west, and the *cardo maximus* that ran north-south, carried traffic across the city. The main pedestrian thoroughfare, originally the processional way leading to the Temple of Jupiter, was now the Souk Al-Hamadiya, abuzz with activity: street vendors plying their trade; small children touting stuffed eagles or playing with plastic air balloons that screeched into the cavernous space below the vaulted corrugated iron roof still pock-marked with bullet holes from the 1925 uprising against the French; tea-sellers in Ottoman costumes and fezes; families chattering happily as they emerged from the Bakdash ice-cream parlour, en route to the Umayyad Mosque. The Roman walls were still intact for almost all their six kilometre circumference, with the original Roman masonry clearly visible at the lower levels, and the later strengthening and 11th century rebuilding apparent at the higher levels.

Ramzi had explained to me how today's Arab names for each gate corresponded to the original eight Roman constructions, all but one of which are still extant. 'The Roman names were called after the gods,' he said, 'like Mercury, Mars, Venus and Saturn, but the Arab names are a mix of Muslim and Christian.' So I learnt that Bab Touma, the Gate of St Thomas, was the main entrance into the Christian quarter from the north, and Bab Kissan, the Gate of Saturn, where St Paul was lowered in a basket to escape the Roman soldiers, was the main entrance to the south, while Bab Al-Faradis, the Gate of Paradise, in the northwest, led to the Shi'a quarter and its new Iranian-funded mosque of Sayyida Rouqiyya, grand-daughter of the Prophet Muhammad. No doubt prices would vary from quarter to quarter. Would the Christian quarter, I wondered, turn out to be more expensive than the Muslim quarter, or vice versa?

In my early wanderings round Damascus two poetic concepts from my days as a student of Arabic, deeply buried inside my head for so many years, now made a surprise re-emergence: the two opposites known as *zahir* and *batin*. The *zahir* was the exterior appearance, the surface which was there for all to see. The *batin*, on the other hand, was the interior, the inside, the unseen aspect that could only be sensed or experienced spiritually. The Old City of Damascus was exactly that: a place that presented one aspect to the street and concealed an entirely different aspect on its inner side. So Bait Nizam, an Ottoman palace with three courtyards that had served as the British Consulate in the 19th century, presented to the street nothing but the simplest of doors. One house I viewed stirred great excitement in me when I saw its superb Mamluk entrance portal onto the street. But behind the door there lay no more than a fragment of a house, two simple featureless concrete rooms approached over an empty garden-like space, run-down and squalid, with an open kitchen in a shed and water drawn from a free-standing tap in the yard. The Old City hid its secrets well. It was simply impossible from the outside to know what you would find on venturing in.

This phenomenon summed up the essence of the city for me in many ways, its timeless quality. Each house was a living microcosm of history, made up of many fragments from different periods, the natural result of a city that has survived so much – earthquakes, invasions, being razed to the ground by fire, riots, and now this revolution – yet has remained continuously inhabited, constantly updating and adjusting to the new realities of each day. Whatever the future holds for Damascus, this process will go on. Mark Twain observed the city's power in *The Innocents Abroad:*

> She measures time not by days and months and years, but by the empires she has seen rise and crumble to ruin. She is a type of immortality … Damascus has seen all that ever occurred on earth and still she lives. She has looked upon the dry bones of a thousand empires, and will see the tombs of a thousand more before she dies.

The depth of the city's history is somehow almost tangible, *zahir*, yet always escapes being truly perceived, and is only truly divinable through its secret inner depths, its *batin*.

At each house the people inside would have no idea we were coming. Often they were not even the owners, just the tenants, but somehow on the grapevine it was known that the house might be for sale. It could hardly have been less like a house viewing in the UK. If there were only women at home, I would be allowed in, but any man who was not part of their family would not be permitted inside unless there was also at least one male, adult family member present to protect the womenfolk. No Syrian woman would ever open the door to an unknown man. Such a thing was culturally unacceptable, irrespective of religion – Christian or Muslim.

In the course of my research I found the Ottoman Yearbook of 1900, which listed 16,832 houses in the Old City within the walls. About half of them were still thought to be standing in some state or other. No other city in the eastern Mediterranean from Athens to Cairo had such a grouping of residential houses. It was acknowledged as being in great danger well before the revolution, and in October 2010 the Global Heritage Fund cited Damascus as one of the world's 12 cultural heritage sites most at risk of irreparable loss and destruction. No doubt it is even higher up the danger list now.

Aleppo is the only other city to preserve Ottoman domestic architecture on such a scale, and has received more funding and outside attention than Damascus, with the Germans heavily involved through the German Agency for Technical Cooperation, GTZ, giving grants to local residents to help them restore and maintain their old family homes. Eighteen months into the revolution, many of Aleppo's historic buildings have been badly damaged. The ancient souks were set ablaze by regime forces targeting electricity generators to start a fire. It was a deliberate policy designed to flush out rebels who had been using a Turkish *hammam* in the souk as a base. Even the adjacent Aleppo Umayyad Mosque, built ten years after Damascus's Umayyad Mosque, was damaged internally by Assad's henchmen, to say nothing of the tragic strike on its unique Seljuk minaret; a thousand years of priceless heritage reduced to rubble in seconds by a mortar shell. Its loss from Aleppo's skyline, equivalent to the disappearance of Big Ben from London's skyline, will have pained residents greatly – part of their identity erased forever. Before leaving, the regime soldiers scrawled the same chilling graffiti on the mosque's water dispenser that was starting to appear all over the country. *Al-Assad aw nahriqhu*, 'Assad, or we will burn it', in other words, the stark choice: either you are with Assad or we will destroy you. Aleppo's mighty Mamluk citadel, a regime stronghold, also sustained some damage from rebel attacks. Heritage is secondary to life for both sides.

In the Arabic sources of the mid-16th century, Damascus proper was described as having about 70 quarters. In Damascus, as in Aleppo, these quarters were the size of small villages, and they functioned like self-contained neighbourhoods within the urban whole. Known in Arabic as *harat, mahallat* or *akhtat*, each one was a specific residential quarter with its own local markets and workshops separate from the main big city markets, similar to today's corner shops in cities like London.

I was intrigued by how these quarters had evolved and what made them group together. Might this help explain the way Syrian society worked and shed light on its complexity? According to the early Muslim sources the reasons were nothing whatever to do with class – unlike London, where Chelsea and Knightsbridge are a million miles removed socially from Brixton and Hackney. They held together in homogenous groupings for safety, each keeping their members protected. Each grouping had a reason to bind together, and this solidarity might be ethnic or might be religious. In Aleppo there was a Turcoman quarter outside the walls, a Kurdish quarter and a street of Persians. Jerusalem had Jewish, Christian and Armenian quarters.

Smaller towns might also have quarters for Turks, Bedouins recently sedentarised or small communities of foreign refugees. A shared village or tribal origin was another reason for communities to cluster in one part of the city. In Damascus and Aleppo refugees from Harran in modern Turkey settled in one area together, thereby maintaining their identity. I wondered how, in the full blaze of revolution, future groupings would evolve as refugees fled the dangers of one suburb or city for the relative safety of another and how the social fabric could survive the levels of stress and destruction to which they were now being subjected.

Religious affiliation, I learnt from the historical sources, was often a further reason behind the groupings, as in Damascus with its Christian, Jewish and Muslim quarters. Within these religious divisions there were frequently further divisions based on sectarian affiliation. So, for example, in Damascus the quarter of As-Salihiya on the slopes of Jabal Qasioun was always associated with the Hanbali sect, thanks to the Hanbali mosque built there, and which drew a community of like-minded Hanbalis. Most of the rest of Damascus belonged to the Shafi'i school of Islamic law. Dubbed the 'City of Tolerance', Damascus is unusual in accommodating all four schools of Islamic law, as represented by the four *mihrabs* or 'prayer niches' in the Umayyad Mosque. In such cases the community built up round the leadership of one shaikh, and was nothing to do with their family, ethnicity or tribal origin. Under the current regime Mezzeh 86 is well known as an area occupied exclusively by its loyalist Alawi supporters. If the regime were to fall, I wonder where they would they all go.

In all these permutations the striking fact was that a quarter and its residents were never unified by social class. Within the quarter, the elite, the *'ulema*, ('learned religious scholars'), functionaries, merchants and craftsmen all lived side by side, rich and poor together, linked together by family, tribe, ethnicity, and lastly, religion. I found this a comforting thought in all the talk of sectarian divisions that were predicted to tear Syrian society apart. Ties of trust were far more important than ties of religion or social status.

The properties I viewed illustrated this classlessness very clearly. They ranged from vast decaying palaces that would have taken hundreds of thousands of pounds and most of a lifetime to restore, to tiny hovels. The tiniest hovel of all had been in the Christian quarter not far from the Umayyad Mosque, a scrappy three rooms, affordable but overpriced and with no architectural features remaining, nothing to recommend it at all in fact – nothing worth saving. At the other end of the scale, but just round the corner from the tiny hovel, I had looked at an enormous twenty-five room rambling place set round one courtyard. The stairs to the upper floor were beyond dangerous, whole sections missing, yet Bassim had run lightly up and I had followed. In the upper rooms beams dangled like matchsticks from the roof and we picked our way through wobbly floorboards. The interior walls bore traces of 19th century frescoes, and careful removal of the modern concrete that had been slapped onto the exterior walls facing into the courtyard would almost certainly have revealed earlier layers, maybe with elaborate coloured stone pastework. At its vast asking price, it would have to wait for a rich Gulf investor to turn it into a boutique hotel.

One house contained a family of tenants who had lived there for the last 25 years at a low rent as the actual owner no longer needed it. But owner and tenants were on good terms, and had agreed to split the proceeds of the sale of the house 50:50. Under Syrian law a tenant who has lived somewhere that long has the equivalent of squatter's rights, so without an incentive of this sort, the tenant would simply stay put. It was therefore vital that the owner and tenant got on well, so that they could reach a mutually beneficial agreement with a sale. The agreement was informal, and in the UK's legal world such an arrangement would have been unthinkable, based as it was on nothing more than total trust between the two parties.

When I reached the stage where I was being shown the same places by my three different contacts, I knew I had reached saturation point – I had seen everything on the market within my price range.

My decision was easy, as there was a clear front runner. It was the only one with that rare thing, a complete courtyard. Even its name felt right – Bait Baroudi, literally the 'House of the Gunpowder Seller'. The Baroudis were a well-respected family of intellectuals and philanthropists, notably including the 20th century patron of the arts Fakhri Al-Baroudi, who had also been a key early nationalist politician devoted to Syria's independence. He had even written a famous patriotic song called 'The land of Arabs is my homeland', with the poignantly idealistic words:

For no border separates us
And no religion divides us.

Especially keen to foster youth education, he had set up several youth movements at his own expense, including the paramilitary Iron Shirts, so-named after the grey colour of their uniforms. Described, despite his known penchant for young boys, as the city's single most popular figure from the 1940s–1960s, he was elected four times to Parliament representing Damascus. My Bait Baroudi had belonged to his extended family rather than to Fakhri himself – there are several Bait Baroudis in Damascus – but I was nonetheless delighted with most of these associations. Even when I later learnt that he had died bankrupt in Lebanon in 1966, my enthusiasm was undiminished.

So now all that remained was to check whether or not its title deed was 'clean'. A 'clean' title was one where no more than four people could lay claim to it. Anything more than that, the lawyer explained, would be a legal nightmare, especially a title where many different relations were involved, following an inheritance dispute. Islamic law is highly complex and proscriptive on such matters, and in cases of family law for Muslims (and Christians, unless they are Catholics), Syria follows the *Shar'ia* Islamic law as defined in the Quran, where a male relation inherits twice the share of a female relation. These same inheritance laws were the reason why so many houses in the Old City had been carved up, their courtyards fragmented as each heir took his or her piece.

Throughout my viewings never once had the owners talked about a different price when chatting in Arabic. It was a surprising insight into their honest dealings. Never once had the price moved up because I was a foreigner, despite all my suspicions.

Later, during that same fortnight of viewings, Marwan introduced me to his lawyer uncle Rashid, who was the expert, he assured me, in getting the *tabou*, as it was called, the old Ottoman Turkish word that everyone still used for their title deed. No foreigners, and indeed surprisingly few Syrians ever succeeded in getting this vital document as proof of title to their house. It was, inevitably, a complicated business, with many stages. Syrian law combines the worst of Ottoman and French law. His last case had taken 16 months to complete, but he assured me that this time it should be less than a year. He was an elegantly dressed man of about 50, pretty much the only Syrian I had encountered who always wore a suit and tie; and smart, black leather shoes. I found his accent a little tricky to understand, as he came from Deir Ez-Zour near the Iraqi border, but he had a competent air about him, and I liked him straight away.

We agreed during that first meeting that if I went ahead with any purchase, I would pay him up front a lump sum that I knew was large by Syrian standards, but which I judged to be worth it if he could succeed in getting the legal rigmarole completed. After all, it turned out there were no other costs, no stamp duty or VAT. Compared to English fees it seemed perfectly reasonable. He explained that I would need to provide various pieces of documentation in the event of a purchase, including my birth certificate, marriage certificate and children's birth certificates, all of which had to be authenticated and legalised in the country of issue. The more peculiar requirement was a letter confirming that a Syrian was entitled to buy property in England, as Syrian law demanded reciprocity. I explained to Rashid that anyone from any nationality is entitled to buy property in England, so it would be an entirely meaningless document. In Syria, he assured me, it was the vital first step.

6

The Dead Auntie

For every bean full of weevils, God supplies a blind grocer.

Arab proverb

I should perhaps make clear that at no point was being a woman a problem – quite the reverse. Of course as a foreign woman I was not subject to the same traditional constraints as Arab women, but even so, the role and position of women in Arab societies is much misunderstood in the West, coloured as it is by regular horror stories emerging from Saudi Arabia and the Gulf.

But in Syria, during my research trips, I was repeatedly struck by how prominent women were in all walks of life. Female labour force rates are the highest in the region and Syria was the first Arab country to give women the vote in 1949. Over half of all university students are female. In 2006 Bashar appointed a female vice-president and even said publicly that he felt women to be more efficient and less corrupt than men. Women hold 12 per cent of seats in Parliament and in ministerial posts and are also well-represented at high levels in the law, in education, in banks – my future bank manager was to be a woman – in hospitals, in journalism and in the arts. At a performance of the Syrian National Orchestra I was amazed at how many women there were, all playing superbly, all dressed just as they would have been in the London Philharmonic. One of them, a violinist, turned out to be Bassim's former girlfriend. Clearly the tradition is a long one, for in the Hama Museum there is even a 3rd century mosaic, found on the dining room floor of a local Roman villa, of six women, each playing a different instrument, on stage, performing to an audience.

Whilst all this sounds excellent, and the Syrian constitution grants equality to men and women, in practice a range of gender discrepancies do exist in Syria's civil, criminal and personal status laws. Labour laws are good for women, with equal pay and generous maternity leave, even including two hours a day at home to breastfeed, but Syrian family law is heavily influenced by Islamic *Shar'ia* law. Reduced sentences exist for 'honour crimes' committed by a male against a female relative for alleged sexual misconduct, and the penalty for adultery committed by a woman is double that of a man. Similarly, rape is seen as a felony, but if the rapist agrees to marry his victim he can avoid punishment. Interfaith marriage is another vexed issue and is not officially recognised unless one party changes their faith. A Christian woman can keep her faith if she marries a Muslim man, but a Muslim woman cannot marry a Christian man unless he converts to Islam. In the event of divorce, custody of children is awarded to the man once the child is over the age of 13 for a boy or 15 for a girl, figures which used to be as low as 7 and 11. Various women's rights activist groups were, before the revolution, fighting ongoing campaigns to reform such discriminatory laws, even getting petitions together on Facebook. Now, such reforms are unimaginably far off.

Young Syrian women can be dressed in jeans and T-shirts or in headscarves. Often it is the man of the household who decides how a woman must appear in public. Conservative women's dress is usually more reflective of cultural traditions than of religious values, and should not be confused with a lack of emancipation: in 2009 a young, Syrian headscarved woman won a major business grant to develop her brainchild of Arabic-language audiobooks. At the other extreme, in the Old City there are several outlets or even street stalls selling outrageous lingerie, all on full display, and women in full-length robes and headscarves will stop and finger the items unashamedly. I remember one pair of underpants with a mobile phone emblazoned over the crotch. Puzzled, I looked more closely and the male stall-owner pressed a concealed button inside them to sound a ring tone. 'A signal to her husband that she is in the mood,' he explained, straightforwardly. More curious aspects of the *zahir* and the *batin* again, I marvelled, thinking of how the underwear sections of our western department stores are generally tucked away in discreet corners on the upper floors, and only ever staffed by women.

As ever it is a complex picture, and of course, there are also many cases of maltreatment and abuse of women, but no matter what they wear, most Syrian women are highly vocal and participative, never more so than now, at street level, during the revolution. A curious exception is at the higher levels, where on the opposition negotiating tables overseas they are still poorly represented, something that may well speak volumes about the Muslim Brotherhood dominance of exiled opposition groups.

Traditionally women do not attend funerals in Islam, but today there is a more active mindset, and women are increasingly taking part, making a political statement of defiance through their mere presence. It is a new phenomenon, breaking the mould. Things will never go back to how they were, though some may wish it. Women of all ages are involved as activists, both pro and anti-regime. At checkpoints only they can perform body searches on other women, and on the streets they can often move more freely and discreetly than men, collecting useful information on roadblocks, general souk gossip or distributing food aid. Women who belong to the traditional Sunni brigades like *Ahrar Ash-Sham* (Free Men of the Levant) wear full Islamic dress which serves as a perfect disguise. But indoors is where women are most engaged in activism, behind their computers, where the virtual world of social media makes their choice of clothing an irrelevance. Facebook and Twitter are not banned in Syria, and cannot be policed since accounts can be held under pseudonyms, a liberating factor for many women whose parents might prevent them from street involvement.

At the other end of the scale, many of the Kurdish rebel groups are known for their female snipers, *muqatilat* ('female killers', literally) – being a good shot does not after all require physical strength. Bashar recruited women into his paramilitary force 'The Lionesses for National Defence', dressed in camouflage and toting rifles to transmit a supposedly liberal and empowered image for the Ba'ath Party, while the extremist rebel group *Jabhat Al-Nusra li-Ahl Ash-Sham* (The Support Front for the People of Syria) rejects the participation of women in fighting roles. Most women fight as part of larger male-led brigades, but there are even some all-female brigades such as Aleppo's Our Mother Aisha Brigade which supports the Free Syrian Army. 'Women are more dangerous than weapons,' says the FSA, 'If you want to spread your ideology, the best way is through women.' Some half-jokingly quipped, even before March 2011, that Syria's future revolution would be led by two million young women unable to find economically independent husbands, forced to embrace celibacy because of rampant unemployment and economic deprivation. Others said the reason Asma al-Assad used to chair a woman's organisation in Syria was in order to gauge the level of their anger.

When it came to the nitty-gritty of negotiations, however, I was not sure how, as a foreign woman, I would be treated. The first time I had viewed Bait Baroudi was with Bassim and Abu Al-'Izz, the wily shopkeeper who sold coffee beans and tea from his stall on the Street Called Straight. Abu Al-'Izz was the self-appointed agent for the district, who kept his ear to the ground and knew who might be selling. It was he who had rung the doorbells, while Bassim and I waited in the street. As soon as I had walked in through the lofty entrance corridor and stepped into the riot of colour in the courtyard, I could sense the scale and perfection of the space. It was like stepping into a semi-tropical jungle.

The young resident, the youngest, as it transpired, of four brothers, took us on a tour that ended on the roof, then pointed down. Hidden by all the foliage, what had not been apparent before was that a concrete wall divided the courtyard, into two-thirds and one third. Two thirds was in the house we had just been shown around, but the other third was behind this wall and looked completely derelict. The young man explained how the entrance to this part of the house was from a separate door in the street. They used it, he said, as a warehouse to store goods for their shop in the souk. His father had put up the wall about 20 years ago, since they did not need the whole house to live in. His brothers already had their own homes, but he, as the youngest brother, could not afford to move out of the parental home, so he was still living here with his wife and young son. Once the house was sold, the proceeds were to be divided between the four brothers and he would buy himself a flat or small house in the suburbs with his share. Set on a proper street just about wide enough to permit parked vehicles outside, the house was located in the Muslim quarter, virtually next door to Bait Nizam, an extravagant Ottoman palace with a trio of courtyards that had been bought by the state in the early 1980s. Bait Siba'i, where I had first met Bassim, was just moments away, the Street Called Straight was one minute's walk north, while the Azem Palace, seat of the ruler of Damascus and even of the whole Province of Syria for centuries, equivalent in some ways to London's Buckingham Palace, was just three minutes' walk away. The Great Umayyad Mosque, spiritual heart of the city and closest parallel to London's Westminster Abbey, was a five minute walk. This was a fine residential area that would equate to something like Knightsbridge in Central London.

'How much are you asking?' I had asked on that first occasion, trying to keep my voice and facial expression as casual as possible.

Umar, as his name was, looked straight back at me and said the figure in Syrian pounds without the slightest hesitation. The sum he gave was the exact amount of my maximum budget. With a bit of luck, I could bargain him down and still have enough left over to cover the restoration and buying costs.

When I returned to Bait Baroudi for the second viewing, I was by myself, and unprepared for the suddenness of events. Umar the young brother showed me round again, while his wife peeped out of the kitchen at me, and their little son played on his tricycle in the courtyard. Standing on the roof, looking down into the derelict part of the house behind the dividing wall that had been built across the courtyard, Umar asked me if I wanted to see that part of the house again. 'No,' I said, falling silent for a few moments, before resuming with feigned nonchalance. 'This house is too expensive for me anyway. How much could you reduce it?'

'My brother Nazir deals with the money. Shall I call him?' I barely nodded, but Umar pulled out his mobile and spoke softly into it. He ushered me downstairs again into the 'ajami (hand-painted wooden lacquer panelled) room where he gestured me to sit in one of the big leather chairs that ringed the outer walls. I scarcely had a chance to adjust to the change in light before a taller, heavier version of Umar stepped in, shook my hand and introduced himself as Nazir, the eldest brother. His shop, it transpired, was close by. Umar's wife brought us coffee on a tray.

Our discussion was simple and to the point. I explained that the house was too expensive and he explained that it was not. I found him surprisingly direct, all small talk kept to a minimum. It felt like a proper business negotiation, the like of which I was used to from my days as an interpreter, when deals were hammered out between the sales team and the Arab client, usually over a period of weeks. This particular negotiation however, took less than an hour, perhaps helped by the fact that I told Nazir I would only be in the country until Saturday morning.

After exploring all the angles and repeating all the points several times, I asked Nazir what his absolute minimum figure was. He gave me a figure, looking me straight in the eye. Up until that point he had not shifted at all from the full price. I had been trying to get the price down, but he rolled his eyes at the impossibility of it, insisting that it was already very reasonable. From what I had seen, I knew he was right. Bait Kurdi, my second choice, which had been originally asking the same price, was now asking 20 per cent more.

'That is my absolute maximum,' I said, looking him straight in the eye, 'my total budget, and I need money left over for the restoration and the lawyers.'

That was how we left it. He said he would need now to consult his brothers, and suggested we had a *jalsa*, literally a 'sitting', here at the house on Friday, in two days' time at 10pm.

Rashid the lawyer was informed, and the next day we met in Marwan's tiny shop close to the Nawfara Cafe. *Nawfara* is Arabic for 'fountain', as in Roman times when the mosque was a Temple to Jupiter, this had also been the main entrance to the temple precinct, complete with colossal nymphaeum. From here the wide processional way had led east to the agora, now lost entirely in the maze of streets and houses. All that remains along the course of today's street is a Roman triple gateway, which you still have to pass through to reach Al-Qaymariya, the 'Little Moon' district, the heart of the busy

Christian Quarter, lined with sweet-smelling bakeries and colourful souvenir shops.

Marwan borrowed three chairs from the cafe and we crammed together inside his shop. Rashid the lawyer produced a pre-printed form, a single sheet of A4 paper, which he explained was a simple Contract of Sale, its set words already laid down, just with gaps where the relevant names and details could be added in by hand. I was taken aback, but he elaborated that if we could agree all the terms at the following day's *jalsa*, a contract of sale would be signed at the end of it, and I would have to hand over the cash deposit to seal the deal. They would both come with me, as would Bassim and Abu Al-'Izz.

It was, of course, completely dark by 10pm. As arranged, Marwan, Rashid the lawyer and I met at Marwan's shop, and together we walked the five minutes it took to reach Bait Baroudi in the Muslim Quarter. We arrived just two minutes after 10pm and Umar opened the door and led us across the dark courtyard to the *'ajami* room.

The formality of the occasion was immediately apparent. Inside the room, thick with cigarette smoke, nine of the twelve heavy black armchairs lining the walls were occupied, leaving just the final three for us. It felt like an unreal stage set which we were walking onto as in a dream, to play our parts in some bizarre drama. We slipped off our shoes at the doorway and glided into the empty seats. Instinctively I headed for the one in the centre, at the curve of the horseshoe if you like, while Marwan slipped into the one beside it. Rashid the lawyer took up the final empty armchair, halfway down one of the sides. The other people I recognised were Bassim and Abu Al-'Izz from my side, Umar and Nazir from their side.

I think it had been entirely unplanned and accidental, but our numbers balanced perfectly. There were twelve identical black armchairs, six of them filled with people from my side: me, Marwan, Rashid the lawyer, Bassim, Abu Al-'Izz and what turned out to be Abu Al-'Izz's cousin; and six from their side: Nazir, Umar, the other two brothers who Nazir introduced as 'Amir and Mustafa, and their lawyer and someone I later learnt was their lawyer's cousin. The symmetry was unintended but perfect.

Nazir was clearly in charge. Once again, there was no small talk, and we got straight down to the business in hand. Everyone knew why they were there, everyone had their role. Trays of coffee and water were brought in at intervals by various women, always in headscarves. It struck me that this meeting, this *jalsa*, was exactly the function for which this room was designed. As the main formal reception room of the house, it was where male guests would be received and matters of business would be discussed. I was of course the only woman present, but no one seemed bothered by that – I was foreign and an Arabic-speaker, and therefore an honorary man. My first such experience had been back in the 1970s when I had stayed during a language-immersion break from MECAS with a Bedouin tribe in Jordan over the *Eid Al-Adha*, the major Muslim religious holiday. Treated as an honoured guest, I was given pride of place beside the shaikh who, refined host that he was, had handed me the tongue, considered the rarest delicacy. As a woman in their midst I never once felt uncomfortable or unwelcome. They accepted me as their guest, their equal even, to be treated with respect.

It was just the same here, and at a very early stage in the proceedings, once it was clear we were all here to do real business, Rashid the lawyer produced the Contract of Sale form, almost casually, from a folder. He entered the names of the brothers first, getting their full details from them in turn, from their ID cards. I was amazed at how readily they cooperated. Somehow I had expected a struggle. Then he looked to me, and entered my name, asking for my passport so he could enter the details. Those basics seen to, Rashid the lawyer began the process of checking with the Baroudi brothers' lawyer about the cleanness of the title.

'Yes, all is fine,' Nazir assured Rashid, 'it is just the matter of the dead auntie, but that will only take two weeks maximum.'

I raised an eyebrow. It turned out that, apart from the four brothers who had inherited the house on their father's death, there had also been an elderly aunt, the father's sister, who, under Islamic law, was entitled to some minute percentage. She had died in the meantime, so it would be a simple matter of tracking down her heirs and resolving the issue. I asked Rashid if this was a problem.

'No,' he said, 'it is a very tiny share of the house, but to be certain it gets sorted out, we will write into the contract that a sum gets held back from the price we pay – three times the value of her share, so it will make sure they do it.' I had no choice but to concur gracefully, and Rashid duly scribbled in an extra clause in the contract by hand.

There had still been no mention whatsoever of the price of the house, the most important thing of all. I had been told by several people – Marwan, Ramzi the Philosopher, Bassim – that it was at this point that most such *jalsa* sessions fail with foreigners, and with Syrians. I was enjoying myself so much I did not even allow myself to think about failure. Shrouded in dense cigarette smoke, which somehow only added to the surrealness of the scene, I was loving every minute. About nine of the twelve people present were smoking – everyone offering theirs instinctively to their neighbours regularly, so that over the course of the evening, most of them got right through their packets.

We were now close to the end of the form. Rashid was sitting with his pen poised over the contract, cigarette in mouth.

'And the price?' he asked, almost casually, looking at no one in particular.

Nazir and I uttered the same words simultaneously, our eyes meeting as we spoke. It was the crowning moment, and I knew then, in that second, that it was all going to work. It was my destiny to buy Bait Baroudi. Rashid scribbled the amount in the relevant gap on the form.

He then produced a second contract form and, chatting with the Baroudi brothers' lawyer, he filled in all the gaps again, but when he came to the gap for the price, he put in a ridiculously low figure. 'This is for the tax,' he explained, as if no further explanation was required, 'so we don't have to pay the real amount.'

'Is that normal?' I asked, in some confusion.

'Totally,' he replied. 'Now we need the deposit.' He stretched out his hand to take the money. I had a moment of panic. The sterling cash I had brought with me from England was still in the bottom of my handbag, where I had been carrying it round for the last two weeks. I had not changed it into Syrian pounds, in case the deal fell through, knowing it would be a one-way transaction – Syrian currency, once converted, could not be changed back to hard currency in 2005, though perversely, one of Bashar's later banking reforms dropped that rule. I reached into my bag and pulled out the wad of notes, held together by rubber bands.

'I only have it in sterling,' I said, thinking how typical it was that, everything having gone so remarkably smoothly, it would now be my own foolishness that caused the deal to fail.

'No problem,' said Nazir, pulling out his mobile phone and using it to summon someone. Within the time it took for him to smoke two cigarettes, a young boy appeared in the doorway.

'Take this to the *sarraf*,' Nazir said, handing him the wad of sterling, 'and bring it straight back.' Banking hours are not an issue in a country with a black market in hard currency, and though the difference between the official and the black market exchange rate in Syria in 2005 was small, with this kind of amount, the difference added up. Nazir made another call on his mobile to establish the exchange rate for sterling, as a kind of check on the *sarraf*. When the boy returned, within an extraordinarily short space of time – no more than five or six minutes – he handed a much bigger wad of notes back to Nazir, who duly counted it out, with the skill and speed of a true shopkeeper. He kept the large pile of notes on his lap, then handed me back a small wad.

'Your change,' he said. The rate on the black market that night was the highest it had ever been – a rate it only reached again during the crisis of the revolution, after the Syrian currency had lost nearly half its value.

Both contracts were then signed by the four brothers, all putting their thumbprints beside their signatures using an ink pad which Rashid the lawyer produced from his pocket. Finally I added my own signature.

It was well after midnight when the *jalsa* finished. Rashid the lawyer and Marwan escorted me through the deserted streets to the edge of the Old City, from where I could return to my hotel. We walked briskly, three abreast, me in the middle, along the full length of the dark and empty Souk Al-Hamadiya, normally crowded with traders and shoppers, our footfalls the only sound echoing up into its cavernous ceiling. There was no need to speak. 'Whatever happens,' I thought to myself, 'even if the deal crashes tomorrow, even if I lose my deposit, it will all have been worth it, just to have experienced this night of the *jalsa*.'

It was a moment to savour, and I will remember it all my life.

7

Insurance against Fate?

Too soft and you will be squeezed, too hard and you will be broken.

Arab proverb

Damascus is in an earthquake zone and there is one due around now. The last major one was in 1879, necessitating major reconstruction. Most buildings within the walls were damaged in some way, including the Great Umayyad Mosque itself, whose repairs are still visible.

The city sits astride the fault line that runs from the East African Rift Valley and passes north through the Dead Sea before it peters out in the Anti-Lebanon Mountains. Given this geographical fact it might be reasonable to assume that earthquake insurance can be taken out. But in practice, no one insures their house, not against earthquakes, not against anything.

Insurance is a vexed issue in Islam. How can you take out insurance against the will of God? As the medieval historian Ibn Sasra wrote in *A Damascus Chronicle 1389–1397*, there is no escape from God's decree, and history is simply the acting out of *qadar* and *qada*: 'God's decree and judgement'. As a result no one in Syria insures their house. When I first mentioned insurance to Rashid the lawyer and Marwan, assuming there would be some local buildings policy I should take out, they both found the idea very quaint. I explained what was normal in England and they listened with interest. Rashid the lawyer said that, yes, he had heard that such things existed, but here in Syria there would be no point, because the insurance company would almost certainly never accept a claim and therefore never make a payout.

Insurance, I discovered, represents a massive contradiction in the mind of the average Muslim. After all, the very word 'Muslim' means 'one who surrenders to the will of God'. If you take out insurance, it means you are not putting your trust in God to look after you. In another irony, Bashar's regime had, pre-revolution, been trying to alter this mentality. After all, car insurance is required by law, though most car owners just take out third party, the minimum requirement, rather than comprehensive. Health insurance was becoming the new big growth area, helped by the fact that in 2010 Bashar's regime gave 750,000 civil servants health insurance, a perk no doubt for loyal employees, with a kickback to loyal businessmen in commissions. However, the concepts of life insurance, travel insurance and general accident insurance remained in their infancy in Syria, a fact that was maybe just as well, since no insurance policy on earth would have covered the disasters that were soon to engulf the country.

The completion date on Bait Baroudi was set for 4 July, giving Umar time to move out to his new flat and me time to extract my total savings from various banks in England and send them out to Syria. International financial transactions to Syria were never straightforward but they were at least still possible in those pre-sanction days.

I flew out from London again on Syrian Air, now something of a regular, and I was even bumped up to first class by the London office manager. Everything was going remarkably smoothly, but then on the morning of the purchase I had an accident. It was the closest I have ever come to death.

On this one occasion, I was staying inside the Old City, at the Dutch Cultural Institute, instead of at my usual hotel outside in the commercial district. The Dutch equivalent of the British Council, the Institute was at that time housed in a slightly run-down courtyard house in the Christian Quarter, close to the Ananias Chapel, where St Paul had been converted. It rented out a few upstairs rooms, generally for the use of Dutch research students, but if they had space, the rooms were available to others. This knowledge I owed to Bassim. He had been given the contract for the Institute's maintenance, and therefore needed to call regularly on the young and dynamic new director, to discuss the building's various ailments – the usual suspects; crackly telephone lines that interfered with internet reception, leaking roofs in summer downpours, malfunctioning fountains and so on.

In size the Institute was similar to Bait Baroudi, with a large courtyard and central fountain, and about five rooms ranged round the courtyard at ground level. Steps led upstairs to a corridor with three bedrooms running off it. It was beautifully peaceful, and despite the heat of an early July night in Damascus, I had slept surprisingly well, with the windows wide open to catch the night-time breeze. It is easy to forget that Damascus, with its high altitude and distance from the sea, enjoys a continental climate and significant temperature drops at night. There were also one or two students staying, friendly enough, but I felt they belonged to a different world. I was old enough to be their mother, and they had the carefree air of youth, having adventures in a strange exciting city, knowing that they would return at the end of the summer to the security of their homes and their universities.

In the morning, as soon as the sun got up, the temperature began to rise quickly. I lay in bed absent-mindedly watching the curtain flap in the last of the dying breeze, thinking about the momentous step I was about to take. I had agreed to meet the Baroudi family at midday for the handover of the balance of the agreed purchase sum, after which I would 'take the keys', as they called it in Arabic. It was the British equivalent of 'completion' but with one big difference. In Syria all such transactions between private individuals are conducted in cash. Syrians are wary of banks, preferring to stay away from them altogether if possible. They do not trust them with their money and only 16 per cent of the adult population has a bank account. Even government salaries are paid in cash. Only ten banks in the country offer Internet banking, and even then, the only facility offered is to check your balance, or at most to transfer money between accounts at the same branch. No bank allows transfers outside to other banks or institutions. Sophisticated customers who use internet banking when overseas would not dream of using it in Syria as they don't consider it secure. The culture of on-line shopping and using credit or debit cards is only familiar to the uppermost echelons, like the President's wife. ATM machines are still relatively new and frequently malfunction or run out of money.

So cash it had to be, and as a result, Marwan had suggested we meet outside the bank at 10am with Rashid the lawyer to withdraw the money from my newly opened account at the Commercial Bank of Syria. Thinking about the best way to transport such a quantity of cash, since a wheelbarrow was not an option, I was considering emptying my holdall for the purpose. The room was getting warmer by the minute, and as I leant out to close the window against the rising heat, the left hand frame, which I had assumed was fixed, burst open from my leaning weight. The window frame was unusually low, so my entire body from the tops of the thighs upwards suddenly had nowhere to go except forward. For a split second I teetered, hanging head-first out of the window frame, waiting to crash my skull against the stone paving of the courtyard.

In that briefest of eternities my entire life was laid out before me. I was exposed. To fall now, of all moments – how could fate be so cruel? *Qadar wa Qada'*. All my strivings had been for nothing.

The brain is a remarkable thing. One second it thought like that, the next it thought quite differently, when it realised gravity was going to give it a second chance. My weight, balanced precariously forward by the suddenness of the window flying open, see-sawed back, and my feet, dangling just a moment earlier helplessly in mid-air, made contact once more with the floor. I had been saved. To what end was far from clear, but I chose to take it as a sign that I had been spared for a reason, after having been quite literally 'weighed in the balance'.

Suitably sobered, I met Marwan and Rashid the lawyer outside the bank at 10am as agreed, and we went in together to find Maryam the bank manager. She was multi-tasking impressively in her usual way, juggling her mobile and the three telephones on her desk, keeping one eye on her computer screen, whilst simultaneously dealing with the various clients in her office and her staff who came and went with papers for her to check and sign. She was a sight to behold, a figure larger than life in all senses, with huge eyes that saw everything, and tight clothing that concealed nothing. A loose gown would have been far more forgiving, but Maryam was not one to be bound by convention. She was her own woman. When I had first opened my account there she had been the deputy manager, but now by a gracious miracle she had been promoted, and since she was a good contact of Marwan's, that, he assured me, would make life very much easier for me in acquiring the legal title to the house further down the road.

Maryam liked me, and it was just as well, because while the first part of my money had transferred out from my UK bank into my Syrian account without a hitch, the second part had disappeared between leaving the UK and arriving here. She thought it had probably got stuck somewhere in the Aleppo Free Zone, where the correspondence bank was denying all knowledge of it. More than three weeks had passed since it had been sent, and the timing was getting desperate, threatening to derail the entire purchase. I was sure it would have arrived by now, and was horrified when Maryam told me it had not. She looked at the expression on my face and did what no other bank manager in the world anywhere would have done.

'Never mind,' she said 'I will let you take the money anyway. It will arrive soon, I'm sure.' And with that, she signed the withdrawal authorisation and swept back into her office, telling us to wait by the cashier's desk. We did as we were told, and what ensued was like something out of a comic farce. Bundles of bank notes started arriving, tipped out of cardboard boxes before our eyes by a succession of bank employees in relays, delegated to bring it up from the basement vaults. The piles of bundles grew and grew. I began to laugh, partly with relief and partly at the absurdity of the spectacle. Could this really be happening? Other bank customers began to laugh too, looking at me laughing, and looking at the mountains of cash. It was turning into a mountain range of money, with peaks and valleys; the Himalayas had come to Syria.

'You need bags?' said the cashier, smiling at me. I laughed more loudly, and he passed the word round his colleagues who then rummaged among their possessions behind their desks, producing about ten plastic bags between them.

'You want to count it?' he continued, handing me the bags. I laughed uncontrollably.

We set off, the three of us – Marwan, Rashid the lawyer and I – from the bank in Al-Nasr St, down into the underpass and up the other side into the main thoroughfare of the Souk Al-Hamadiya, clutching our plastic bags brimming with the bundles. It needed all three of us to carry their sheer weight and bulk. No one gave us a second glance. We were just normal people, carrying our shopping.

At 12 noon, the appointed hour, we stood before the door of Bait Baroudi and knocked ceremonially. What a moment. It had all gone like clockwork – sort of. Against all the odds, everything had fallen into place. Umar, the youngest brother, opened the door, smiled in friendly fashion and led us into the courtyard, now strangely empty, cleared of all the pot plants that had previously cluttered it. All the rooms were empty too, and the only furniture left was a set of four grubby white plastic chairs set out in the least hot of the main down-stairs rooms. All the Baroudi brothers were there, and Umar's young son rode about on his tricycle, weaving between the chairs like an obstacle course. The only other object in the room was an electronic banknote counting machine, which they had hired and were very proud of, but it malfunctioned all afternoon and they eventually aban-doned it, reverting instead to good old-fashioned hand counting. It took them six hours, and I sat and watched and waited patiently on my plastic chair. As at the *jalsa*, I was the only woman present.

Time takes on whole new dimensions on such occasions. I felt it deserved to take that long; if it had all been over in a flash it would not have felt right. During those six hours of waiting, I learnt how to accept time and its passing, how to accept that there are some things you are powerless to control. With that realisation I came to truly understand the meaning of the Arab proverb '*Al-sabr miftah al-faraj*', which, translated simply, means 'Patience is the key to happiness', except that the Arabic conveys so much more than that. Sabr is not just patience, it is one of the cardinal Bedouin virtues, conveying for-titude and perseverance in the face of obstacles and the ability to cope with adversity, be it deserved or undeserved. It conjures up pictures of the resilient nomad enduring the hardships of the desert. *Miftah* is just the key, literally 'the instrument of opening', but *faraj* is far more than happiness; *faraj* is the release from suffering.

As I sat and waited, I felt a deep inner calm. It was hot, over 40°C, it was sticky, and there were no distractions beyond watching those around me, observing their actions. I was thirsty, I was hungry, but I felt strangely insulated from those mundane discomforts. I had learnt not to focus on them. Whatever was coming next, I was ready for it.

Soon after 6pm, the counting exercise complete, Nazir Al-Baroudi stood up and handed me the key to the house. Marwan and Rashid the lawyer had left long ago, returning to their own lives and duties, but Rashid had left me a document for the Baroudi brothers to sign, confirming their receipt of the money. This completed, we shook hands, then all four brothers processed ceremonially out into the street. The little boy had been collected earlier by his mother. I went back inside, passing again from the darkness of the corridor into the brightness of the courtyard, just as I had done when I met Bassim for the very first time a few months earlier. But this time I was alone, alone in my own house, the house of my dreams, and it was real.

In the Arabic language there are only two tenses, the past and the imperfect. Only these two states exist; either an action has been completed, or it has not. Our strange English convolutions of could, would, should, might are irrelevant to the Arab mind. With the closing of the door, with the taking of the key, my action had passed from one state to the other. It was complete.

8

Revelations

Circling about to reach Paradise is better than going straight to Hell.

Arab proverb

Flying out to Damascus the next time was truly different. This time I was staying in Bait Baroudi, and the dream was tangible. No more hotels, no more Dutch Institutes. This time I was putting my head down in my own courtyard house in the Old City, though I would, of course, be camping. The house was totally empty, all furniture gone, so Bassim and I had agreed beforehand on a minimal list of things he would buy in advance of my arrival. I have the list still. It was the first invoice I ever received from Bassim, the first in a long line. He prepared his accounts beautifully.

I think often about the magic of that first stay, and its echoes of what was to come. It was August 2005, and when I stepped out of the airport terminal building, the heat hit me full in the face even though it was ten at night. I hailed a taxi, then realised with a shock that finding Bait Baroudi at night by myself in the depths of the Old City would be well nigh impossible. Street names mean nothing in Damascus, people navigate using landmarks, and though I had a detailed cadastral plan of the city I knew that no taxi driver in Syria understands maps. The one-way system for vehicles was complex, and as we weaved our way through endless narrow lanes that any western driver would have considered impassable, I realised just how little I knew the place. I had no idea where we were, and recognised nothing in this dark rabbit-warren-like maze of streets. My eye was caught by a large poster of Bashar in a suit, smiling and waving paternally at me, with the slogan *Mnuhabbak*, 'We love you.'

At last the moment came, when after lengthy wanderings on foot in the confusing alleyways near Bab Al-Saghir, I finally arrived at the familiar door of Bait Baroudi with its comforting hand of Fatima knocker. Trembling as the key turned in the lock, I stepped over the worn marble threshold and glimpsed, beyond the unlit corridor, my first sight of the courtyard by moonlight. The space I was entering no longer seemed like a house, but more like a small palace, grand but intimate. The dream was taking on new dimensions.

Six weeks beforehand, after taking possession of the key in July, I had agreed with Bassim that he should immediately go ahead and arrange to have the modern white cement fascia removed from the courtyard walls. Not only that, but we had also agreed that, as the first big structural change, the dividing wall across the courtyard should be removed, in order to reunite the two parts of the house as one. The result, especially after the time spent lost in the labyrinthine lanes of the *hara*, made me feel I had arrived at some kind of sacred sanctuary.

Exclaiming with child-like pleasure, I discovered the things Bassim had bought. In the kitchen I found an enormous old-fashioned fridge, a local make I had never heard of. It stands there still, serving the many residents who now crowd the same space and for whom it is also a sanctuary. There was a simple gas-ring, a kettle and a smattering of cutlery and crockery. Under the shelter of the *iwan* stood a round bamboo table with a piece of circular glass as its top, and a pair of deep comfortable bamboo armchairs to go with it. Now, these same chairs are supplemented with tens of plastic chairs. I dragged the mattress he had bought into the *'ajami* room so I could wake up to a view of the painted ceiling. Today many mattresses cover the floors of several rooms where extended families sleep, waking up to the sound of gunfire and distant shelling, just as I had been woken by the very first bombs in Damascus in November 2011, straight after the dawn call to prayer.

Even though it was by now close to midnight, I was pretty sure a few shops in the Old City would still be open, so I set off to find some provisions – bottled water, juice, milk, yogurt, cheese, bread, jam, tea and coffee, eggs, tomatoes and oranges – meeting the friendly shop-keepers of the neighbourhood who gradually grew to know me well. Today a curfew imposed by armed 'People's Committees' keeps everyone indoors after dark.

Every inch of the place was a discovery during that first trip. Everything was rich with promise. The way the sun fell into the court-yard, its shadows moving softly from one side to the other, the way the vibrant leaves from the bougainvillea fell leaving a magenta trail, the way the palm doves swooped down from their nests in the heavy foliage to peck at invisible delicacies on the ground, the way the bats flew silently in and out of the *iwan* catching mosquitoes; all of it bewitched me. Empty of the cluttering furniture, I now noticed all sorts of things I had not seen before: the deep white marble window-sills, the exquisite shapes of the window frames, the tiny insets of blue coloured glass, the mouldings on the doors, the magnificent proportions of the *iwan*. The white-painted cement cladding had previously covered the vertical courtyard surfaces with a hideous uniformity, but now the spectacular original stonework was revealed, with its inlay in shades of red and green, exactly as Bassim and I had hoped. It was the *zahir* and the *batin* again.

Each of the four courtyard walls was revealed to be different, the first clue to the different ages of each part the house. Each was beautiful. Three out of the four were built of alternating bands of black and white masonry known as *ablaq*, a distinctive style that started in the 14th century under the Mamluk empire and continued well into Ottoman times here in Damascus. I later noticed that even in London's Bedford Square the arched frames of all the doorways had alternate black and white bands painted on to mimic this masonry – Damascus in Bloomsbury. The white was a local limestone, not true white but more like a soft golden yellow, and not one uniform flat colour, but many shades, some deeper, some paler. The contrast with the black was dramatic, as dramatic as volcanic stone should be, because this is the stone of the Hawran, spewed out by scores of volcanoes south of Damascus eons ago and still scattered over the once fertile plain. Tough and rugged, the black basalt conveys massive strength and power, while the softer limestone is altogether warmer and gentler. They are necessary contrasts to each other. On the outer wall of the 'ajami room a delicate niche was now visible, formerly covered by the concrete, just beside the door, where I imagined an oil lamp would once have burned to light the courtyard. Running round the top of the ablaq masonry I noticed a strange zig-zag pattern in red, black and green, a mysterious design with echoes of Mesopotamian merlons. I felt as if the house were trying to speak to me, to tell me its secrets.

But the most exciting discovery of all was still to come. In that derelict part of the house where there was no electricity, some areas were so murky I had never really been able to see them properly. On the occasions when I had viewed the house before, the winter reception room, with its six-metre-high ceiling, had been piled high with boxes of tea and rice for the Baroudi shop in the souk. It had been impossible to see behind them. Now the room was empty, I noticed a square hole in the wall, stuck my head in and shone my torch upwards. Above me a multi-coloured wooden ceiling was painted in exquisite hues of gentle blue, grey, green, pink and beige, designed like a carpet with an elaborate border frieze, a perfect fit for the space. Protected by a liberal coating of cobwebs, it was in immaculate condition. Clearly the Baroudi family had never known it was there – the price of the house would have shot up if they had – and presumably the owners before them had not known about it either. The likelihood was it had remained undisturbed since the time of the French Mandate in the 1920s, a relic, maybe, of when the last Ottomans had lived in the house. I called it 'the secret ceiling' and came to see it not simply as an attractive addition to the house, but as a potent symbol of Syrian society, in its tapestry-like blend of many elements. Round its fringes it even had fantasised buildings like those created out of green and gold mosaics on the walls of the nearby Umayyad Mosque.

Later Bassim and I speculated that the mysterious space inside the hole might have been the treasury of the house, where valuable possessions were hidden. Bassim wondered if it might even have been a kind of priest's hole, where the eldest son would have been hidden away from army recruitment in Ottoman times. The entrance was just about big enough for a normal-sized person to wriggle inside. In the current revolution it would have made the perfect weapons cache or hiding place for rebels when regime soldiers broke down doors in the Old City to search houses as part of their regular patrols.

⁂

One of the things I did during that first stay in Bait Baroudi was to call on the neighbours and introduce myself. The patchwork of how the houses fitted together was an inscrutable jigsaw puzzle, impossible to judge from the street, so I had studied Bassim's copy of the cadastral plan prepared by the French during the Mandate in the 1920s to work out who the neighbours were and where their respective entrances might be.

There were a total of four immediate neighbours, only one of whom had their entrance in the same street as mine. I decided to start with that one, calling round early one evening. The door was opened by an elderly man in a traditional, long, white robe, and when I explained who I was, he immediately invited me in for tea. He led me across a tiny courtyard, up a couple of steps and into his surprisingly spacious reception room. The furnishings were hideous, with enormous ugly armchairs, plastic flowers and the usual photos of Hafez and Bashar. Neon strips provided all the light, giving off a harsh glare, but the ceiling was magnificent, with inlaid stone patterns that must have dated back to early Ottoman times. It was a curious mix, as was his family, a wild-eyed son of about 40 and two young girls, whom he summoned to introduce to me. His wife did not come in, but he shouted instructions to her to make the tea.

It transpired over the course of our conversation that he was looking to sell his house, and hearing of my recent purchase, wondered if I might be interested in buying it. It was a novel thought – here I was, fresh from buying one Damascus courtyard-house, when along came the chance to buy another. The sum they were asking was on the high side, given the square metreage when compared to the much larger Bait Baroudi, but whatever the price, I did not have the money. There was no harm in looking though, and since he was keen to show me round, after tea I followed them on a tour of the house, the elderly father leading the way. It was a veritable jumble of a place, cluttered and dirty, but the fact that the house was in such a state did not cause them the slightest embarrassment. There is no shame culture in the Arab world, only honour, a completely different concept. Why should they feel ashamed about the way their house looked? It was their house after all. They took me onto their roof, completely enclosed and at a much lower level than mine, something I was relieved to see since it guaranteed the privacy of my extensive open terraces.

Later, when I told Bassim about my visit, he said that of course the neighbour's house would be worth more to me than to anyone else because of the way it fitted so neatly with mine – it even had a blocked-up connecting door. 'Let him wait a while,' he said. 'He may drop his price when he realises no one else will pay him this amount.'

Among the other neighbours the biggest surprise came in the house that lay to the east, behind my 'ajami room, when I discovered it belonged to the Qabbani family, and was where Syria's most famous love poet, Nizar Qabbani, had grown up as a boy. He had since died in exile in London in 1998, but had named Damascus the 'City of Jasmine', and in his will asked to be buried there, calling it 'the womb that taught me poetry, taught me creativity and granted me the alphabet of Jasmine.' His grave is now in Bab Al-Saghir cemetery, less than 500 metres away from the house of his childhood. I had not studied him as a poet at university, but had always known his name.

Nizar Qabbani had begun as a love poet, writing his first poetry aged 16, and then publishing his first book of poetry at his own expense while still a law student at Damascus University in 1944. He was the first Arab poet to write poetry that demonstrated an understanding of women, in awe of their strength and beauty, acknowledging their emotions, admitting them as equals of men. His own sister had committed suicide aged 25, when he was just 15, rather than be forced to marry a man she did not love. The young Qabbani blamed Syrian society for its restrictive ways and vowed to try to fight for freedom.

'Love in the Arab world,' he once said, 'is like a prisoner, and I want to set it free. I want to free the Arab soul, sense and body with my poetry. The relationships between men and women in our society are not healthy.'

His poem *On Entering the Sea* is the most powerful expression of mutual, equal love between a man and a woman I have ever read:

Love happened at last,
And we entered God's paradise,
Sliding
Under the skin of the water
Like fish.
We saw the precious pearls of the sea
And were amazed.
Love happened at last
Without intimidation... with symmetry of wish.
So I gave... and you gave
And we were fair.
It happened with marvellous ease
Like writing with jasmine water,
Like a spring flowing from the ground.

Extraordinary though this translation is, one critic described it as 'like drinking coffee that has been diluted ten times', so distant is it from the Arabic original. The idea of symmetry and mutual desire between two people is beautifully conveyed in the original through the use of a special form of the Arabic verb – the VIth form, for those who are interested – which means to do things to each other equally. No other language has such a verb. Arabic may only have two tenses, but it has 12 forms of verb, expressing all shades of meaning from the same three root consonants.

As Qabbani grew older he became increasingly political, especially after the Arab humiliation of the 1967 Six Day War when Syria lost the Golan Heights to Israel. Voicing his despair with the Arab world and its political leaders, he wrote: 'Each day we regress a thousand years.' What would he have made of Syria today? His father, who owned a chocolate factory, had fought against the French Mandate authorities, and had been imprisoned on many occasions – another big influence on his revolutionary tendencies. Threatened with arrest and exile, he declared:

'No regime could arrest my poems, for they are dipped in the oil of freedom.'

As a diplomat who was posted to Beirut, Istanbul, Madrid, London and finally China, Qabbani resigned in 1966, by which time he had established a publishing house in Beirut in his own name. He settled in Beirut, and it was here that his beloved second wife, an Iraqi schoolteacher, was blown up in a terrorist attack on the Iraqi Embassy during the Lebanese Civil War in 1981. The poem he dedicated to her, 'Balqis', summed up his despair with the entire Arab world.

After her death he left the Arab world, moving between Paris and Geneva, finally settling in London for the last 15 years of his life.

With all these associations I was a little nervous about ringing the doorbell of the Qabbani house, the house with which I shared the largest boundary. I need not have worried, for the door was opened by a delightful elderly man, dressed in the traditional long white robe, who ushered me in as if my calling round was the most natural thing in the world. His courtyard was enormous, at least half as big again as mine, with a large central fountain and many mature trees and plants. It was, however, surprisingly devoid of original features – no *ablaq* on the outer walls, no stone inlay above the doors – everything was covered up by the same ubiquitous white plaster that had covered my courtyard until recently. Even his main reception room, a space of considerable size, had no *'ajami* and no decorative paintings on the walls or ceiling. The house had clearly been untouched for a long time and was still relatively unmodernised. He had lived there more than 25 years, it transpired, only having essential repairs done, so not much had changed in that time. It was even possible therefore, that Nizar Qabbani and his beloved Balqis had stayed in the house, and seen it exactly as I was seeing it now.

Studying the cadastral plan after my visits to all the neighbours, combining it with what I had now seen with my own eyes, I worked out that my courtyard must have been the original *salamlik* of a much bigger house. The house of the neighbour who wanted to sell was clearly the much smaller *khadamlik* courtyard, and the Qabbani house was the much bigger *haramlik* courtyard. The hierarchy of the courtyards was always for the *haramlik* to be the most richly decorated and beautiful, which meant that the modern white cladding at the Qabbani house must be concealing some extremely beautiful decoration that would have far outshone mine at Bait Baroudi. I wondered how many years it had been since the trio of courtyards had been divided into three separate dwellings. All I could know for sure was that it would certainly have been before the French Mandate in 1920, but how much before remained a mystery. Who might have been the original owner of my house? Some Mamluk prince? Bassim had at my request obtained from the relevant government office the *tasallsul mulkia*, a list of its previous owners, but such lists only went back to the start of the French Mandate. Even so, military ranks loomed large, and my utility bills were all in the name of a Syrian brigadier, so the house must have had some sort of military pedigree. The bills still carry his name today, whoever he may be. Might he even suddenly reclaim his property, since Rashid the lawyer has not managed to this day to get the *tabou* or title deed in my name?

These were the sorts of questions I pondered as I sat in the courtyard. After the initial adjustment to being alone: I began to appreciate the silence of the place rather than to fear it. I saw things and noticed things I might not otherwise have done, tiny things, the way the light moved across the stones of the courtyard, the way the breeze moved and rustled in the foliage, the way the insects and butterflies hovered around the fountain. I heard every sound as if magnified by the four walls of the courtyard and relished the beauty of the call to prayer, the voices of children playing in the street, the occasional sound of a bicycle ringing its bell or a street vendor's call. I was in my own magical world, and experienced here some of my deepest moments of happiness and peace.

I wondered what it was that gave this space its power, its level of supreme tranquillity. My undergraduate studies of the Arab world, its language and literature, history and culture all those years ago had not prepared me for the beauties and spiritual qualities of Islamic art. I wanted to try to rectify this ignorance and perhaps even undertake academic research to explore its mysteries. I felt that somehow, something very deep about this place was just beyond my grasp, just outside my comprehension.

Whatever it was, I had to learn to perceive it for myself, to see beyond the individual perfections of the geometric patterns, beyond the specific shapes of the graceful arches, beyond the marvellous colours of the stone pastework, to understand something infinitely greater.

Engulfed by the courtyard that surrounded me, I felt embraced as if by some archetypal womb, so safe, so utterly removed from the cares of the world. Although nothing in the house would have predated the early 1600s, making it entirely Islamic, the courtyard style house as a concept went right back to the Egyptian and Sumerian civilisations, and to Asia Minor, evolving throughout the Bronze Age. It continued through into the Hellenistic-Roman-Byzantine traditions – I thought about the open courtyard houses of Pompeii I had visited. This courtyard style served as the inspiration and model for the Umayyads, the first dynastic Arab caliphate, the first settled Islamic civilisation. They made Damascus their capital; before that they had been a largely nomadic society, building a string of castles and palaces in the desert, all with courtyards – Mushatta, Kharraneh, 'Amra, Azraq, Khirbet Al-Mafjar – scattered across the northern deserts of Jordan. Syria's deserts had a few too, though less well-preserved: Al-Hayr Al-Sharqi and Al-Hayr Al-Gharbi, and, of course, the Umayyad city of 'Anjar, just over the border in Lebanon. I had explored all of these places in past years, so maybe now, subconsciously, I was dimly aware that here in this courtyard house, Islamised by the later Arabs and the Ottomans, I was sitting in a multi-layered fragment of history.

'In its countless alveoli space contains compressed time. That is what space is for,' wrote Malcolm Quantrill in his *The Environmental Memory*. 'The entire skeleton of the city becomes its collective memory through the spatial memories of its constituent parts.'

But it was not just that. Above and beyond that sense of the house's antecedents, that awareness of its evolution through the ages to reach this point, there was an unmistakeable sense of the sacred, and I vowed to probe it further.

My struggles to find the meaning behind Islamic art continued to haunt me long after I completed my MA studies into Islamic Architecture. 'You Christians are all obsessed with symbols,' my Egyptian professor would say disparagingly, whenever I ventured to ask in seminars whether there was any meaning behind a particular shape or design. Why did the domes in Cairo's City of the Dead suddenly develop elaborate lacework patterns, and what was the ultimate purpose of the *muqarnas*? She would give me a withering look.

Nothing, she insisted, anywhere in the literature, no textual references suggested that any particular shapes had hidden meanings or that there was any symbolism driving the designs and patterns of Islamic architecture. Could she really be right? In her book *Beauty in Arabic Culture* she talks of how Paradise is described in the Quran in physical terms. Sunnis, she says, believe in this physical resurrection of the body, and the enjoyment of all physical pleasures in Paradise. It is not thought of as an allegory. Hell too is physical torment. The promises are taken literally, not symbolically. Spiritual and bodily happiness are compatible in the eyes of Sunni Muslims. Eating and drinking are part of this life of luxury in Paradise, where the Quran tells the believers: 'You shall be served with golden dishes and golden cups.' (43:71), and, '... arrayed in garments of fine green silk and rich brocade.' (18:30) and, 'From both seas you eat fish and bring up orna-ments (pearls and coral) to deck yourselves with.' (35:12).

From such words you can begin to understand why death might even seem attractive, the entrance to a world where all physical com-forts and finery are to hand, especially if earthly life is degraded and difficult. Yes, of course it is true that Islamic art seems at first glance to be concerned with nothing more than providing a beautiful backdrop to such visions of Paradise, pure ornamentation, decoration for deco-ration's sake. There is even a verse in the Quran: *li-kull shay zayna* – 'everything has its ornament' – which Western-educated art histori-ans wheel out in defence of their argument. But what does that mean? Simply that everything can be beautified? Surely there was more to it than that.

Sitting in that space, whether in my *'ajami* room or in my court-yard, looking at the shapes, colours and patterns that surrounded me, absorbing them, feeling them, sensing them intuitively, I could not accept so shallow an explanation. Muslim philosophers and theologi-ans have devoted extensive thought in their writings to the nature of matter, the nature of the universe. They reject, almost to a man, the Aristotelian concept of an eternal cosmos. What they believe instead – and this is an entirely Muslim theory, not derived from anything in the Greek or classical world – is that the world is in a constant state of recreation by God. So, what we explain away as the laws of nature for cause and effect, such as hunger and eating for example, are not laws of nature at all, but laws by which God chooses to control the world. So when God chooses to alter the usual pattern of cause and effect, someone can feel full without eating or can eat without being hungry. Miracles can, therefore, be explained as God's divine intervention to change the ordinary course of events in nature. Man can exert his will to try to make certain things happen, but whether or not they do is ultimately up to God. How else can you explain the 'accidents' of daily life? Each day you embark on some project, full of intention, with no control over how it will turn out. On one day you will succeed and everything will go according to plan, and the next day you will be randomly thwarted and obstacles will appear to have been put in your way, to see how you will respond. Sometimes God will reward your perseverance and grant the completion of your goal, and at other times an 'act of God' will prevent it – an earthquake, a car accident, for example. Ibn Sasra related numerous accounts of how people tried in vain to avoid their fate. One story tells of a mother who tried to stop her son going off to war, hiding him in a room of her house to keep him safe, rather like my 'secret-ceiling room'. In the night, lightning strikes the roof of that room only, and it falls in, killing the boy in spite of all her efforts. *Qadar wa qada*'.

Modern philosophers labelled this theory of the early Muslim theologians 'Occasionalism', and traced it back to 9th-century Iraq, where its original proponent, Al-Ash'ari, first expounded his theories to a group of fellow Muslim philosophers at the religious colleges of Basra. The universe, he said, was composed of particles that were constantly changing according to God's will as the universal creator. Shape, colour and luminosity are subject to continuous change, according to the Ash'arites. In any kind of decoration the quality of the light has a huge impact on how something looks.

People have observed the same phenomenon inside Islamic domes of the 10th and 11th centuries, where the architectural device of the *muqarnas* is used to effect the transition from the square of the ground plan to the circle of the dome, often via an octagon. The effect when viewed from below is to give the dome a certain weightlessness. The play of light on the *muqarnas* as the sunlight changes to moonlight throughout the day dissolves its mass, making the dome appear to stand unsupported, as heaven is described in the Quran: He created the skies without pillars...' (31:10).

Muqarnas have sometimes been described as stalactite or beehive vaulting, with enthusiasts saying they must represent the honey promised to true believers in Paradise, a theory that made my Professor scoff aloud. *Muqarnas* are undeniably a purely Islamic artistic creation, first found in Iraq in the early 11th century in funerary monuments, then later in mosques, hospitals, fountains and even palaces.

I puzzled over what might have been in the minds of early Muslim architects, what their aims would have been. Any religious building is seeking to express deep truths about religious beliefs, just as Christian architects designed churches with triple aisles to represent the Holy Trinity, and domes to represent heaven, painted with Christ Pantokrator or biblical scenes such as the Last Judgement. Muslim architects were not permitted to go down that road so their task, instead, was to create a spiritual space without recourse to human or figurative representation. They wanted to express theological concepts about the nature of the universe and its relationship to God, the intrinsic cosmological patterns affecting all Creation. Medieval Islamic scholars studied the laws and patterns of the cosmos to create a cyclic numeric order. Al-Jabr, whose name gives us the word 'algebra', deduced mathematical laws, patterns and shapes from astronomy, concluding that the circle was the parent of all polygons. The circle holds deep meanings, a symbol of eternity, without discernible beginning or end. For Muslims and Christians alike, the circular dome would always represent the heavens, the realm of the spirit. And from the circle the three fundamental shapes of Islamic art are derived: the triangle, the square and the hexagon. The six-pointed star found in the paste work decoration above the doorways of my *iwan* was simply two overlapping triangles. Suddenly I saw these shapes all around me.

The square featured in all early cultures, the symbol of earth, physical experience, the material world – *al-dunya*, in Arabic, meaning literally the 'lowest level'. Muslim intellectuals recognised in geometry the unifying intermediary between the material and the spiritual world, which they expressed in the doctrine of *tawhid*, 'divine unity'. Through the abstraction of endlessly repeating decorative patterns, the eyes and the mind are led to a contemplation of the infinite, and are led ever further upwards towards the *muqarnas* in the transitional zone between the square of the floor plan and the dome. There were often windows in the base of the dome, allowing the light to enter and to reflect off the intricate and complicated surfaces of the *muqarnas*, giving the impression of a rotating dome of Heaven. The device spread quickly from Iraq to Syria and North Africa, and in Damascus the earliest example is, fittingly, in today's Arab Science and Medicine Museum, the Maristan Nur Ad-Din, with its 11th-century dome using *muqarnas* as squinches (corner supports) to make the transition to an octagon, and then on to the circular dome.

Yet somewhere along the way all the symbolism of these shapes was lost. Their highly charged meanings gradually disappeared, and by the 16th century they were simply accepted as decorative devices and no more. Some things can be so profound that people eventually become oblivious to them, an almost archetypal, instinctive knowledge buried deep inside the subconscious. People forgot that these devices and patterns were in fact a uniquely Islamic approach to express the theological thinking of the time, to enhance the sanctity of a place and to help induce a meditative state. In this state the believer could feel closer to God, in the same way that the Sufi *dhikr*, the whirling ritual dance, could enable him to experience a mystical union with God. People forgot that, not only in mausoleums and mosques, but also in private houses, it was considered desirable to create an atmosphere conducive to serenity and equilibrium. Maybe Goethe, keen admirer of Islam and its philosophies as he avowedly was, had a similar thought when he called architecture 'frozen music'. Even my *'ajami* room had its own *muqarnas* niche, made out of wood, not stone or stucco, its own small representation of celestial infinity. Its scenes of gardens, trees, flowers and stylised buildings painted on the wooden lacquered walls conjured up images of Paradise, designed to lift the mind from the literal mundane world up into a world of underlying spirituality. In the coloured stone pastework of my courtyard, it could be no accident that the geometric designs were always placed within outer frames of circles, each one like a miniature cosmos. Islamic scholars believed the cosmos to be created upon the principles of arithmetic, geometry and music, and the basic aesthetic of Islamic geometric design is a rhythmic movement starting from and returning to a centre. It must therefore be, I instinctively felt, a reflection of the cosmic rhythm, enabling us to reach our own centre through our awareness of being at the centre of a greater whole.

My Professor would have reprimanded me for such thoughts, but sitting quietly and alone in my *iwan* and in my *'ajami* room, watching the changing light throughout the day as it played on the geometric shapes, I could get inklings of such things.

9

Friends and Brides

Bring your hearts together, but keep your tents separate.

Arab proverb

Disturbing such reveries a few days later the phone rang and it was Tariq, a wealthy, young Syrian I had met on my flight out from London in July. It was the one and only time I had travelled first class, bumped up by the kindly Syrian Air manager. We had by chance sat next to each other and ended up chatting the whole five hours. Now he was inviting me to visit him and his family in Homs. 'Why don't you come today?' he said with that wonderful immediacy which is so charming in all Arabs. 'My mother has been cooking and loves to feed extras. I have been busy until now renewing my id.'

'Renewing your id?' I exclaimed, all sorts of crazy visions running through my mind, 'That must be challenging!'

'Certainly is,' he continued, 'it took me hours, sitting all day in this tiny office yesterday, until I bribed the guy, then it speeded up.'

Even in Syria, I thought, it cannot be possible to bribe someone to renew your id. 'Is it expensive?' I enquired, wondering if it might be worth my while too, 'Should I try it?'

'What are you talking about?' he retorted, 'You can't get one. You aren't a Syrian citizen.'

'No,' I said, 'Is it only for Syrians then?'

'Of course. You are foreign. All you need is your passport.' Only then did I realise he was referring to his Identity Card and was mispronouncing I.D.

I jumped into a taxi on Straight Street and asked the driver how much he would charge to take me to Homs. He looked a little surprised, then said, 'One way?' We agreed a price the equivalent of what I would have paid in England to get from my house to the train station. I was happy and he was happy.

As the taxi laboured in the afternoon heat up over the pass that led north from Damascus on the two-and-a-half-hour drive to Homs, it was hard to believe that in winter this road was often closed by heavy snow. I had only ever travelled through Homs before, never stayed there, though I had heard that Homsis are to Syrians what the Irish are to the English, the butt of jokes like: 'Why did the Homsi stare at the frozen orange juice? Because it said "concentrate"' and 'How do you keep a Homsi busy all day? Put him in a round room and tell him to sit in a corner.'

The journey was quick and uneventful, but rendezvousing with Tariq in Homs turned out to be highly complex and time-consuming. I had suggested as our meeting point the Al-Nouri Mosque, which I knew from my ancient *Guide Bleu* to be the oldest mosque in the centre, so I imagined it must be straightforward. What Tariq had not admitted to me, however, was that he did not know where the Al-Nouri Mosque was, thinking it must be some obscure place I knew about from my guidebook writing. He was, therefore, suitably mortified when his father told him it was another name for Al-Jami' Al-Kabir (literally the 'Great Mosque'), the main mosque by the old souk, right next to their family shop. The shop has since been destroyed by heavy shelling in the siege of Homs in early 2012.

In the balmy warmth of the evening, we sat outside in the jasmine-scented yard of his parent's house, a modern block of flats in which each son had his own floor. The parents lived on the ground floor, and the four sons progressed upwards in order of seniority, with Tariq, as the youngest, on the top floor. I had been put in the third-floor flat, as Adnan, the third son, now lived abroad, and rarely came back. Today their house, like Bait Baroudi and so many others, is lived in by many displaced families whom they have given refuge, after they themselves fled to England in August 2011. Contrary to media reports whole areas of Homs are still inhabited.

Tariq had warned me that his father was a man of few words. He was perfectly content to sit smoking his *nargile* water pipe, gazing into the middle distance, and it seemed almost wrong to disturb him by speaking to him. Tariq told him I spoke Arabic and he glanced at me and grunted. Both his parents spoke only Arabic, despite having lived for many years in London, where, I was amazed to learn, they owned a similar set-up to this one, with a flat on each floor, in Regent's Park. They also had another such place in Beirut. How on earth had his father managed to build up such a successful clothing company, even buying and running a mill in Manchester, without English? His skill in the clothing trade, it turned out, was legendary. He had a real nose for it, and in the early days had been prepared to take considerable risks. When he left Syria in 1960 to avoid having much of his land sequestrated by the Ba'ath Party, he had first moved to Beirut, then, when the Lebanese Civil War broke out in 1975, he had relocated to London, arriving with a cash sum of just £35,000, enough in those days to buy him either a house in Chelsea or a house in Regent's Park. He chose Regent's Park because it was better value, and he lived in this the same house until his peaceful death, aged 93, in October 2013 while war raged in his homeland. All the brothers were now fully employed in the family business, except for Tariq, who had broken with tradition, instead attending an American business school. Most of them lived in London, but came to Syria to visit the parents every summer in relays.

It had the potential to be very awkward, Tariq inviting this much older woman to stay, but it was not. Everyone was entirely natural and normal, making me feel very welcome as if I was part of the family. I genuinely liked them all and found them excellent company. The evening meal was served by a couple of resident Filipino maids. I did not take Tariq to task over it then, in front of his family, but later when we were alone, I asked him why they did not have Syrian maids. 'We used to have locals,' he replied matter-of-factly, 'but the supply started to dry up in the 90s.' 'You mean as the Alawis got richer,' I said, 'they stopped sending their daughters out of the home?' 'Something like that,' he conceded.

The next day Tariq drove his father to view the orchards, taking me with them. It was an outing they made every day, to check on the fruit and the workers, his father putting on a special hat for the occasion. Right up to his death, Tariq's father had telephoned Homs every few days to check on the workers and the orchards. We dropped him off, leaving him to discuss agricultural matters with the workers, then drove on to the place which Tariq had told me about when I had first met him on the plane. It was a huge mock caravanserai, built from black basalt, and on entering the big open space, through the gate, there it was, exactly as he had described it, a beautiful blue swimming pool. In each corner was a separate changing area, one for each brother's family, except for Tariq, who, as the fourth brother and still unmarried, had to make do with sharing one of theirs. It was like their own version of an Umayyad desert palace, an inspired idea of his father's, he explained. It reminded me of a stage set, something like a Hollywood movie of a Mills & Boon novel in which we were the stars, and we enjoyed a unique day, never again to be repeated, lazing and swimming beneath a magnificent blue sky.

My *Guide Bleu* had spoken of a Christian quarter in Homs, and I asked Tariq if we could visit it. 'Of course,' he said, 'I like going into the churches because it gives me some extra *baraka* ('blessing').' It was the first time I had come across this fluidity between Islam and Christianity, the idea that a Muslim could gain spiritually from entering a church, and vice versa. It was certainly something I had often felt on entering a beautiful old mosque, that sense of otherworldliness which only a holy place can give. One of the 30 houses I had viewed before buying Bait Baroudi even contained the tomb of a *wali*, a Muslim holy man, which had been proudly shown to me as bringing extra *baraka* to the house. There was no suggestion that it added anything to its price, only to its spiritual worth.

As we drove into the old part of Homs I was surprised to see it had walls, like a miniature version of the Old City of Damascus, and even a few old gates. Unlike Damascus' Christian quarter where most residents were quite wealthy, it felt poor and a little run down. Homs was 30 per cent Christian, though most of them were not just in this quarter, but fully integrated throughout the districts of the city. In the revolution, during the famous fight for Baba Amr where the Sunday Times journalist Marie Colvin was killed, Christians fought alongside

Muslims, Tariq later told me, united in their struggle against the regime. In the souk, both Christians and Muslims owned shops side by side and had done for centuries. This social cohesion is the main reason why Homs, Syria's third city, rose up as one against the regime early on, unlike Damascus and Aleppo.

Homs has two main churches, about 300 metres apart, each one like a beautifully kept oasis of calm, both with fine biblical frescoes that ranged from the 6th to the 12th centuries. As ancient Emessa, Homs was an important early Christian centre with its own bishop. Even the Al-Nouri Mosque where we had met, it turned out, had once been a 12th century church dedicated to St John, on the site of a pagan temple, following the same pattern of evolution as the Great Umayyad Mosque of Damascus.

The larger of the two churches was the unfortunately named Church of the Holy Girdle, girdle being a mistranslation of belt, as legend had it that the long textile belt found below the altar in 1953 was used by the Virgin Mary. It is part of a complex of buildings which serve as the Syrian Orthodox Archbishopric and even has a small souvenir shop selling rosary beads which can double as worry beads. I have mine still. We were shown a tunnel and steps down into an early crypt and a special well of cool water, said to dispense *baraka* to all who drank from it. Tariq wolfed down three cupfuls with gusto.

Today it is on the front line, and has had its windows blown out, though the priceless frescoes are mercifully unharmed. They are even guarded by Muslims. Little heralded to the outside world, there are 35 Christian families who continue to live inside the city, either too poor or too old to leave. Tariq supports some of them financially, families his family has been intertwined with for generations. Homsi humour has helped them cope with the tragedies. 'Every joke is a tiny revolution' wrote George Orwell in 1945, and it was fitting that Homs, dubbed 'Capital of the Revolution', should fight back with its own jokes. Spoof Facebook pages such as 'Homs Tank Wash Services' have sprung up, offering washing and lubrication services to tanks cracking down on protesters. Posters were produced parodying the regime ones of Bashar with his paternally raised hand, but changing the slogans to things like 'I am free', 'I lost my shoes', 'I am with Syria.' Homsis posted pictures of themselves on Facebook with aubergines, zucchini and potatoes hanging from their belts like mock grenades, after the regime accused them of being armed gangs with sophisticated weapons. When the regime said they were all Islamists who shouted 'Allahu Akbar' (called the '*takbir*' in Arabic), they threw it back in their faces by changing the slogan to '*tahwil*', meaning 'bank transfers', a reference to regime figures thieving from the state coffers.

At the end of my stay Tariq announced that he would give me a lift down to Damascus, as some of his friends had suggested that he meet with a girl they felt he might be interested in. Normally, it would have been his mother who performed this service of finding him potential brides, as she had already done successfully for all his brothers, but she was currently all out of ideas, the last ones having been summarily rejected. He felt he might as well see what his friends could line up for him. 'In fact,' he said, 'why don't you come along? Then you can see the kind of thing I am up against.'

The date was set up for 10pm the following evening on the roof terrace of Leila's Restaurant. In recent years the rooftop restaurants of the Old City have become extremely fashionable with the in-crowd of wealthy Damascenes, as they are highly atmospheric and romantic venues where boys and girls can meet up in groups and get to know each other. On this occasion, to my surprise, there were ten of us, on a large pre-booked table in the corner, directly under the illuminated Jesus Minaret of the Great Umayyad Mosque, from whence, according to both Muslim and local Christian traditions, Jesus will descend on the Day of Judgement. The setting was breathtakingly surreal. Tariq and I arrived together, purely by chance, as he had driven into the Old City from a relation's place out in one of the fancier residential districts, and virtually run me over in the street. It was good not to be arriving alone, but instead to be more like Tariq's protégée, and he introduced me to them all. They were a mixed bunch of young Syrians, most of them students studying overseas, whose parents were paying for them to enjoy themselves back home here, over the summer. The girl it was all about was called Sara. She was stunningly beautiful, with cascading jet black, glossy hair; large, green eyes, and a slender but shapely figure shown off to perfection in tight, blue jeans and high heels, with a clinging, shiny, red top. Tariq appeared mesmerised from the start, and slid into the seat opposite her to begin the session.

It was like a business meeting, and each party knew exactly what it was about. There was no beating about the bush, and, encouraged by the presence of her friends, Sara began questioning Tariq, enquiring after his birthday, his star sign, his wealth, his prospects, his views on marriage, his views on children and much much more. It was fascinating, like something out of an Arabic version of *Sex in the City*. I was mesmerised too. She started producing photos of herself as a baby, passing them round, and began talking about what she was looking for in a husband. It was nothing if not to the point. It turned out she was 22 and studying business in Houston, Texas, where she lived with her brother in a flat their parents rented for them. Now she was here visiting them for the summer.

The discussion turned to fate, *qadr*.

'What do you think?' said Tariq, turning to me, 'Do you believe in what is *maktoub* (literally, 'written')?'

'Not on the whole,' I replied, 'but just sometimes, something happens that is so extraordinary, so unlikely, and in such amazing circumstances, that it is as if it is *maktoub*. Like with my house, I feel that must have been *maktoub*, there is no other explanation.' I told them the story of how I came to buy the house, and they agreed.

The meal came to an end and we all stayed on in high spirits until midnight. There was no alcohol. Leila's did not serve it, being so close to the mosque, but no one minded. No one needed it. Tariq never drank, despite his playboy image. Coke and fruit juice was all he ever had, the same as the others.

'Well,' said Tariq, after everyone had said their goodbyes down in the street. 'What do you think?'

I took a deep breath. 'Do you really want to know?

'Of course.'

'If I were you, I would run a mile.'

It was not the answer he had hoped for.

♦

All through the next week back in Damascus I enjoyed myself, spending lots of time with Bassim, Marwan, Rashid the lawyer and Maryam the bank manager. Ramzi the Philosopher was away out of Damascus touring the country with various foreign groups. Maryam seemed to have developed a soft spot for me, and was very keen that I meet her family. She invited me to join them for the day in the place they had recently bought jointly as a weekend getaway in the hills. 'It will be lovely and cool,' she said, 'we always catch the breeze there.' I felt I should accept, since she had been so good about letting me withdraw all that cash before the transfer had even been processed. Without her kindness, I would have had to default on the final payment and might well have lost the house. The money eventually turned up in the right place three weeks later, having got stuck in the Aleppo Free Zone correspondence bank, exactly as she had suspected.

She had never herself learnt to drive, but said her brother would take us in his car. It was about an hour's drive west towards the foothills of the Anti-Lebanon range, so they arranged to collect me from Straight Street late morning on a Sunday. It was a special feast, she said, the Feast of Mariam. I had not realised until then that she was Christian, Maryam being both a Muslim and a Christian name. It had never arisen or been relevant. When I mentioned it to Marwan, he too was surprised. Syria's Christian population, estimated at about 10 per cent of the total 22 million, had on the whole integrated seamlessly into the broader Muslim population. It was something the secular Ba'ath Party system of the Assad regime was keen to list among its achievements – protection of religious minorities – though it was questionable if they should take the credit, since religious harmony had existed in the country long before them.

Maryam and her brother chattered to us amiably on the drive, windows rolled down for the breeze as the car had no air conditioning, hair blowing in all directions. I sat in the back, amid huge piles of provisions for the day's events. As well as being the Feast of Mariam, it transpired it was also the birthday of Maryam's niece, Ruby, who was three. The whole extended family was going to be there, from her parents down to her sisters and all their children. She, it turned out, was the only unmarried sister. 'I cannot find a Syrian man who is not frightened of me,' she laughed, and I could believe it. She was a force of nature. Her mind was sharp as a razor and she switched subjects effortlessly from politics to women's clothes, from Syria's banking system to the food she liked. She was a live wire, and men must have found her truly intimidating. 'Can you find me an English man who will not be frightened of me?' she asked tossing her hair back and laughing even louder. 'I'm not sure,' I answered.

The car approached a bare hillside with a string of new developments laid out along a small ridge. The roads leading up to it were still just dirt tracks and many of the concrete houses were half-finished. We pulled up outside the end one. 'Isn't it beautiful?' she said proudly, 'We have just been planting the garden. It will be like Paradise.' I admired her vision, for what lay before us to my mind looked like a badly executed housing complex, built of ugly grey breeze blocks, sold on before the infrastructure was properly in place. She led us into the tiny earth garden, still muddy from recent watering, and introduced me to her parents and the rest of her family, including the birthday girl, little Ruby, who was dressed up for the occasion in a white frilly dress. None of them spoke English. 'Ruby is top of her class,' boasted Maryam, caressing Ruby's cheek and giving her a big kiss. 'She knows lots of words in English and can count to 20 already … can't you, Ruby, you clever girl. You will grow up to be a government minister and help our country to develop, won't you?' Ruby jumped up and down gleefully at the prospect. She did seem remarkably advanced for three – Syria's first female prime minister perhaps?

It was a wonderful day. They were clearly all delighted to have me there and to share their celebration. All had brought contributions of food, and I watched wide-eyed as the feast was laid out on folding plastic-tables and paper plates, beginning with red jelly and chips, and ending with pizza and ice cream, all washed down with Coke and fizzy orange. It was like a giant picnic, and there were high spirits all round. Maryam's father talked about his Kurdish ancestry and recounted stories from his childhood. Her sister, Ruby's mother, who was a pharmacist, chatted about her work and her customers, while Ruby herself spilt jelly and pizza all over her dress, squatted in the muddy water pools around the newly planted trees, and danced in circles, enchanting all the adults. I was genuinely sad when it started to grow dark, time for her brother to drive me back to the city.

10

The Donkey between Two Carrots

To taste is to know.

Al-Ghazali

'With the time came the man', runs the saying. One of Islam's greatest thinkers, Al-Ghazali, was born into a turbulent world in 11th century Persia. He resigned from his well-paid teaching position at the court in Baghdad, where he had been a towering figure as a highly respected jurist and theologian, made arrangements for his family, sold his possessions and disappeared into the Syrian wilderness. Seeking peace and refuge in Syria, he eventually regained his mental health in Damascus. Writing in Arabic, he went on to produce over 70 books on Islamic philosophy and the sciences. He withdrew from formal academic life and shunned involvement in the networks of power, saying he needed a period of *'uzla*, 'isolation'. The period was to last ten years, two of them spent in a Damascus minaret.

For much of his life the Muslim world was locked in a bitter sectarian struggle between the Sunni Abbasid caliphate in Baghdad and its rival Fatimid Shi'ite caliphate in Cairo. A radical group called 'the Assassins', today's equivalent of Al-Qaeda, were carrying out targeted killings of high-level figures, intent on undermining the political status quo. The 14th-century jurist As-Subkhi wrote of him: 'he taught at a time when people had more need of the truth than the darkness has of the light of the heavens and the barren land of the fruitful rain. If there had been a prophet after Muhammad, it would surely have been Al-Ghazali.' His achievement was to bring the Sunni orthodoxy of his time into a closer alignment with the tolerance of Sufi mysticism. How desperately Syria needs an Al-Ghazali now.

Among the stories Al-Ghazali told to illustrate his thinking was that of a donkey between two carrots. The donkey agonises over which carrot might be juicier or bigger for so long that it ends up dying of starvation in the middle. The moral of the tale is to show how indecision is a form of decision and its consequences potentially deadly. Such indecisive donkeys have been tragically abundant in the Syrian crisis. America could not decide what its course of action should be until 30 months into the revolution, and even then, poised to strike against the Assad regime in reaction to their use of chemical weapons, Obama handed the 'hot potato' decision back to Congress. The subsequent unanimous UN Security Council agreement to dismantle Syria's chemical weapons arsenal allowed indecision on the war itself to continue.

Syria's 'silent majority' has also been unable to choose between the two extremes on offer – the regime or the rebels: 'You are either with us or against us.' The reason Khalid, as an apolitical environmentalist, had left for Amman in the early days was to avoid having to make that choice. It was the same reason that so many refugees had felt compelled to leave their country, not just to escape the fighting. Had there been a moderate alternative in the middle, a carrot so obviously juicier and bigger than the others, all parties would surely have chosen it long ago. Instead the two carrots have been getting further and further apart, making it harder and harder for the silent majority to decide.

Al-Ghazali, I recalled from my distant studies, arrived in Damascus in a state of crisis, and was given the uppermost apartments of a minaret. Not just any minaret, but the Great Umayyad Mosque's Minaret of the Bride, Islam's earliest minaret. He was even living up there during the First Crusade, when Jerusalem fell, though he makes no reference to it. His concerns were spiritual, not worldly.

'I turned to the way of the mystics,' he wrote, he who had turned from orthodox Sunni Islam to Sufism late in life, making the latter respectable even. As a student I had read his *Al-Munqidh min Al-Dallal* ('Deliverance from Error'), a kind of autobiography. Written a few years before his death in 1111 and often compared to St Augustine's *Confessions*, he describes his spiritual and physical breakdown, despite all his learning and fame. 'I realised that what is most distinctive can be attained only by personal experience (Arabic *dhawq*, literally 'taste'), ecstasy and a change of character ... I saw clearly that the mystics were men not of words but of personal experience, and that I had gone as far as I could by way of study and intellectual effort, so that only personal experience and walking in the mystic way were left.'

Who could fail to recover, after two years of living in such a building? Regaining his faith through discovering the power of Sufism, Islamic mysticism, he realised that the Sufi experience was the highest form of knowledge and that beauty was created by God for humans to perceive and enjoy: 'Pleasure is a type of perception' *(al-ladhdha naw' idrak)*, he realised, 'to taste is to know' *(man dhaaqa 'arifa)*. He compared the world to a big house decorated with the most precious materials, and explained that we have been given our five senses to see, taste, feel, smell and hear the beauty all around us. That is a reflection of God's light and power. By perceiving this beauty through reflection and contemplation, humans will be led ultimately to God, he believed. Perception of beauty leads to God, and perception of this beauty gives us a taste for the eternal bliss of the hereafter. Thus, the simple acts of daily life, like eating and drinking and listening to music have behind them a mystical level, through which we can perceive the divine.

I was struck by the huge contrasts between the rich spiritual life of Islam's devout early mystics, the current intolerant extremism of its *jihadi* fundamentalists and the secular scholarship of modern times. Our Westernised, materialistic society has largely lost its capacity to perceive not just the superficial 'outer' beauty absorbed by the senses of sight, smell, touch, hearing and taste, but also the higher level of beauty, the 'inner' beauty perceived by the heart. In Al-Ghazali's *The Alchemy of Happiness* he explains how the more that people can abstract and discipline their faculties, the closer they will come to the apprehension of exalted things, to the attainment of supreme happiness. Is this the beauty that some people see in suffering, I wondered? Is this what helps a Muslim accept even death? It is a common concept in Arabic thought that beauty has the power to free people from sorrows. No wonder it is so cherished.

Al-Ghazali, in his greatest work *Ihya 'Ulum Al-Din* ('The Renaissance of Religious Sciences'), made the point that man should sanctify all aspects of life, aware at any moment that he may die and meet his maker. He even described how to eat and drink, how to lead a married life and any number of other worldly activities. All his writings are preparations for death, often exploring the relationship between death and dreams, and between reality and dreams. In *Al-Munqidh* he has a dialogue between sense-perception and intellect-judge, where he downgrades intellect as being inferior to intuitive knowledge. Sense-perception, talking about dreams, says:

> Do you not see how, when you are asleep, you believe things and imagine circumstances … and so long as you are in that dream-condition, have no doubts about them? And is it not the case that when you are awake you know that all you have imagined and believed is unfounded and ineffectual? Why then are you confident that all your waking beliefs, whether from sense or intellect, are genuine? … perhaps life in this world is a dream by comparison with the world to come; and when a man dies, things come to appear differently to him from what he now beholds.

He also wonders whether maybe the trance that Sufis reach during their *dhikr*, their 'special state', when they achieve *fana*, 'oblivion' or 'annihilation' of the self, is the closest thing man can ever achieve to union with God, short of death itself.

'The happiness of the drop is to die in the river,' he said. Is this what suicide bombers believe at the moment of their death, that they are merging with God? The *jihadi* rebel group Jabhat Al-Nusra even talks in terms of 'martyrdom-seeking operations' and declares in its propaganda videos posted via its own media outlet: 'We are a people who will either gain victory or die.' Such an extreme ideology could hardly be more different to that of the moderate Al-Ghazali.

How curious that Al-Ghazali had arrived at his carefully considered conclusions whilst on retreat in Damascus. And how even more curious it is that one of Islam's most famous mystics, Ibn Arabi, after wandering through North Africa, Egypt, Mecca and Turkey should also choose to settle in Damascus for the final 17 years of his life. He died here in 1240. Born in Andalusia he found in Damascus a freer environment and a more receptive audience for his teachings than in Cairo or in Muslim Spain. He was greeted as a spiritual master and given a spacious house by the grand qadi (judge) to live in with his wife and son. Saint, philosopher, mystic, sage, poet and traveller, his writings focussed on the seven stages of man's journey to union with God, the mystical ascent to the final stage where he becomes the 'Perfect Man' (Arabic *al-insan al-kamil*) and is filled with love.

He experienced several religious visions whilst in Damascus, including one in which he saw Jesus, Moses and the Prophet Muhammad together. In another the Prophet passed him the book *Fusus Al-Hikma*, 'Bezels of Wisdom', a book of 27 chapters in which each chapter spoke of a different prophet and a different aspect of wisdom. None of it, Ibn Arabi insisted, had come from his own learning.

In another vision Ibn Arabi saw himself on a nighttime journey (like the Prophet's *mi'raj*) ascending to the outer limits of creation. There, in a garden, at the furthest boundary of the cosmos, he hears the discourse of a 'Universal Tree' and four spiritual birds whose charming tales and elaborate speeches mask the fact that they are none other than the awesome images of the Perfect Human Being with his four cosmic faculties. His supreme command of Arabic and all its complexities shows itself in many intricate plays on words, but his message of unity and inclusiveness to all shines through:

> *O Marvel! A garden amidst the flames,*
> *My heart has become capable of all forms:*
> *A pasture for gazelles, a monastery for Christian monks,*
> *A temple for idols, the Ka'abah for Muslim pilgrims,*
> *The tablets of the Torah, the Book of the Quran,*
> *I profess the religion of Love.*
> *Whatever direction Love's camels take,*
> *That is my religion and my faith.*

With such visions of the hereafter, who would fear death? There are far worse things than death. Sons going out on protests would say to their mothers: 'Pray that I am killed rather than captured.' Death was infinitely preferable to torture in captivity. A six-year-old boy tried to hang himself after witnessing the torture of his parents: 'I want to die this way,' he said to his rescuers, 'rather than let Bashar's armies kill me slowly.'

Today in Damascus, every Friday a little after the Maghreb prayer, a Sufi *dhikr* is still held at Ibn Arabi's tomb in the Muhyiddin Mosque in As-Salihiya under the shadow of Jabal Qasioun. It used to be led by a sufi shaikh, formerly Mufti of Sweden, then living in Damascus, called Shaikh Muhammad Al-Ya'qoubi. 'All are welcome, all denominations, all sects,' he used to say. I attended it once. 'Ibn Arabi,' he declared with certainty, 'is present in the tomb and listens to the prayers of pilgrims who visit him. Some believers even claim to see a beam of light leading from his tomb to the *dhikr*. But for most, the light is hidden, concealed behind a series of veils, veils which represent the layers of ignorance in men's perception. As the mystic progresses through various levels and stages of understanding to higher levels of perception, the veils begin to lift away and become more translucent, allowing him to be closer to God. Every life is, whether consciously or not, a voyage of discovery towards what unity with God really means.' The teachings of both Ibn Arabi and Al-Ghazali were addressed to all, everyone was welcome. It made me think of the English composer John Tavener's piece, 'The Protecting Veil', inspired by the mysticism of the Eastern Orthodox Church to which he himself converted from Presbyterianism.

In June 2011 Shaikh Muhammad Al-Ya'qoubi was expelled from Syria by the regime. He had openly criticised the government for its violent response towards peaceful protesters and had called for Bashar al-Assad to resign. From exile in Morocco he has been actively engaged in fundraising for the victims of violence personally leading convoys of food, aid and blankets in December 2012 to help displaced Syrians in Turkey get through the winter. Men such as him will be much needed in Syria's future and he feels strongly that after the war, the role of Islamic scholars will be vital in helping to heal the rifts in Syrian society, to reach out to everyone. He began by supporting Kofi

Annan's Six-Point plan for peace by diplomatic means, but when I met him again in London in January 2013, invited by him to speak at a fundraising event, he had become deeply frustrated at the inertia of the international community and was lobbying energetically for foreign intervention by Jordan, Turkey, NATO, the UN and America. His attempts to join the Syrian National Council as its first major Sufi representative were also thwarted by powerful Muslim Brotherhood figures who dominate that body in exile. Having been informed of his appointment in April 2013, the offer was promptly withdrawn the following month before it went public. Qatari intrigues behind the scenes were to blame, it later emerged, as they wanted more power for their own Muslim Brotherhood protégés. Men like Shaikh Muhammad Al-Ya'qoubi were too outspoken for the regime, and too conciliatory for the rebels. Neither side wanted him to be the moderate carrot in the middle, and the silent majority stayed silent, too frightened to have a voice.

What a mess the Syrian opposition has become. Far more extreme than the Muslim Brotherhood elements, fanatical fundamentalist groups like Jabhat Al-Nusra and the Islamic State of Iraq and Sham (ISIS) with their black flags and black balaclavas have been increasingly hijacking Syria's revolution. Spearheaded by religious extremists, some of whom were even released from Assad's own prisons, and sponsored by wealthy individuals in Saudi Arabia and the Gulf, they are affiliated with Al-Qaeda and believe all aspects of Islam need to revert to the 'purity' of the time of the Prophet, which is why they are also called *Salafis* (from Arabic *salaf,* meaning ancestors). Will they destroy and loot the beautiful shrine of Ibn Arabi, just as their *Salafi* co-ideologists have already looted and destroyed the Sufi shrines of Libya? Their numbers are increasing all the time and most of them are not even Syrian.

Jabhat Al-Nusra was created in January 2012, nearly a year into the revolution, and was initially welcomed as an organised and well-armed fighting force by the Free Syrian Army (FSA), in the absence of support from America and the West. The FSA was therefore very angry when America and Britain designated Al-Nusra a terrorist organisation, considering this to be a basic misunderstanding by the West of the realities on the ground inside Syria. It is a confused picture as ever. The well-respected Institute for the Study of War has even speculated that Al-Nusra's origins are linked with the Assad regime, from the days when it was funding militant Islamist groups to cross the border into Iraq and to fight against the Western coalition troops after they had toppled Saddam Hussein in 2003. What an irony that these same fighters, most of whom are Syrian, should now be fighting against the very regime that had sponsored them in the first place. Their stated aim in entering the Syrian conflict was to topple the Assad regime, then create an Islamic state ruled by *Shar'ia* law. In practice, as time goes on they seem more interested in the latter than the former, much to the alarm of ordinary Syrian citizens. In the early months of the revolution they accounted for no more than 3–4 per cent of the rebels overall, maybe reaching 10 per cent around Aleppo. The well-armed regime troops are getting worn out, but fighting, they feel, to stop their country becoming a '*Salafi* kingdom.'

While most fighters in Al-Nusra are from Syria, the extremist group ISIS which appeared over a year later in April 2013 is both foreign-led (by an Iraqi) and foreign-dominated. Its fighters come mainly from Saudi Arabia, Libya and Tunisia, though there are also Chechens, Kuwaitis, Jordanians and Iraqis as well as a few Pakistani Taliban and even Chinese. Dressed in their Pakistani-style tunics and menacing black balaclavas, brandishing their weapons, they form a stark contrast to the conservative but moderate Sunni Muslims who make up 74 per cent of Syria's resident population. Typical communiqués use language like: 'Our army is full of hungry lions who drink blood and eat bones.' It is hard to imagine their ideology ever taking root in Syria, despite their ceaseless propaganda videos on YouTube and their thousands of tweets – all the rebel groups have their own highly active Twitter accounts.

Many Syrians told me long before the revolution that the Syrian brand of Islam is close to the tolerant Sufi Islam of Ibn Arabi and Al-Ghazali – open to all and with no coercion. Yet groups like ISIS are so intolerant they even started to ban tobacco as un-Islamic in areas they controlled in Syria's north, not just alcohol and what they called 'immoral entertainment'. The kind of Syria they are trying to usher in would end up destroying the country's very identity, its tolerant character. Moderate Syrians have begun social media campaigns against them with slogans like: '*DAESH* [Arabic for 'ISIS'] GO OUT. Bashar and DAESH are one. We didn't have a revolution against a tyrant for another tyrant to come and control us in the name of religion! Those who belong to Syria, Syria is for all of you. Those who belong to Al-Qaeda, go to Afghanistan!' Dozens of Arabic language Facebook pages have been set up rejecting ISIS, its Islamic credentials and its brutal tactics. Ordinary Libyans have finally ejected their extremist fighters; ordinary Syrians will eventually do the same, given the chance.

Apart from Shaikh Muhammad Al-Ya'qoubi, one or two other candidates have tried to be that moderate middle-ground carrot of Al-Ghazali's: men like Muaz Al-Khatib. When the election of this remarkable man – the former imam at the Damascus Umayyad Mosque and from a highly respected family of imams – as the new head of the SNC was announced, many including myself were filled with hope that all would be well. His pedigree was perfect, and like Shaikh Muhammad he had spoken out against the regime early on and been expelled. He exuded charisma, authority and wisdom, but sadly such men are ill-equipped to survive dirty political intrigues where the requisites for success are over-arching ambition and greed rather than any genuine concern for the Syrian people. His only mistake was never to mention, in any of his otherwise statesman-like speeches, his commitment to regaining the occupied Golan Heights from Israel, a serious omission in the eyes of most Syrians. In March 2013 he resigned, saying he could not accept the many conditions outside foreign powers were placing on aid to the opposition, nor their manipulation of events for their own interests. Earlier he had made a direct offer to the regime, saying he was ready to talk to the Vice-President Farouq Al-Sharaa in a neutral country in return for the release of political prisoners. No response came, hopes were dashed, a good man was lost and another possible avenue towards reconciliation was blocked.

❦

As for me, I was another of Al-Ghazali's donkeys, unable to decide, now that I had bought the house of my dreams, what on earth to do with it. Acquisition had been the goal, but now that the goal was realised, what direction should the restoration take? Bassim had already launched the process by obtaining a *rukhsat tarmim basit*, a 'simple restoration licence' from Maktab Anbar, the headquarters of the Directorate of Old Damascus, and was now awaiting instructions. He had drawn up proper architectural scale drawings, so I could spend hours poring over them. Beyond restoring the house to its former grandeur, saving it from dereliction and collapse, I had no very clear idea what I wanted to do with it. Was it realistic to think I would ever live in it myself? It was impossible to say.

Finances were the overwhelming constraint. Everyone told me the obvious thing was to turn it into a boutique hotel. There was a very clear demand for good quality rooms in the Old City and I played on my calculator, trying to forecast running costs and room rates, coming up with some startling profit margins. I even went to see a senior engineer recommended by the Ministry of Tourism for guidance on the technical requirements, since I had no idea what the rules were. The pioneer was a businesswoman from Aleppo, Maya Mamarbachi, who had spent years restoring a house in the Christian quarter, and had now turned it into Damascus' first boutique hotel, Bait Al-Mamlouka. Bassim had worked with her on that project as a trainee architect, and had introduced me to her. I decided to pay her a visit and find out about the realities of running a small hotel. Maya was very obliging and invited me in to sit with her over the course of a morning, so I could observe what she did.

The alternative option was to convert the top floor of the house into a self-contained flat for renting out, either long-term or short-term, whilst keeping the ground floor for myself or for friends to stay in. There was plenty to think about.

Sitting in Maya's office I observed as she dealt with a succession of issues. First there were the complaints from the guests, saying the night-watchman had kept them awake by talking on his mobile in the courtyard all night long. She raised her eyes to heaven and said she would have to sack him, as this was the third time it had happened. Then there were the employees' health issues. A cleaner came in complaining of a pain in her arm, saying she thought she needed to go to hospital. After a bout of questioning, Maya gave her some money and told her to catch a taxi there, but to return as soon as possible.

Next came two government officials, saying they needed to do another health and safety check, a particularly absurd pretext, since health and safety regulations in Syria are non-existent. The world's finest Crusader castle, Krak des Chevaliers near Homs, didn't have a single safety rail in sight along its spectacularly sheer ramparts, and in Hama I used to watch young boys leaping into the Orontes river after dark, launching themselves with impeccable timing from the highest point of the groaning ancient waterwheels, beside a sign in Arabic which translated as: 'Swimming and approaching the waterwheels is forbidden.'

Maya told me these same officials had already come two weeks earlier and done all the safety checks, and that they simply wanted more bribe money. In their position they could randomly close her down anytime they felt like it, so it was worth her while to pay them off each time they called. It was the accepted practice. She told me how she longed for the good old days during the restoration phase, when life had been simple. Then, she said, it was just a question of paying off the neighbours. 'You must add at least 10 per cent of your budget for your neighbours. They think you are rich because you are renovating your property, and they come forward with all sorts of things they insist you pay for because they say you have caused damage. I ended up paying to repair the chimney of one neighbour, installing a new bathroom for another, and repairing the roof of a third. It was just expected, so I did it to keep the peace and to stop them complaining and making life difficult for me.'

This helped me decide: I needed to keep it simple. By turning the upstairs into a flat I would avoid the headaches of having to employ staff or mess about with adding en suite bathrooms. It had never seemed right to think in terms of altering the proportions, to destroy the centuries-old layout of the rooms. I wanted to keep the house as close as possible to its current structure; minimal interference, I concluded, would be the guiding principle.

The donkey and the carrot story is not so far-fetched, because this decision took, in reality, a full 18 months of agonising. Dying of starvation along the way did seem like one of the options. There were all sorts of complications, most of them unforeseen. The financial one was obvious. I knew the golden rule of restoration: get a quote, then double it; not just the actual budget but also the timescale. It was unlikely to be any different in Syria – who knows, probably worse.

What I had not reckoned on was the matter of the *mukhalafas*, literally in Arabic, the 'violations.' Syrian property law, it transpired, is based on the way each house in the Old City has been recorded in the exhaustive property register carried out by the French under the mandate in the 1920s; the French were particularly keen on cataloguing, also compiling the first ever catalogue of Syria's antiquities. For residential property, a meticulous record had been made in 1925 of exactly what each house consisted of. Any deviation from that written record was considered a *mukhalafa*, a violation or breaking away from the position as laid out in the French cadastral plan, no matter how absurd or irrelevant it now seemed. Consideration of the number of potential *mukhalafas* in a house was, along with a 'clean' title, one of the likely obstacles I had been warned about when buying a house in Syria. Bait Baroudi, Bassim had said, did not have many *mukhalafas*, so obtaining the restoration licence should not be too difficult.

In the event, when the committee from Maktab Anbar came round to inspect the house, they found four. One had been expected: the makeshift bathroom on the roof that had clearly been added after 1925. It would simply have to be removed, like all *mukhalafas*, since it should never have been added. But the other three were completely unexpected: the kitchen ceiling and the downstairs bathroom ceiling both turned out to be made of concrete and concrete was a violation, not in use before 1925. Neither of us had noticed these ceilings before, as they were so filthy it was impossible to guess their age. At some point since 1925 these ceilings must have needed repair and the easiest and cheapest thing to do had been to slap concrete up there. The fourth violation was the most ridiculous and could not have been foreseen, as it involved the door from the street into the derelict part of the house. This, we had worked out from our study of the house layout, would have been the original door into the courtyard, yet by the time the 1925 French records were compiled, it had been walled up. Therefore the law required this original door to be blocked up again, even though the other street door was clearly a later addition. It was typical of the absurdities of the system under which everyone had to labour.

When a system imposes so many constraints, it is only human nature to try to find ways round it, as all Syrians have been forced to do for decades. Maybe this outside-the-box type of thinking has made Syrians more ingenious. Maybe it is no coincidence that Steve Jobs' birth father was a Syrian from Homs. We racked our brains to come up with novel solutions, and it required all Bassim's powers of ingenuity to overcome the problem of the two ceilings, and all of mine to overcome the problem of the blocked original entrance. Bassim had the brainwave of covering the kitchen ceiling with a fake old wooden beamed one. Then he would get a different engineer back to inspect the property and ask him to redo the report. The ceiling was so high, he assured me, no one would notice that the fake ceiling was new not old. It would be like a reverse *mukhalafa* – the irony appealed to me. And it worked. An entire inspection team came and never noticed. Back in England, I received Bassim's text message:

> Dear, just yesterday the committee come to the house, they fanded everything ok. Hope during 10 days we have the licence.

Bassim could have started a business in fake old ceilings. For the bathroom ceiling he had another brainwave. He would remove the concrete and replace it with a dome, so that it looked like a Turkish *hammam*, and would even put in fake holes with lights, to replicate the traditional style of Turkish baths, lit by many tiny circles of bottle glass. It was a stroke of genius. Steve Jobs would have been proud of him. My own contribution to solving the problem of the last *mukhalafa* was to turn the area inside the blocked up doorway into a large bathroom. Today it is the world's most beautiful bathroom, a joy to ablute in, with stone flooring and heavy beams. The original Mamluk fountain is perfect for washing dusty feet, and the Syrian toilet is like a throne, obtained from the Zenobia Company, the local sanitary ware firm named after the rebellious desert queen of Palmyra.

I was in my element during the chaos of restoration. The house was a total mess. There was mud, filth and debris all over the place, in the courtyard, in all the rooms. But I did not see it. Scaffolding held up the painted ceiling in the *'ajami* room while the roof was dismantled and repaired. But it did not worry me. We cleared out the sand and dirt that had accumulated over the centuries above the roof beams, stripped off the damaged plaster exposing the *adoubi* ('mud brick') and poplar-tree poles of the original construction. Scratching around in the dirt of an Ottoman palace, fingernails black with the dust of history, hair caked with sweat and filth, I did not see the turmoil all around me. I only saw the vision we were striving for. In my mind's eye, all was clear.

Syria too was on a high during that summer of 2006. Next door in Lebanon, Hezbollah had dealt the Israelis a severe blow and the atmosphere in Damascus was euphoric. The Street Called Straight was decked with celebratory yellow and green flags and banners of Hezbollah and T-shirts with the smiling face of Hassan Nasrallah. I bought mine along with everyone else. Bassim, Marwan and Ramzi, along with hundreds of other ordinary Syrian citizens, drove to the border every day after work to collect thousands of fleeing Lebanese refugees and bring them to their own homes for shelter. Schools opened specially to house them for the summer. Over a hundred slept in the *iwan* of the Danish Institute.

From morning until night I was in Bait Baroudi with the workers. Most of them were Palestinian, as it turned out, living in the unofficial refugee camp of Yarmouk, indistinguishable to the untrained eye from Damascus' other southern suburbs. Largest of 59 refugee camps, it was dubbed Palestine's capital in exile, yet after rebels poured in, it became one of the many targets of regime bombardment, and subjected to a siege of such length that the shaikhs in Friday prayers eventually gave the desperate residents permission to eat cats and dogs. 'Surrender or starve,' the regime told them, whilst ignoring international calls to allow humanitarian aid agencies in or to allow civilians out. Bassim said the Palestinians were the best workers, especially the carpenters, plumbers and stonemasons.

Whenever I had to make trips back to England, Mas'oun the electrician actually lived in Bait Baroudi like a guard, very tidily, in a corner of a downstairs room, the rest of the space piled high with tools, radiators and boiler equipment. He would talk of how much he had grown to love the house, and how he loved it most of all after dark when he was alone. On Fridays he would visit his family in Deraa, near the Jordanian border, then known to everyone only as the place where TE Lawrence had his notorious encounter with a Turkish soldier, and now known to everyone as the place where the first demonstrations and deaths took place in March 2011 in Syria's revolution. It is one of the poorest areas of Syria, home to thousands of displaced people from the northeast of the country because of an acute water crisis after four years of drought in the Jazira region. Mas'oun would talk of the beauty of Deraa, its waterfalls, its gorge of the Yarmouk river.

The other workers, Abu Mahmoud the stonemason, Faadi the painter, Muhsin the plumber and Faadil the plasterer came and went according to the need for them, but there were always at least three or four of us sitting together for tea breaks, perched on the fountain edge or on battered plastic chairs. In Bassim's lists of accounts tea and sugar featured separately as entries, it being accepted local practice for the employer to provide refreshment for his workers. Their daily wage was SY400 for the unskilled and SY600 for the skilled workers, the equivalent of £4 and £6 in the currency of the day. Bassim would pop in regularly to give instructions, but otherwise I was alone with them. They accepted me and I accepted them – it was the VIth form of the verb again, the verb of doing things mutually. Sometimes, towards the end of the day, when Mas'oun was out shopping or praying, I would go up on the roof and just sit and watch the palm doves whirling in the sky or listen to the sounds of the city. The music of the call to prayer from the myriad mosques echoed round the walls and on Sundays the church bells were distantly audible from the Christian quarter. The city was entering my soul.

It was a marvel that all these craftsmen still existed, taking a pride in their work in a way that scarcely exists in the West anymore. In Damascus these crafts were alive and well, and normal. A metal-worker would work for seven months on one bronze vase and think nothing of it. The men in the souk who sold the silk to cover the cushions of my 'ajami room seating would explain to me the meaning of the different patterns and colours. The design on the Damascene embroidered tablecloth I bought, they explained, was a stylised pomegranate, dating back to Roman times when it was a common fertility symbol. I was living steeped in history, which enriched the simplest of everyday activities. Surely the very act of sitting down on such a fabric would bring with it a special pleasure, as would the very act of eating off such a cloth; it was Al-Ghazali's *dhawq* in action.

I wondered what thoughts were in the heads of the craftsmen as they worked for months, maybe even years, on these extraordinarily beautiful walls and ceiling. Mysterious panels, coloured green, ran all round the room at a height of about three metres, and written on them in golden paint was an exquisite, cursive Arabic script. Had anyone studied the writing in these 'ajami rooms? My Arabic was good and I had studied a great deal of obscure Arabic literature as an undergraduate, but I could make out very little of these strange inscriptions. I even wondered if it was Arabic at all – maybe it was Ottoman Turkish which is written in Arabic script? I later discovered, with Ramzi's help, that the inscriptions were a Sufi incantation, its words chosen by the original master of the house to create a world within a world, a search for immortality through union with God.

The final discovery in Bait Baroudi, on stripping out the accumulated debris of decades, was a trio of vertical clay pipes suddenly emerging from the gloom – we had inadvertently stumbled upon the original water system that had led into the house from the street. They would certainly have dated back to Ottoman times, but might have been earlier than that, Byzantine or even Roman, since the building material had not changed. The Roman water system in Damascus was thought to have survived more or less intact into Ottoman times. Each house of significance in the city had its own water supply running directly inside, feeding the courtyard fountain, and running out again, in a circular system. Above the three vertical clay pipes we uncovered a small carved niche and alcove, where an oil lamp would originally have lit the space. Bassim suggested it would be wise to block off the tops of the pipes with a wire netting to make sure snakes and scorpions did not find their way into the house. After all, the pipes would certainly lead to dark underground passages that were now dry, perfect lodgings for such creatures.

Following these discoveries I sometimes regretted my decision not to go ahead with an idea to dig down under the courtyard to create my own *hammam*. Bassim had even drawn up plans based on my specifications – just big enough for six. Who knows what we might have found? Would there have been more traces of the early water system? Roman mosaics even? I had ruled it out for financial reasons. *Hammams* have a long tradition in Damascus, begun by the Romans. The object was not simply to get clean, but to gossip, to network, to discuss the latest goings on, the markets, the prices, both for Romans and for Arabs. Arab men would go, not every day like the Romans, but perhaps every other day, after work. But while Roman women were not allowed entry to the baths, Arab women were given designated times during the day when the baths were made over exclusively to women and the staff would be female. If a husband refused his wife bath money, it was grounds for divorce under the *Shar'ia*. For women it was almost their only social opportunity to mix with women from other families. Even the shopping was done by men, the market not being viewed as a seemly place for women to appear in public. But they were permitted into the closed world of the *hammam*. Here prospective mothers-in-law would eye up potential brides for their sons, as all was on view, and bargains were struck. Not so long ago Tariq's mother would have found him a suitable bride from the *hammam*, gaining a view of her he would have no chance of getting until the wedding night.

When water shortages in the Old City were very bad, lasting more than a day or two, I too reverted to Ottoman ways, visiting the Hammam Al-Nasiri, my neighbourhood *hammam,* and emerging like a new species that has shed its top skin layers. Even before the revolution, mains water would usually only flow between two and four hours a day in summer, and the rest of the time everyone had to rely on the water tanks on their roofs. Syria suffered four years of drought in a row until winter 2011, with rainfall levels far lower than usual. On every visit I would discuss the water situation regularly with Abu Ashraf, my faithful caretaker. It was one of the first things I would ask him about on arrival, how full the water tanks were, and what time of day the cuts were. Once I said to him I wished England could give some rain to Syria. We have *akthar min al-lazim*, 'more than necessary', I assured him, we could afford it. That is *shughl Allah*, 'God's work', he replied simply.

Tony the Yorkshire stonemason, a later tenant in my upstairs flat for two years, told me that had I built my own *hammam*, it would in fact have been the safest place to take shelter in the event of an earthquake, an event he was sure was imminent. 'When it comes,' he said, 'I'm heading for the fountain pool. That'll be the best place since you stupidly didn't build the *hammam*.' Today it would have made a good bomb shelter.

11

The Law and Educational Corruption

May God protect the vineyard from its watchman.

Arab proverb

Legal nightmares, I was soon to discover, were part of normal life in Syria. Most people seemed to have had direct experience of court cases somehow or other. Throughout the restoration years of Bait Baroudi I had regular meetings with Rashid the lawyer to get bulletins on the progress of my ownership documents through the quagmire of Syrian bureaucracy. We would always meet in the same place – Marwan's tiny shop – since the house itself was not yet in a fit state to hold meetings.

Inevitably there were times when, because of work and family commitments, I had to be back in England during the interminable process, sometimes receiving text message updates from Rashid in Damascus via Marwan which brought such welcome relief from tedious English paperwork that I wrote them all down verbatim just for the sheer entertainment value of re-reading them whenever my spirits needed lifting.

One day I got a text from Marwan:

Today all thing's went very well at the court and he get his money. take care.

Unaware of any court case I had no idea what he was talking about, so texted back:

> That is good. What happened at court and who got his money?

The reply came:

> That mean the house is your's by acourt order so it's done and the house is all your's now by law.

That seemed like good news, so I was therefore even more puzzled when his next text, some weeks later, ran:

> Hi sorry to say that there is no news but Rashid told me that there is some thing he can do with the court so you do not loss the kiass all the best.

I asked for clarifications and he obliged:

> Hello! How r u? The papers still in the scurrity [security] even doumnek's papers still the same. Anyway the low [law] has edited by the coverment [government] 2weeks a go w r still I waiting 4the details.

This was getting alarming, and I texted back:

> Is the kiass the difference in price before and after restoration? Am frightened at how the law may change! Could they still take the house away from me?

The reply came moments later:

> The change wuld be better and about after the restoration we could manage it anyway don't be afraid no one will take ur house from u.

The law relating to house ownership by foreigners inside Syria was in a constant state of flux, as were many other laws. In 2006 it was suddenly announced that non-Syrians were banned from ownership, but by that time my papers had already entered the system. The reason for that change in law was not to prevent people like me from buying, but to prevent Iraqis. Over two million of them had fled Iraq as refugees from the fighting that followed Saddam's fall, and the wealthy ones started buying up property, especially in Damascus, distorting the market by pushing up prices so Syrians could no longer afford to buy. By 2009 another law had come in permitting ownership under certain conditions; any property with a ground area of more than 200 square metres could now be bought by a foreigner, leaving the smaller places available for Syrians. Bait Baroudi was comfortably in the bigger category, so I assumed my paperwork would finally progress through the system. Instead, my documents remained 'frozen' in the security headquarters for the next year, no doubt awaiting the requisite level of bribery before any progress could be made. Rashid did his best, trying court case after court case, but lots of Iraqis were caught like me in the system, and only a few of them got through by devising complex appeals. By the time my case came to be heard, the female judge had lost patience with the appeals and ruled against me. Today I still have no ownership papers, just the original contract of sale, though Rashid tells me that among Bashar's raft of reforms rushed through after the revolution broke out, there was a new law permitting all foreigners to buy again – a perfect opportunity for a future risk-taking investor.

Text exchanges with Bassim when I was back in England tended to involve money and negotiations with Nazir Al-Baroudi. Since all the house ownership papers were still in Nazir's name, we needed power of attorney from him every time we had to apply for restoration licences, extensions to restoration licences and suchlike.

Once or twice, when I happened to be in Damascus at times that coincided with the various court cases, Rashid the lawyer took me with him to attend the hearings. The fine, old court building dated back to the French Mandate and stood on Al-Nasr Street just outside the city walls, more or less opposite Maryam's bank. There were always crowds outside the building, milling about in groups, but the inside was like a scene from Dante's *Inferno*. Shouting hordes were everywhere, pushing, straining to get up the stairs and into the various offices, frantically waving pieces of paper in the air. Rashid was a maestro, and I was forever impressed at how deftly he dodged the crowds, weaving to and fro until he got to the head of the queue and then with a toss of his head, caught the eye of the relevant official behind his desk or at his *guichet*. Once we also had to go to a police station for me to sign various papers on the ownership of the house, and the multi-stage process took minutes rather than the customary hours, thanks no doubt to the previous greasing of palms that had taken place.

My only successful court case, and this was totally without bribery, was against the neighbour's son, who seemed to have become slightly unhinged. He would appear at the door of Bait Baroudi with wild eyes, often late at night, ranting and raving about the damage the restoration work was causing, and about how his father was becoming ill from the noise and disruption. Sometimes I found him quite scary and intimidating, and Bassim told me I should complain to the *mukhtar* ('local mayor') on grounds of harassment. Eventually I did, and the effect was dramatic – peace at last, and the judge in the court case found against him thanks to the *mukhtar*'s evidence, so that was that. He never bothered us again.

৯৫৬

In the usual pattern of events, the speed of any transaction is a direct result of the size of the bribe paid to the official involved, but in a climate of censorship and stifled political debate, attempts to air such topics have until recently had to be disguised in clever satires, like the musical *Sah Al-Noum*. In the story, a scathing critique of the bureaucracy and authoritarianism of the Arab world today, the governor wakes up once a month to stamp just three requests from his people. The Lebanese diva Fairouz played the leading lady at Damascus' Dar al-Assad Opera House as part of the inaugural event after the city's nomination as Arab Capital of Culture back in 2008. The heroine steals the stamp, approves all projects and throws the royal seal down the village well, after which the community flourishes. When the governor awakes to find the royal seal missing, the village informer betrays her. All ends happily, however, when she is saved by unanimous popular support and a change of heart by the governor, who becomes an enlightened benevolent. Sitting in the audience were Vice-President Farouq Al-Shara'a and former defence minister Mustafa Tlass, on whom the message was surely not lost.

Today activists are less circumspect. The banners of Kafr Nabl in the rebellious province of Idlib openly lampoon everyone, including the president. Bashar has been shown as Gollum from Tolkien's *The Lord of the Rings*, the scrawny, obsequious creature corrupted by the ring in his vicious pursuit of power. The title is given as 'The Lord of the Thrones' and in a speech bubble he even says 'My Precious' with a lisp, like Bashar's lisp. Punishment ensued through regime shelling, leading the townspeople to beg the banner-makers to stop their work. They did, but two months later the townspeople regained their defiance and asked the activists to start again. The cartoonist Ali Ferzat depicts Bashar's awkwardness by showing him sitting on a giant throne wearing an oversized military uniform. By making him the object of ridicule, the oppressed can feel, albeit temporarily, a little more empowered.

Everyone knows that Syria's institutions are inefficient and corrupt, but many of the employees working within them feel stuck, not daring to defy their political masters, whilst hating the system they have been forced to tolerate. The bribery culture is deeply engrained and will not change overnight no matter what laws are passed or no matter what government is in power. I used to have regular conversations about this with Syrian friends, when I complained about how long it was taking me to get my paperwork sorted out in Damascus. 'The thing is,' they would say, 'there are two kinds of corruption in Syria: the first is a kind of nepotism, where privileged people around the president get projects approved while others get them turned down. That can be dealt with; the president needs to get rid of these people because they create a lot of bad feeling.' We all knew the key culprit was Bashar's cousin, Rami Makhlouf; 'the big thief' as he was known inside Syria.

'The second kind of corruption,' they would tell me, 'is the petty corruption. This is much more difficult because everyone is involved, everyone has to do it – otherwise nothing works. This kind of corruption will take at least a generation or more to eradicate.'

My own experience certainly bore that out. Any document you

needed from any government office would not be forthcoming unless money passed hands. It was simply the accepted practice. At the border crossing from Lebanon to Syria you could either stand in line for hours or put a few notes inside your passport to facilitate the processing of your visa. Everyone who could, chose the latter approach.

At Maktab Anbar during the restoration period of Bait Baroudi, there was a point when my file, which held all the restoration licences and approvals of the *mukhalafas,* mysteriously disappeared. When the official who 'lost' it was given an incentive, he miraculously found it again. Bassim was brilliant at this game and knew just how much to give to make sure things happened, yet also knew never to give too much. It was an art, one which I as a foreigner could not hope to master.

Sometimes, as I discovered, it was more a case of total incompetence than of bribery. People often held their jobs through connections (*wasta*), not through having won the position on merit, and were therefore utterly useless in their work. In the Ministry of Tourism before the revolution I had been in discussion with officials about the possibility of setting up long distance walks among the Byzantine Dead Cities in the hilly countryside north and west of Aleppo. They were very keen and asked me to come up with a range of proposals. In one of our many meetings to discuss the project, I talked about the pamphlets they would need to design to publicise the routes. A junior headscarved employee suddenly piped up: 'We already have pamphlets.' Everyone turned to her incredulously. She had never uttered a word before in any meeting.

'Where?' said her boss. The employee scurried off and returned a few minutes later carrying some very impressive and beautifully designed pamphlets. Her boss had clearly never seen them before. 'Where on earth have these been and who did them?' she asked in bewilderment. We had by this point been discussing the project over a period of months and the same employee had been present throughout, but only when I mentioned the word 'pamphlets' had she remembered their existence.

It gets worse, because it transpired the pamphlets had been sitting in that same cupboard for a full three years, forgotten and unused, a moribund relic of the Swiss attempts to get projects moving inside

Syria, just like the depressing Jboul scheme Ramzi had told me about on our first trip together and which had also ended up on the scrapheap. Syrian inertia is even a match for Swiss efficiency, and when the Swiss ambassador, a keen walker who had been pushing for the project to get off the ground, reached the end of his posting, his beautiful pamphlets disappeared into the cupboard and that was that.

Once the processes of law and order broke down with the start of the revolution most people saw it as an opportunity to break the rules, especially with illegal building projects. Why bother to apply for planning permission now? Once your house had an extra floor on it, the chances of the authorities ever asking you to take it down later were nil. There was a veritable building boom in the early months, and best of all, no need for bribes.

Civil disobedience was also on the rise. *Karama*, Arabic for 'dignity', was the key watchword, hugely important in Syrian culture. Shopkeepers in Damascus pulled down their shutters and wrote 'dignity strike' on them; anti-regime graffiti appeared overnight on the walls; main highways were blocked by burning tyres; red dye was put in public fountains to symbolise the blood of martyrs; loudspeakers were put in Damascus' main squares playing revolutionary songs; the independence flag, symbol of the revolution, was simultaneously raised in several prominent places round the city. The idealistic protagonists were mainly young Syrians, men and women, politically independent and with no financial backing. They were at their most active in spring 2012, and appeared to be gaining popular support by mobilising resistance in the big cities where security was tight. But by 2013 the regime had tightened its grip on the capital still further, squeezing almost all such activities to a standstill.

Challenging the status quo never went down well on any level. Back in England I was once invited by the Syrian ambassador to give a talk to British tour operators, to encourage them to run tours to Syria. I spoke at length about the beauties of the country, all the sites it had to offer visitors, then finished with a plea to the Syrian state to end corruption and free up its bureaucracy so that foreign businesses could operate more easily. I was never invited again.

Corruption, sadly, also now pervades the education system. Ramzi the Philosopher used to tell me many fond stories about his student days studying English literature at Damascus University – the respect for the professors, the rigour of the exams, the love of learning. He was in despair when, the year before the revolution broke out, he and all tourist guides were told they had to sit an examination to test their knowledge in order to get their tour guide licence renewed. The test was a farce.

'They failed me and the university professors, but they passed their own people who know nothing,' he said, trying to maintain his usual calm. In the end he had to bribe his way to his licence.

When Farida, the girl who was later to become Bassim's wife, told me about her experiences at Damascus University, I did not believe her at first, and just thought it was an excuse for dropping out. She had always been a good and diligent student at school, she said, so when she set out on her journalism course she worked hard, expecting to get good grades. Instead, after handing in a few assignments, she suddenly started to get bad marks, with comments warning her she was going to fail. Confused and upset, she went to see her professor to ask why.

'What is your name?' the professor had said, looking at her knowingly. 'Think about it. With a name like yours, you will never succeed here.'

That was the point at which she fully understood the Assad Ba'ath Party. If you didn't toe the party line, you had no hope, no chance to get on. It didn't matter how good you were at your course. What mattered was your loyalty to the party and the regime. If you were not with them, you were considered against them, and punished accordingly. Her family name was Azem, the powerful Ottoman family which had given Damascus no less than five of its governors between 1725 and 1809. Azem Palace was the grandest and most splendid palace in all Damascus, built on the site of the governor's palace from Roman times onwards. Today it houses the Museum of Popular Arts and Traditions, having been confiscated from the Azem family in 1951 by the Syrian government, just as Bait Mujallad, the next most magnificent of all the palaces in Old Damascus, was expropriated by the Ministry of Culture in late 2013 saying they wanted it converted to a cultural centre. Owned by Nora Jumblatt, Syrian wife of Lebanon's Druze leader Walid Jumblatt, and restored by her at vast expense, it has been kept locked up and empty since the start of the revolution. She fears it will now be trashed as revenge for her husband's vocal anti-regime stance. In Hama, where Farida is from, the Azem Palace was badly damaged by regime shelling to quash the Muslim Brotherhood rebellion of 1982. The Azem family name, therefore, still holds strong associations for Alawis and other regime loyalists. They equate it with the privileged wealthy elite of Ottoman Sunni Muslims who used to persecute them.

The Students' Union at Damascus University has long been run by the socialist Ba'ath Party, and the rewards for joining it are considerable. Membership is not compulsory, but with incentives like an extra five to ten grade points immediately added to their totals, Ba'athist students can get into the better faculties. Ba'athists are also guaranteed a good room on campus, much cheaper than any room you can rent in the city. The Ba'ath Party MP in charge of the Students' Union is reported to be a close friend of Maher al-Assad, Bashar's violent brother, commander of the elite 4th Armoured Division. The Students' Union has to give permission before any event can take place on campus, and aware that the student environment has traditionally been the source of unrest and dissent, the one-party Ba'athist police state has made it its business for some years now to monitor the activities of the students carefully.

Dozens of students have been arrested simply for speaking out against the regime, voicing criticism of it. Plainclothes secret police patrol the campus and students are encouraged, through a system of rewards like getting a better room or being given money, to report any fellow student who, for example, uses his mobile to film protests taking place on campus. The informer would then be paid, and would get to keep the mobile phone as a bonus.

Ba'ath Party interference is also evident abroad, when students are sent overseas to study at the government's expense. By chance, I met an old acquaintance from my undergraduate days at a party, now a professor of Arabic at one of the many universities in Paris. She was complaining bitterly at the low calibre of the students sent to her from Syria. 'I tried my best with them,' she said, 'but in the end I realised the fault was with them, not with me. They should never have been sent in the first place, they were not even interested in studying, just in shopping.'

Paradoxically, education is an area where Bashar, on first becoming president in 2000, introduced a number of reforms designed to move away from the military indoctrination that was prevalent under his father. Bashar did, for example, get rid of the military uniforms in schools, to encourage a more normal environment for learning, and even modernised the syllabus a little. Since its rise in the early 60s the Ba'ath Party did make some beneficial changes: electricity across the country, subsidised fuel, water and bread, health clinics and free education. A cynic might observe that Hafez had other motives for extending eligibility for free schooling; by controlling the national syllabus, he successfully controlled what many young minds were fed at an impressionable age in a form of brainwashing designed to create the national psyche that accorded with his vision – another reason why Syria has stayed stuck so long in its Ba'athist rut. It was quantity at the expense of quality.

In 1973 university education became a right, free of charge and guaranteed by the state, and in those early days when Ramzi the Philosopher had been a keen young student, numbers were still relatively small and education had been a government priority. But over the course of the 1980s and 90s numbers shot up without the parallel investment required. Overcrowding and minimal interaction with teachers became the norm, sacrificing critical thinking and student development. With class sizes of 50 or more, rote learning and memorisation were the easiest options, and many professors were still products of the rigid Soviet era, using out-dated teaching methods and textbooks. On the eve of the revolution spending on higher education accounted for just over 1 per cent of GDP, compared to the 33 per cent spent on defence, even though in 2010 the government's Five-Year Plan had been to increase enrolment from 20 per cent to 30 per cent by 2015. No wonder those families who could afford it sent their children abroad to study. Few returned, and under-skilled labour remains the biggest barrier to Syria's future growth. Soon after becoming president in 2001, Bashar allowed private universities to open, teaching a slightly broader range of subjects, and by 2010 15 such institutions had opened to supplement the five state universities, though only the wealthy elite could afford the fees and the Ba'ath Party still controlled the syllabus. Even so, across the country female enrolment rocketed and by 2008 women graduates outnumbered men. Some of the students who benefitted from these changes may well be the very ones now demonstrating against Bashar and orchestrating the protests. Researchers have estimated that roughly half of all students have been forced to drop out of their studies since 2011, pushing the country further and further backwards, further and further behind its neighbours.

A priority in post-Assad Syria will be a complete overhaul of the education system. Before he gave up and left in 2011, Tariq had tried to start up a new school in Homs following the example of the English public schools he had himself benefitted from as a boy. He had the land, he had the money, but he did not reckon with the constraints of the system. He could bribe his way through the initial bureaucratic procedures to make sure building work actually began, but then he hit a barrier. The Ba'ath Party insisted on total control of the syllabus and would not budge one iota. It made Tariq's vision pointless. There was a huge market, he told me, for such a school, with a good ethos and work ethic, along with rugby pitches and tennis courts for the team sports he believed fostered such good practice in children. 'You will be the headmistress,' he said. Who knows, in a post-Assad Syria, maybe I will be.

12

Completion and the Caretaker

My bread is baked, my jar is full.

Arab proverb

The restoration of Bait Baroudi took a full three years, but finally, in summer 2008, it was complete. I could barely believe it.

The place was magnificent, not in the sense that everything looked new, but rather the reverse. 'The place is old,' I had said to Bassim, 'so I want it to look old.' He knew what I meant, and so, unlike most restorations in the Old City, which had ended up looking so perfect they might as well have been new, the house looked and felt as if the inhabitants of earlier centuries had only just left. It was exactly what I had wanted, exactly what I had tried so hard to achieve. The stone walls of the courtyard still had cracks, and there were still sections missing in the paste inlay above the doors.

Everything that needed to be new, was: plumbing, pipe work, electrics, central heating, telephone wires and TV points. Otherwise, wherever possible, Bassim and I had used old materials from the salvage yards. Where stones were missing from the courtyard, we went in search of them. On the roof, we had lightened the load by removing the heavy parapet walls and replacing them with a filigree set of railings from the salvage yard, their quality of workmanship far exceeding anything new we could have found.

Where fitments had to be new, such as lights, door handles, kitchen and bathroom ware, I had discovered a hierarchy of nationalities. The best and most expensive kit was from Germany or Italy. Bassim knew I wanted wherever possible to buy local, but for things like taps or central heating, he advised it was worth splashing out. 'If you buy Syrian or Iranian or Chinese,' he warned, 'it will be cheap, but you will always have problems.' For lighting, I was delighted to discover that there were still craftsmen making traditional metal lamps in all shapes and sizes, and at remarkably cheap prices. In my *iwan* arch I hung a gigantic mosque lamp that looked as if it had been tailor-made for the space. They would gladly have designed me a lamp specially, had I come up with a different design, for no extra cost. Not only that, but because they were local shops, they delivered a huge selection of my choice to the house as a matter of course, so that I could try them all out in situ. It could hardly have been easier. Door handles, I discovered, were best from Saudi Arabia or Egypt, while saucepans and kitchenware were best from Turkey. The souks of the Old City were full of choice, reflecting both Syria's home-grown skills and its trade relationships with its neighbours and allies at that time. Today's choice is more limited; the produce of Syria's own ingenuity has become more prominent, supplemented largely by Iranian and Russian goods. War economies develop fast.

For simple furnishings I looked in vain in the shops, even in the new Gulf-funded shopping malls that were starting to spring up to serve the insatiable consumerism of the wealthy new suburbs like Ya'four where anyone who was anybody lived in Dubai-style villas competing in vulgarity. Everything was either ultra-modern or hideously ornate. In the end Bassim designed some tables and wardrobes, and had them built for a fraction of the usual cost by a carpenter whose workshop was round the corner. For colour choices, I drew inspiration from traditional Damascus products such as tiles. Local craftsmen still produced decorative tiles in the typical Damascene colours of blue, green, turquoise and black, on a crackly white background; and tucked away at the back of dusty shops in the Old City, I found a series of remarkable tile panels to set in the walls of the kitchen and bathrooms. Thanks to the hand-painting, they looked old. Everyone who saw the house after restoration assumed the panels had always been there.

I do not know what drew me to buy the particular tile panels I chose. I had stumbled upon them very early on in the restoration process, before there was anywhere to keep them safely away from damage caused by the builders. I fussed about them almost as much as I fussed about trying to preserve the plant life of the courtyard, about the vine and the bougainvillea and the myrtle and the wisteria, trying to make sure the scaffolding did not obscure them from light. I had wrapped the tiles carefully in newspaper and put them in a small chest in a corner of the room where Mas'ud slept, but the day finally came when I had to get them out and show them to Bassim to explain where I wanted them all set. My favourite design was composed of a nine-tile panel which I told him I wanted on the wall above the Mamluk fountain of my *mukhalafa*-inspired bathroom.

'About the tile panel,' Bassim said, 'do you realise what it is, the big one with nine tiles?' I looked at him blankly, and he realised I did not. 'It is a copy of the tile panel from the tomb of Muhyiddin. The plumber will never put it in the bathroom; it would be disrespectful.'

'Muhyiddin Ibn Arabi?' I said in disbelief. It was the very tomb I had already visited twice, where I had met Shaikh Muhammad Al-Ya'qoubi before his expulsion from the country. How strange that I should have chosen these, from among all the others.

The nine tiles, three by three, form a panel of about one metre square. In the centre is a kind of cartouche with '*Izzat Allah*' written on it – the 'Might of God'. Along the top are the names, written in cursive script, of Allah, Muhammad, and Abu Bakr and Umar, the first two caliphs to follow Muhammad. At the bottom, also in cartouches, are the names of Uthman and Ali, the third and fourth caliphs after Muhammad, the so-called 'rightly guided' ones, *Al-Rashidoun*, both of whom were murdered. After this, the stage was set for Islam to split into its main Sunni vs. Shi'a division, between the Umayyad Caliph Mu'awiya and Ali, the Prophet's son-in-law, a division which has been the source of so much trouble and sectarian strife ever since. What I now understood, looking at it properly, was that the tile panel was designed as a Sufi message, emphasising the unity of Islam before this damaging division. The central motif is a vase of stylised flowers, flanked on either side by a pair of stylised cypress trees, in turn flanking a palm tree and a mosque lamp hanging from a chain, and the trio of images are set in an architectural triple arch supported on twisted columns of cobalt blue and turquoise. The ensemble was an image of harmonious and evocative beauty, and made me think again of *tawhid*, literally in Arabic 'making into one, bringing together disparate elements into a whole'. Nine, I subsequently learnt, is seen in Sufi circles as the perfect number – in the nine times table, the sum of the individual numbers in each multiple of nine always adds up to nine – where the sum of the parts always equals wholeness. Clearly Ibn Arabi could not be in the bathroom, within view of nakedness and bodily functions, and that was that. He went in the kitchen instead, where he could cast harmony on the cooking.

Taking my cue from the dominant blues and greens of the tiles, I chose an immense slab of dark green marble for the kitchen work surface, an object of beauty that turned the chore of chopping food into a delight. Today this same kitchen will be serving anything up to 30 people each mealtime, spilling out into the courtyard under the bougainvillea.

Still influenced by the tiles, I plumped for a strong green on the walls of the *mukhalafa*-inspired bathroom. Achieving this colour turned out to be surprisingly straightforward. Fadi the painter was a wizard. A young man in his twenties, he lived and breathed colours. All I had to do was to point to a colour in the tiles or in the *'ajami* room or in the secret ceiling, and he would set off into the souk to buy the powders, return within the hour and mix it with the oils before my eyes. Within days, the entire colour scheme of the house was settled by this method. He was a living sample-pot creator with an instinctive sense of how to reproduce a colour, like a musician who could hear a tune once, then recreate it impromptu on his instrument.

In the *'ajami* room I asked the carpenter to make low-level benches, designed like chests for storage, then had the cushions made in traditional Damascene richly coloured silks. How did I ever afford all this? Three years' worth of work, with five to six workmen's wages, plus Bassim's fees as architect, not to mention the court cases and the bribery money – it should have bankrupted me, and it would have done if the crash in sterling had come any earlier. But by 2008, when the sterling exchange rate slipped from 100 to 63 Syrian pounds, most of my bills had been paid. The world was mad but my timing was perfect.

It was to get madder, for when, thanks to a contact of Bassim, I secured long-term tenants for the upstairs flat, the house began to produce a reasonable income stream. The Aga Khan Development Network had decided to rent it as a guesthouse for their visiting experts. Just round the corner from Bait Baroudi they were embarking on a giant restoration project to convert a trio of Ottoman palaces (Bait Siba'i, where I had first met Bassim, Bait Nizam, the former British Consulate and Bait Quwatli, residence of the former president Shukri Al-Quwatli) into a luxury hotel, and, Bassim told me, the mere existence of such a project had just doubled the value of my house overnight. He subsequently became their project manager, timed exactly for when my own restoration was completed. The rent, of course, was in Syrian pounds, so my agonies watching the exchange rate like a hawk were finally over. Until then I had monitored its every twist and turn, trying to judge the best timing for converting my transfers of money out from the UK into Syrian pounds. No one, I reckoned, knew more than me at that time about the vagaries of the Syrian exchange rate. My savings exhausted by the end of the restoration, I had not allowed myself to worry much about the future. And now suddenly I was starting to get money coming back. It was a miracle, as I had never done it for financial reward.

So the upstairs was rented out, but the downstairs I kept for myself, my family, and friends; and when I was not there, I employed Abu Ashraf to look after the place. Some might have said he was idle and useless, but to my mind Abu Ashraf had many sterling qualities, chief among which was his total honesty. He was illiterate, like many Syrians of his generation, and therefore had a phenomenal audio memory. He knew and understood the value of time and how to spend it. He knew that time was most definitely not money. He knew instinctively that too much exertion was fruitless and would ultimately be damaging to his health and equilibrium.

I had stumbled upon him in a small and rather run-down hotel where he worked as a caretaker and general cleaner. It was pretty much the cheapest place to stay in the Old City, and was run by a friend of Ramzi's from his university days on a semi-illegal basis as it had no permit to function as a hotel. But the friend was a shrewd operator and knew how to get round such obstacles. He had a system of bribery in operation whereby once a month, an official from the *mukhabarat* would call round, be given a cup of coffee and collect SY1000 for his trouble. The deal was that he would be given photocopies of the passports of the guests who had stayed over the course of the month, all foreigners, often students. 'The authorities know we are here,' he had explained, 'but they let us function, as long as we cooperate with them.' Later, when the *mukhabarat* started to get greedier, he was less sanguine about them. 'Last time they took the canary as well as the SY1000, 'he complained. 'I'm fed up with it. Just because we don't pay taxes, it doesn't give them the right to take whatever they feel like.'

At the time this complaint had made me laugh, but later, when it started to happen to me, I was less amused. All sorts of things started to disappear from the house. Luckily they were not interested in the things that mattered to me such as my paintings or prints of Old Damascus, preferring instead any new bits of ironmongery that were around, such as secateurs for pruning the vine.

As for the taxes, Rashid the lawyer – to whom I had given power of attorney in all legal matters concerning the house so he could act in my absence if I happened to be in the UK – would take the Aga Khan rental contract, filled out with fictitious figures, to the *Muhafaza* (the Governorate Building), bribe the official, then pay a low figure up front on the year's rental, generally about a tenth of what the legal figure would have been. When I queried this practice, I was dismissed as a hopeless innocent. It was what everyone did, he told me.

Abu Ashraf's duties at his former employer's run-down hotel were not especially onerous. Cleaning the communal kitchen and bathrooms and sweeping the courtyard were tasks he interspaced liberally with sessions of lying in the hammock on the roof, sleeping or smoking. The original idea was that he would find someone from his village to look after my house, but when I asked him about it, to my surprise he said he would do it himself while the house was empty, as it was not enough work for someone younger to do full time. He was a grandfather, with four grown-up children, and lived with his family out in the Ghouta, Damascus' famed oasis, now much shrunk and shrivelled up, where he had a small house and *bustan* ('orchard') in Kafr Batna. The area is now even further shrivelled by regime shelling and the chemical attack of August 2013. Like many men of his age, he was highly religious and conservative. As well as his hammock breaks, he would stop work for prayers, performing his *wudu'* ('ritual ablutions') in my Mamluk fountain, for which it was intended, before going out to pray in the mosque on the street corner. Every street corner had its mosque in the Old City, making the call to prayer at dawn, noon, afternoon, dusk and evening a cacophony of sound, each mosque slightly out of synch with its neighbour. When he returned, he needed a period of calm, so he would sit in the courtyard for a while, with a cup of sugared black tea and a cigarette.

I learnt early on that there was no point in trying to impose my standards of cleanliness on Abu Ashraf. There are levels of cleanliness, just as there are levels of understanding, or even indeed levels of honesty. People can look at the same thing, but all see something different. To some it may look clean, to some it may look dirty; it is simply a matter of perspective. In the same way, people can look at a building, and for some it will be composed of all its tiny details, while for others it is just a building. In some ways, his habit – standard practice in this part of the world – of changing his shoes when he came in from the street, was much cleaner than the Western habit of bringing the street dirt into our houses on our shoes. He had his outside shoes and his inside shoes, just like he had his smart clothes that he arrived in, and his work clothes that he kept in the house and changed into before getting started. The way it worked best, I discovered, was to let him do his own daily routine, namely the things he felt were necessary: sweep the courtyard, empty the bins, make his tea and sit in the courtyard smoking his cigarette. Once he had accomplished those tasks, I could give him other specific tasks. One day it might be washing the woodwork of the courtyard doors and windows, another day it might be beating the carpets in the courtyard. If he strayed too far out of his comfort zone, things tended to go wrong. So when my favourite pale blue Egyptian cotton sheets were ruined, because he had put them in the washing machine with a red towel, he could not see the problem, since everything was clean. It was pointless getting angry or annoyed with him. After all, at the end of the day, it was only some sheets. He had things in proportion.

In addition to his sense of proportion, Abu Ashraf's knowledge of unlikely matters never failed to impress me. I once consulted him about where I should go to buy a tortoise for the courtyard. I had by chance seen a 19th century painting called *The Tortoise Trainer* by Osman Hamdi Bey set in a courtyard house, in which tortoises were being schooled to stroll about during fine banquets with candles waxed upright and lit on their backs, a silent lighting system whose eccentricity appealed to me. Childish fantasies about hosting such an occasion filled my mind. The idea of having a creature of immense calm and patience living in the courtyard struck me as being somehow fitting, and during my later researches I discovered that the tortoise is seen in Arab societies as a symbol of good luck and long life for the owner of the house. So tortoises in courtyard houses were not so far-fetched after all.

The day after my consultation with Abu Ashraf, he appeared at the house carrying a large plastic bag from which he proudly produced a tortoise. 'From my *bustan*,' he announced, beaming. I was taken aback, worried that the poor creature might be traumatised by this dislocation from its habitat, but Abu Ashraf pooh-poohed my concerns and assured me it did not mind or even notice. As a result we entered into a pattern whereby the tortoise, Zulfikar as I named it, after the twin-bladed sword of Ali, would migrate by plastic bag, arriving whenever I was in residence in Bait Baroudi, and departing after I left, to return to Abu Ashraf's *bustan*.

In the pre-revolution days, when I was once obliged to be back in England for a while, I had allowed an English tenant to stay in the downstairs part of Bait Baroudi. She arrived with her own set of rules, which she expected Abu Ashraf to obey. I ended up having to ask her to leave, not Abu Ashraf. She never really forgave me, or understood that he was part of the city and she was not. And he could do things none of us could. He knew how to pay the electricity and water bills at their complicated ministry premises, he knew how to get the phone line fixed the same day by tipping the telecoms engineer, and he knew how to keep the *mukhabarat* men sweet by making them tea and sitting with them to chat. He even made tea and took it outside for the street-sweeper, explaining that the poor man was *miskiin* ('wretched'), and earnt very little, so it was his duty to look after him. Sometimes, at the religious holidays or *eids*, he would give him a few Syrian pounds from his own modest salary. Charitable giving is deeply embedded in Islam, and Muslims give readily to the poor, especially street beggars who have no one to look after them.

I have been impressed many times by Islam's admirable network of social care, and by its duty of *zakat*, 'alms tax', where two and a half per cent of capital is taken and distributed to the poor. *Zakat* is one of the Five Pillars of Islam, an obligation for every Muslim. There are no old peoples' homes in Syria. Every family looks after its own weak and vulnerable relations, and the uprising has strengthened these bonds, which are very necessary to cope with the horrors of war. No one can rely on the state. Yes, without doubt, Abu Ashraf had his priorities right, and the straightforward kind-heartedness of his approach to everything was an example to all us foreigners who thought we knew best, who considered our values superior.

But even he was afraid of the regime, of the powers of the *mukhabarat*. I once allowed some friends to stay on the ground floor when I was away, not realising the problems it would create for Abu Ashraf. The *mukhabarat* happened to do their rounds, and on finding new people in residence, took him to task, saying they would return with their superior. He fled to his village and was not seen for days, lying low, until my friends had gone. He took no unnecessary risks and his simple faith accompanied him at all times. He would say '*Ya Rabb!*' each time he climbed on a chair to water the hanging plants, addressing his Lord and Master, invoking his protection. In shops the same invocation – *Ya Rabb* – was spoken aloud to God before climbing up to reach something from the top shelf.

'*Tawakkul 'ala Allah*', was the great Sufi concept. It was even written on one of the inscription panels of my *'ajami* room – not that Abu Ashraf could read it. He did not need to. He felt it, he sensed it, he lived it. If you look it up in the great Hans Wehr Arabic dictionary, it says 'to trust in God, to put oneself in God's hands'. It implies giving up any idea that your own actions might control the outcome of a situation. It implied complete surrender to the will of God. The early ascetics and mystics of Islam adhered to this way of living, shunning worldly concerns, but while we westerners might see that as a total abdication of responsibility for the consequences of our actions, people like Abu Ashraf lived by a code where they did their best, tried their hardest, but still recognised that not all things could be controlled, that some things would simply be '*fi yadd Allah*', 'in the hand of God'. When his village of Kafr Batna, a hotbed of rebel activity, came under heavy shelling in early 2012, he brought his family to the safety of Bait Baroudi. I was happy it could serve as their refuge. In between, when things quietened down, they would go back to their own house and live in it again, since leaving it empty would have exposed it to looters, or even squatters.

No, *tawakkul* was emphatically not a matter of giving oneself up, hopelessly, to whatever came along, and saying that it must be God's will. It was, rather, a state of mind, and there could be degrees of it according to the strength of someone's faith. It was achieved through what the mystics called *zuhd*, the renunciation of worldly concerns and preoccupations. It was the ultimate test of faith, and the Syrian revolution has forced everyone to challenge their faith, to examine their honest beliefs, in the way that only a confrontation with death can do.

13

No Return

If we have been pleased with life, we should not be displeased with death, since it comes from the hand of the same master.

Michelangelo

The timelessness of the city was almost overwhelming when seen from the roof of Bait Baroudi. The view was over the minarets and gables of the Great Umayyad Mosque, and beyond to Jabal Qasioun, the mountain that watched over the city, guarding it from harm. Often Ramzi and I would sit in silence there, just absorbing the spirit of the city. Its resilience, its confidence, and its power felt tangible. It had a way of reducing everything to essentials. Neither of us ever dreamt those days might end.

Of course, if you chose to look at it differently, in specifics, the city was a mess: the sea of rusting TV satellite dishes, the cluttered water cylinders and discarded debris on the flat dusty roofs. But somehow none of that mattered. The practice of sitting up high to look beyond your walls, where you might also be on view yourself, was an alien one in this part of the world. Your home was your haven, and you focused inward, on the *batin*. If you wanted to focus on the outside world, the *zahir,* you left your haven and entered the street. Every time I left or entered Bait Baroudi I felt that sense of transition from one world to another. How much more so that would be now, when each leaving would be like a farewell to the haven, with no certainty of safe return, now that random arrests, car-bomb explosions and lawlessness had become daily occurrences in the capital.

It was difficult to credit that this mountain had turned now from guardian to attacker, with the regime stationing artillery on its heights to shell the neighbourhoods they wished to punish. Bassim had said, when he saw the guns pointing down at the city, he knew it was time to leave: 'They could shoot at me any time, even though I have done nothing,' he said. 'I feel life has become cheap. It means I can no longer sleep here, in what used to be my refuge.' His flat was on the top floor of a tall block in Abu Roumaneh, once the safest part of town, but now regularly subject to bomb attacks by the rebel Free Syrian Army brigades, targeting the many state security buildings in the area. He had chosen the area for its safety when he moved there four years earlier, but now it was getting to the point where the previously safe regime areas were targets for the rebels.

On the night of 18 July 2012, when the huge bomb at the National Security Headquarters killed Assef Shawkat and four other top security chiefs, Bassim packed one suitcase and left with his family, driving straight to the Lebanese border, less than an hour from central Damascus, along with two thousand other families all trying to leave the country. Beirut was overcrowded and difficult, and he still felt unsafe, even though he was able to stay with friends. He decided to fly to Istanbul and start a new life with his family. He had wanted to stay in Damascus for as long as possible, to conserve his savings, knowing that life would become expensive once he left. As ever, his judgement had been spot on, and he chose exactly the right moment to leave.

As for the rest of us, we had no idea what was coming. After that, the July 2012 bombing of Shi'a neighbours in Al-Amin Street told us the regime had distributed guns to ordinary Alawis in Damascus so that they could defend themselves against the Sunni Islamist rebels who had perpetrated the bombing. At the same time rumours were spread among the Sunni residents that regime thugs were coming to kill them in revenge for the attack. They armed themselves with big sticks, metal bars, whatever they could find. Nothing happened, no one came, but the regime had sown the seeds of paranoia, setting neighbour against neighbour, and destroying trust in the community.

In the peaceful days, before the revolution, Ramzi and I often used to make day trips in his old Lada out of Damascus, when he had gaps in his commitments to his tour groups. Looking back, one such trip stands out in my memory and served as a warning. Our destination had been Qal'at Jandal, marked as a citadel/castle, a site of archaeological interest on the tourist map of the Damascus countryside (*rif Dimashq*) produced by the Ministry of Tourism. It was only about 35 kilometres outside the city to the southeast, and we estimated this would give us plenty of time to explore and even go for a walk in the cool air, since it was shown as quite high up in the mountains. We had not, however, reckoned with its being in the Golan Heights. Every time we approached the mountains, we encountered a checkpoint. We tried a number of different approaches, and each time it ended, frustratingly, in a barrier manned by Syrian army officers, rifles hanging casually over their shoulders. Wasn't it possible to visit the castle? Ramzi would ask. They would inspect our passports, look at us, then say, no, it was *mamnou*.

The weather was good, so we decided to continue south, trying to find another route up towards Mount Hermon. Against the odds, one small road allowed us to get higher and higher, without a single village or checkpoint. It was beginning to make quite an ascent and we started to feel hopeful we might get into the mountains after all. Rounding a corner, there in front of us was a checkpoint. Ramzi stopped the car and fumbled for reverse gear, visibly shaken. Peering forward, I said: 'It's ok. It's a UN checkpoint. We can go through it.'

'Are you sure?' he said, anxiously. The idea that we might actually be able to go through a checkpoint in this part of the world had not occurred to him.

'Go closer. Look. Do you see? The notice says it is forbidden for Syrian military vehicles to pass, and we are not a Syrian military vehicle.' Ramzi was very uncomfortable, and clearly not happy about the idea of going any closer. Never had I seen him so agitated. Very much against his better judgement, Ramzi was persuaded to drive slowly forward. 'I'll do the talking,' I said, winding down the window. 'Don't worry – look, the soldier is from Austria, I can tell from his colours, and he's wearing the UN blue beret.'

Sure enough, the Austrian soldier greeted us smilingly: 'Go on,' he said, waving us through, 'it's fine, you are welcome.' In a state of semi-disbelief Ramzi drove on as the road wound higher and higher into the mountains towards the ridge. If it carried on, soon we would cross the ridge and be able to look over into Israel, we joked, not really sure where we were on the map any more. On and on the road wound, Ramzi getting increasingly anxious, until, just before the ridge, we rounded a corner and there before us was another checkpoint. 'I knew it,' said Ramzi, sweat breaking out on his brow, 'we must turn back now.'

'No it's fine,' I said again, 'it's another UN checkpoint. Look, the soldier is Polish.'

Sure enough the soldier waved us forward, 'You are welcome,' he said, not even asking to see our passports. We began to laugh, it all seemed so incredible, as Ramzi's ancient Lada struggled up the last section of the road before the ridge.

'My God,' I exclaimed, 'we are going to Israel after all!'

The car crossed the brow of the hill and we gasped. There before us lay a landscape of unimaginable beauty – green, lush, tended, with a prosperous and well-organised-looking town nestling a little below us. There were fields and factories, all immaculately maintained and watered. It was like looking down onto the Promised Land. Somehow, without plan or intent, we had stumbled into the one place where it was indeed still possible to look down into Israel.

'It's Majdal Shams,' cried Ramzi suddenly. 'I recognise it from the TV!' We got out of the car and stood looking down on it in disbelief. How could it look so totally different, from one side to the other, from Syria to the Occupied Territories? 'Money,' said Ramzi simply. Israel was in receipt of vast amounts of American aid to settle these lands, and the Golan Heights were fertile and well-watered.

What remained with me above all from that day was not the wonderful picnic we then enjoyed as the reward for our accidental excursion to the Golan, but Ramzi's fear, and the degree of it. Why was calm Ramzi, of all people, my wise philosopher, so afraid? Later he explained: 'You have to understand. They can arrest me any time they want, throw me in prison. My family would never even know where I was or whether they would ever see me again.' It made me realise for the first time how normal law-abiding citizens like him felt afraid of any encounter with the military or the security services, thanks to their powers of immediate arrest under the Emergency Law – and this was in November 2010, before Bou Azizi set the Arab Spring alight in Tunisia, and before anyone had any premonitions of what was shortly to erupt across the region, no one that is, except Bassim.

That same month he had said to me, as we sat on the bamboo chairs in my *iwan*, 'I feel something will happen, I feel a lot of tension in the air.'

'What do you mean?' I had asked, 'I don't feel anything.'

'I think there will be a war …' he had said, on 20 November 2010.

※

Bassim is now in Istanbul, struggling to learn Turkish, after finding that no one would employ him without it. His savings are running out, although many friends have helped him get a cheap flat where he, his wife and two small children can live. His instincts told him it would be a long time before he could go back.

For those who decided to stay, or who did not want to leave, things soon went from bad to worse. Marwan's mother was a typical case. She lived very simply in a small flat in Zamalka, a northeast Damscus suburb that was to become a rebel hotspot and suffer regime reprisals. It was also affected by the massive chemical weapon attack of 21 August 2013. She was at her happiest when she could squash her grown-up sons and their families into her tiny living room and feed them. A devout Sunni Muslim, she had nevertheless completely accepted Marwan's marriage to a Western woman, welcoming her wholeheartedly and unquestioningly as the person who made him happy. She could have continued to live, after her husband had died, in the more spacious family home, but she decided to sell it in order to distribute the money between her sons, just keeping enough left over for her own modest flat. The building in Zamalka was still unfinished, the stairs were littered with rubbish and the neighbourhood was scruffy, but she chose not to focus on that. Her status did not come from where she lived but from what she did.

It made me think of the passage in Mark 10:25: 'It is easier for a camel to pass through the eye of a needle than for a rich man to enter the kingdom of heaven.' The similarities between Islam and Christianity are sometimes very striking. Many Muslim scholars think highly of Christianity's ethical teachings, and Al-Ghazali often quoted Jesus and the Gospels to support his arguments. The Quran mentions Jesus by name more times than Muhammad, in 90 verses of 15 Suras, describing him as a great prophet chosen by God to spread the word – just not as the son of God. It also teaches the virgin birth, and venerates Mary for her piety and chastity.

Marwan's mother had invited me for the *Eid Al-Adha*, along with all the rest of her family. It was a bit like being invited for Christmas, and I had felt I might be intruding, but Marwan assured me his mother would love me to be there as well. There would be lots of wonderful *Eid* food – she had been up most of the night baking special pastries – and we would all watch the climax of the annual *musalsala* together, a TV soap that the whole country was addicted to. During Ramadan and the run up to the *Eid* the episodes would be screened nightly, in the build-up to the grand finale over the *Eid* holiday itself.

Often these *musalsalat* were period dramas set in Damascene courtyard houses, a Syrian version of *Downton Abbey*. In the summer of 2012, just before Bait Baroudi became a haven for refugees, I was approached by a local TV company wanting to rent it for such a series – *Revolution in Damascus* maybe. How absurd. I refused.

At the *Eid* everyone dressed more smartly than usual, so I put on my 'Sunday best' of white trousers and a dark jacket. *Eid Al-Adha* means Feast of the Sacrifice, and always begins with the sacrifice of an animal, usually a sheep.

It was the first time I had been in Bait Baroudi for this particular *Eid*. If I had thought about it in advance, I might have made the connection between the ritual sacrifice and the butcher's shop at the top of the street, and realised that red trousers might have been the best decision. To reach The Street Called Straight where Marwan was waiting in his car to drive me to his mother's place in the suburbs, I had to negotiate rivers of blood running down the street. The carcasses of several sheep were lying inert outside the shop, and the butcher and his helpers had scattered sawdust on the cobbles to try to soak some of it up, without much success. Just sometimes it was the differences between the two religions that were most striking.

Maybe it was a symbol of what was to come, of the killing and destruction that was to engulf Zamalka, forcing Marwan's mother out of her flat. In August 2013 a huge car bomb exploded in that exact spot where Marwan had waited in his car on a Street Called Straight at sunset on the last day of the Ramadan *Eid*, timed to cause maximum casualties. My neighbour and his wild-eyed son were killed in the blast. No one claimed responsibility and no one pointed the finger. Fear and chaos were starting to engulf the city.

᠅

When the demonstrations had first begun in March 2011, I asked people how they thought things might develop next. Abu Ashraf had heard nothing about them. 'If there had been any demonstrations,' he said, 'they would have been in support of Bashar, not against him. No one would dare to demonstrate against him.' Abu Ashraf was, after all, old enough to remember only too well how brutally Hafez al-Assad had dealt with dissent in Hama in 1982. Ramzi the Philosopher was touring in the north of the country with a Far Eastern tour group, one of the few that had not cancelled when the Arab Spring broke out in Egypt. We spoke by mobile: 'This regime is too strong,' he assured me, 'no one will have the power to stand up to it.' Other Syrian friends, all Sunni Muslims, called round at Bait Baroudi and were equally sure it was nothing, just a few youngsters with too much time on their hands. 'Nothing will come of it,' they said.

Later in the day Rashid the lawyer came round. I asked for his reaction and told him what Abu Ashraf had said. 'Abu Ashraf *majnoun!*' he laughed ('Abu Ashraf is mad!'). He went on to explain that his worry was not about a few harmless demonstrations here in Damascus, but about the Kurds in Deir Ez-Zour where his family had their roots. Nawruz, the major Kurdish festival was coming up, and he feared they might mobilise then, because of their very real grievances about lack of citizenship. It was an issue Bashar al-Assad had repeatedly said he was looking into, but nothing seemed to change on the ground. After the revolution began, he rushed through legislation granting them citizenship, but it was too late.

Rashid was right to worry. Syria has two million Kurds, about 15 per cent of the population though exact figures are notoriously unreliable in this part of the world. Now, taking advantage of the regime vacuum in the northeast, the Kurds were seizing control of the northeast areas round Al-Hasakah and Qamishli, even seizing some of the border crossings into the Kurdish parts of southeast Turkey. Kurds have historically been bad at uniting, with seven dialects and seven political organisations to bring together, but some of Syria's Kurds have linked up with their fellow Sunni Kurds in Iraqi Kurdistan, and are openly receiving military training from them. Turkey's government is horrified, fearing the effects on their own restive Kurds, whose guerrilla activities under the Kurdistan Workers' Party (PKK) recently flared up again after ten years of near stability. Ankara is engaged in a delicate peace process with its Kurds, giving them greater freedoms and rights in return for them laying down their arms and withdrawing to Iraqi Kurdistan. Turkey knows how easily Kurdish ambitions could derail plans for the economic expansion of its southeast regions, and part of its thinking in supporting Islamist rebel groups in Syria is as a counterbalance to the Kurds.

But it was not only the Kurds, as Rashid explained to me. Another source of unrest was the power of the tribes in the eastern regions of Syria. The Shammar and the Jabour had well over a million members with strong ties across the border to Iraq. The Egaidat had one and half million, with links to Saudi Arabia, Qatar and Kuwait. Many leaders of what would become the Free Syrian Army, when it sprang up spontaneously that first revolutionary summer of 2011 to defend demonstrators against regime attacks, were senior members of these tribes. Tribal loyalties remained strong, even under the Ba'ath, and were often underestimated by the authorities. When chaos comes in this part of the world, people revert instinctively first to family, then to extended family, then to clan, then to tribe, and only then to religious grouping. Large numbers of Syrians are descended from tribes in the Arabian Peninsula who moved north with the Muslim conquest in the 7th century. Despite the artificial borders drawn by French and British colonialists to create Syria, Lebanon, Jordan and Iraq, after World War One, the tribal links remain strong, with tribal elders appealing to their relatives across the region for help.

I spoke with Bassim many times in March 2011 when demonstrations first erupted, expressing my concerns about what might happen in the future and warning him to be prepared. 'You do not know what will happen. When a crisis comes it is very sudden and there is no time to react. Even in England,' I said, 'I always keep a spare five litre flask of water under the stairs for emergencies, lots of candles and matches, and plenty of tins and dried food in the pantry. I also fill up my petrol tank as soon as it goes below half, as you never know when you might have to drive a long distance unexpectedly. Avoid the panic and prepare yourself.' That was my advice to him.

He in turn advised me to take out my Syrian currency while exchange rates were still stable and while banks were still functioning normally. The thought had already crossed my mind too, but I did not want to rush into unconsidered action. On the afternoon following those first riots, we arranged to meet at the fruit market roundabout where he would collect me in his car and take me to the salvage yards to look around. I had long wanted to visit them again and had heard that they had now been moved from their previous location, but I did not know to where. Neither did Bassim, slightly to my surprise. He was late, as usual, and I stood in the sun waiting for him, alongside a group of teenage schoolgirls waiting for their bus. They were in the uniform of one of the UN-run schools.

Palestinian children are educated at special UN schools that have a very good reputation, and I did not mind Bassim's lateness since it gave me a natural chance to chat with the schoolgirls. Their transport was also late. They were happy and bubbly, saying how much they enjoyed their school life. Would schoolchildren in England ever say such a thing with sincerity? Their bus arrived and whisked them off, as they grinned and waved goodbye. Syria has historically treated its Palestinian refugees well, far better than Lebanon, for example. Now it was different, with their unofficial camp in Yarmouk besieged and suffering from heavy bombardment, many were forced to flee to Jordan's Zaatari Camp and become refugees for a second time.

Bassim showed up shortly afterwards, apologising profusely, with a string of reasons why he had been delayed – it was always the same: too much to do. He insisted he wanted to find the salvage yards, so I climbed in without guilt and we set about trying to locate them. He drove to where he thought they had moved, on the edge of the

Ghouta, where we instead found a sheep slaughterhouse. We asked whoever we could find in the streets and were redirected many times, eventually driving a good half hour out of the city, east to 'Ain Turma, where we found the first storehouses with the tell-tale collection of old beams, stones and tools outside. Ancient fragments of stone or marble were what I was really after, and the owner instructed his son to lead us on his moped to an old villa deep in the Ghouta, to an area near Kafr Batna, Abu Ashraf's village, now a rebel strong-hold subjected to frequent heavy shelling. We followed as he led us along narrow dirt tracks through small orchards, until we arrived at a crumbling villa.

It had clearly once been the weekend retreat of a wealthy family, and stood in its own plot of land bordered by trees. The grounds were bursting with relics of a bygone age, many stone fragments of marble or limestone, dating back to who knows when, maybe even to Byzantine or Roman times. Round the back there was even a derelict swimming pool, long empty, full of dirt and debris. We wandered round in morbid fascination. Inside, the villa was crammed with yet more stuff, all salvaged from wealthy people's houses: old crystal chandeliers, antique china, a hotchpotch of oil paintings, even vintage clothing covered in the dust of generations. It was like a frozen relic of a bygone age. Standing there in the warm sunshine of the late afternoon we sensed we had stumbled into a lost world. I did not know for sure, but already suspected that it might well be our last outing together, after all the countless outings we had made together over recent years. Bassim felt it too, that moment slipping away, never to return.

In the neglected gardens I found two ancient limestone grinding stones with hollowed out centres, which I could immediately visualise serving as bird baths in the courtyard of Bait Baroudi. They cost almost nothing, and I arranged for them to be delivered the following afternoon. The boot of Bassim's old Mercedes would have easily taken them in his pre-children days, but now it was too full of prams and child seats to be an option. I paid the son in cash without hesitation, never doubting his honesty, and asked for them to be delivered the next day.

On the drive back I asked Bassim whether in his opinion anything more would happen in the country, now after those first demonstrations. He took a deep breath. 'You really want to know?' he said. 'I think these first demonstrations are just testing the water. The revolution will come to Syria, for sure, and when it comes, it will not be peaceful. What do you think?'

'I think as long as there are no killings, it may be fine,' I said, 'but if people die, then it will all change.'

The last thing I did that day was to make a trip to the bank. A flustered and distraught Maryam greeted me. 'It is good you come today,' she said, struggling to fight back the tears. 'If you came tomorrow, I would not be here. I have been sacked and transferred to Branch no.12 in Jisr Al-Abyad, a horrible small branch with no good clients.' The story she told about why this had come about filled me with horror. She had made enemies, she explained; people in the regime did not like her because she had refused to comply with a corruption scam for which they needed her cooperation. As a result they had invented a story about her, and filed it as a report, saying she had taken down a photo of the president and stamped on it, then thrown it from the roof of the bank. It was preposterous. 'Do they think I am mad?' she wept, 'Who would dare to do such a thing? It would be like asking to be thrown in prison!'

While I sat with her, she promised she would take my account with her to the new branch. 'I will take all my good clients with me,' she said. 'They will all want to come.' I did not know what to think or what to do. I told her I needed to check on some transactions that Rashid the lawyer had made on my account and asked for a full print-out of my statement. She dispatched her assistant, and in a few moments the statement was brought back into her office.

'But you have done so much for this branch,' I comforted her. 'You have made everything so efficient, you have brought in the computers, the CCTV, everything works so well since you have been manager.' I meant every word. It was true. She could see I meant it and was grateful. 'Is there a crisis here, in the financial sector?' I asked. She looked at me with her enormous bulging eyes. 'Of course,' she said, 'there is a huge crisis, but the government does not want to admit it. There will be very bad times coming.' She was summoned out of the room by an official, and while she was gone, I thought about her words. When she returned, I said, 'I have decided to withdraw half my money and take it now. I will leave the rest for another time.' She arranged it, and moments later, after signing a few permissions, the wads of cash were placed in front of me. I put them to the bottom of my canvas bag. We said our goodbyes, and hugged and kissed each other. I never saw her again.

There had been unexpectedly heavy snowfall in the mountains around Damascus overnight, on the day of my departure. It was Friday 18 March 2011 and from the airport departure lounge I could see the snow still on the hills. According to the local news channels it had been very heavy up in the Anti-Lebanon range and in the Jabal Druze to the south. I did not know it then, but sitting sipping tea and gazing out at the snow, this was to be the last day of relative peace in the country. Later that same day, serious demonstrations broke out in Deraa, after noonday prayers, the first such Friday of many. A few people were killed by regime troops firing indiscriminately into the crowd. Syria's revolution had begun, exactly as Bassim had predicted four months earlier.

Now as the war grinds on into its fourth year, two key questions remain: how much more time will it take and how many more will have to die? Tragically the answer to both remains the same – more than anyone thinks.

14

Monasteries and Desperation

If God did not forgive, Paradise would be empty.

Arab proverb

Christians, whether they like it or not, are peripheral players in Syria's revolution, partly because most have chosen to stand on the side-lines, and partly because they have no power base. They are scattered all over the country in pockets. Most of the wealthier ones have left, and the ones that are too poor to leave must manage as best they can, taking their chances with the rest. Syria's Christian sites are both dead and alive, and in my years of research all over the country I have visited most of them. Today both categories are under threat.

The 'dead' ones are by far the most numerous, as Syria contains some 700 sites with the remains of over 2,000 churches scattered in the hills to the west and north of Aleppo, a legacy so significant that a process began in recent years to get the whole area declared a UNESCO World Heritage site, a status it finally achieved in 2011 just in time for the revolution. Forty villages, *'villes mortes'*, as UNESCO calls them, grouped together in eight archaeological parks, form a unique illustration of the transition from the ancient pagan world of the Roman Empire to Byzantine Christianity. The ensemble of dwell-ings, pagan temples, churches and Christian sanctuaries, funeral monuments, bathhouses, public buildings, wine and olive-presses, gives a glimpse into the rural lifestyles of late Antiquity. In summer 2013 UNESCO, watching helplessly as more and more of the country's cultural heritage was either damaged, destroyed or put to use as regime or rebel strongholds for their strategic and defence value, did the only thing they have the power to do: add them to the World Heritage in Danger list, along with Syria's other five World Heritage sites.

Such classifications are worthless in time of war, as UNESCO knows full well. Krak des Chevaliers, the world's finest Crusader castle, sits on its peak guarding the Homs Gap, the only flat route to the sea from both Homs and Damascus between the mountain ranges. Once filled with 2,000 Knights Hospitallers, and until early 2011 bursting with a similar number of tourists, it is now the strategic lair of a rebel group, making it the target of a series of bombardments by the regime's air force.

Before the revolution I had been discussing with the Ministry of Tourism a plan to create a series of walking trails in these hills, complete with maps, linking some of the most romantic and hauntingly beautiful ruins, such as Serjilla and St Simeon's. The plan had been to involve local communities, who would benefit by providing accommodation and selling hand-made crafts. The Turks, the Lebanese and the Jordanians had devised such walks, so why not the Syrians? The ambitious Abraham's Path had already been plotted on the map, starting in Turkey's Urfa, the city of Abraham's birth, and running through Syria all the way to Hebron in Palestine, the city of Abraham's death. One day it will be possible to walk such a trail in its entirety, when the country is at last able to focus on its future. Ramzi could lead the walks – he loves hill walking – and his gentle manner would coax the villagers into participation, building trust and hope in their communities, without fear of reprisals.

But those were the so-called 'dead' Christian ruins. Beyond them I also visited monasteries that still had communities of living monks and nuns, not big communities admittedly, but communities nevertheless. The convent of Our Lady of Saydnaya in the Qalamoun Mountains north of Damascus with its famous icon attributed by tradition to St Luke is like a kind of Syrian Lourdes, visited by Christians and Muslims alike seeking cures. Saydnaya is also well known, as are the two monasteries of Mar Sarkis (St Sergius) and Mar Thekla (St Thekla) at nearby Ma'loula, for being one of the few places left on earth where you can still hear Aramaic, the language of Christ. The nuns and monks oblige by singing the Lord's Prayer in Aramaic, then selling you some of their sweet wine.

Confusion reigned when reports suddenly hit the world's press about fighting in Ma'loula, with Christians terrorized and forced to flee to Damascus. It was just before America was expected to launch air strikes against Syria in September 2013 in retaliation for its chemical weapons attack in the Ghouta. For the previous two and half years of the revolution Ma'loula and its residents had stayed out of the war, remaining neutral. It was not in any way strategic; it lay in a narrow cleft tucked under a cliff, and the revolution had simply passed it by until there was an attack on its regime-controlled checkpoint by Jabhat Al-Nusra fighters.

Conveniently, the BBC's Middle East correspondent had been granted a regime-sponsored visa and was on hand to interview the distressed and fleeing residents as they arrived in Damascus. A day or two later he was taken up to Ma'loula to accompany the regime troops so he could see them 'in action', re-taking the town from the rebels. The regime was cleverly presenting a narrative of Ma'loula as a Christian catastrophe, accusing Islamist rebels of persecuting the local residents for their faith. It also gave the regime another chance to air the Sunni extremists' slogan: 'Alawis to the grave, Christians to Beirut', to reinforce their line that minorities were being persecuted by Islamist groups like Jabhat Al-Nusra. The true picture of what happened at Ma'loula is still not fully understood, though there were three Christian deaths that received worldwide media attention.

In late 2013 the regime began a major push to displace the rebel fighters from the Qalamoun mountains above the Christian villages of Ma'loula, Saydnaya and Qarah, in a determined effort to cut off the rebel smuggling routes into the country from Lebanon. Helped by well-disciplined Hezbollah fighters, they took the Cherubim Monastery on its strategic peak at 2,011 metres and turned it into an army barracks. I well recalled the monastery's commanding views over the oasis of Damascus to the south and over the plain of Baalbek to the west, and struggled to imagine the soldiers camped in the beautiful stone church, once a Roman temple, watched over by the 11th century icon of St Nicholas. Had its Greek Orthodox monks been escorted elsewhere or had they fled in terror to Damascus, like their fellow Christians from Ma'loula? No one mentioned them and no foreign journalists were on hand to report.

Media coverage of the revolution tends to portrays Syria's Christians as too fearful to be involved in the rebellion, either remaining silent or pro-regime, but I discovered this was not necessarily the case.

Far from fearful is one of Syria's most surprising monasteries, which allows both Christians and Muslims to stay the night in basic dormitories. Mar Musa al-Habashi (St Moses the Ethiopian) is about an hour's drive north of Damascus, the brainchild of an Italian Jesuit priest, Father Paolo dall'Oglio, who believes passionately that religion should not be a barrier between peoples.

Reconciliation was Father Paolo's life's work and driving force. 'Victory without revenge' is what he sought for Syria, his beloved adopted country. Considered by many an 'icon' of the Syrian Revolution, larger than life in both physique and character, Paolo took it upon himself to battle not just for reconciliation between Christians of different moulds. 'I am fully engaged,' he said, 'in Islamic-Christian harmony-building, but today I'm also in the service of Islamic-Islamic harmony-building. We want next Ramadan to be a time for prayer and action for the reconciliation between Sunnis and Shi'ites.' This commitment is what led to his imprisonment in Ar-Raqqah, the only 'liberated' provincial capital in Syria, by the Al-Qaeda-linked group ISIS in summer 2013.

Expelled from Syria in June 2012 for his outspoken anti-Assad criticism, and for his equally outspoken support of the opposition rebels, a man like Paolo has never been one to shy away from difficult tasks. As a young man he studied Law in Rome, Arabic and Islam in Damascus, and completed a PhD in Naples on the 'Value of Hope in the Quran'. In August 1982, when his mission as an Arabic interpreter for the charity Caritas was ending, he chanced upon a reference in a 1938 Syria Guide to a ruined stone monastery on a cliff reachable by mule in three hours from Nebek, the nearest village. Seeking a retreat before his return to Rome and his Jesuit community, he decided on impulse to go and spend ten days there alone in communion with God. The course of his life was changed, as he knew then that he had found his mission: to found a new community in Mar Musa. As a six-year old, Paolo recalled being captivated by the stone in the cell of St Francis of Assisi. As a teenager in Rome he was mesmerised by the stone in the catacombs and declared his wish to become a 'priest-archaeologist'. In Mar Musa he found that same stone, in which he saw a symbol of poverty, of simplicity and of closeness to the essential. I knew exactly what he meant, thanks to my experiences in Bait Baroudi.

Before offering his life to the priesthood, Paolo had flunked his Bac, and gone to work in a shipyard in Fiumincino, a two-hour journey from his parents' house in Rome. There he learnt, he said, the fraternity of a close community and the rewards of manual labour. As a Jesuit scout he also spent a few nights on the streets with dropouts, sharing their poverty and squalor, another experience that changed him profoundly: he moved out of his parental home to care for an elderly woman who lived alone.

In Mar Musa he made good use of all these skills, helping to restore the monastery with his own hands, caring paternalistically for the small community that slowly built up around him, living simply and self-sufficiently. The monastery collected its own rainwater, and kept goats and chickens; for milk, cheese and eggs. Pigeons occasionally provided meat. When visitor numbers gradually increased, reaching 50,000 a year in 2010 – mainly Muslims – these meagre resources were stretched to breaking point, but Paolo never turned anyone away, not even backpackers who clearly just saw it as a free night. He advocated the importance of bringing people together, rejecting occidental divisions between religious orders. 'For me there is no east or west,' he said.

Already quadri-lingual, the decades he spent in Syria made his Arabic flawless. After his expulsion, incapable of being a bystander, he started to appear on the opposition Arabic TV channel Orient News in a weekly programme talking with refugees outside the country, exhorting reconciliation. He toured internationally, calling on world leaders to help the opposition rebels fight the Assad regime, predicting the rise of Islamist extremism if a vacuum were allowed to develop. Starting in February 2013 he entered Syria a number of times and even met with 'militarised extremists' (he did not like the term *jihadis*), trying to mediate between the various opposition factions. 'We need to prepare the ground for reconciliation,' he said. 'Take the Alawi clan of the Assads. They are not all criminals ... They too are victims of the regime.' Syrian State TV accused him of being 'embedded with Islamic extremists and paid by Al-Qaeda'.

Days after the kidnap, Pope Francis mentioned him openly in his prayers.

'I believe my mission,' Paolo had said in 2009, 'is to create some sense of understanding between Muslims and Christians. Today the idea of a 'clash of civilisations' has become more popular, unfortunately, because it is not true. Islam and Christianity are branches of the same religion and I recall a time when Christian women wore covers over their heads.'

From peaks of 500 visitors a day, numbers plummeted once the fighting began. On my last trip there in November 2011, I was driven by Abu Ashraf in a taxi he had borrowed from his village, and we were the only visitors. Thankfully we encountered no road-blocks on the 100 kilometre drive north from Damascus on the Homs highway, a relief since Foreign Secretary William Hague had just announced Britain's support of the rebels and it would not have been a good day to have a British passport. Beyond Mar Musa to the east we learnt from Father Paolo that all the villages had been free of regime control for months, running their own councils and affairs. 'They are too small for the regime to bother with,' he explained. The monastery laid on a generous lunch for us, a welcome reward for Abu Ashraf, who, to my surprise, had laboured up the 350 steps with me, breathless from his cigarettes. Father Paolo greeted us both equally, speaking perfect Syrian Arabic to Abu Ashraf and perfect English to me. Knowing it would almost certainly be the last time for us, and the first and only time for Abu Ashraf, he showed us round the monastery church, explaining the meaning of its ancient biblical frescoes, followed by a tour of the immaculate cheese factory.

Abu Ashraf was very taken with the place, and especially admired the ingenious wire and pulley system used to transport the milk from the goats high up on the mountain down to the factory within the monastery. Soon after our visit I heard the Syrian authorities were trying to expel Father Paolo for his explicit anti-regime statements, and the monastery even suffered a night-time raid by an armed gang looking for money and weapons. Paolo happened to be away at the time of the raid but I later met one of the young Syrian Christian women who had been sleeping there, staying on a retreat. She told me how she had calmed the invaders down, having seen the fear in their eyes, as the rest of their faces were concealed behind balaclava helmets. She had not panicked, but had appealed to their mercy, asking them not to kill everyone for nothing, since they had nothing worth stealing. She even took them round the monastery, showing them all the cupboards where they could search. They left after trashing the place but harmed no one.

Paolo refused to be silenced. Some months later the regime exiled him and he left for Lebanon, then on to Rome. At the time he said he would rather die in Syria than live outside it. He may indeed have had his wish granted, for in August 2013 he was reported to have been executed in his prison cell in Ar-Raqqah by ISIS *jihadis*. He had re-entered the country illegally through rebel-held territory from Lebanon, intending to negotiate between Kurdish groups and the Islamists who had started to fight each other, just as they had in Ras Al-Ayn. He had hoped to persuade them of the futility of such infighting when their shared enemy was supposed to be the Assad regime. Nothing has been heard of him since. Today Mar Musa remains open without him, designated a 'protected area' for birds.

Just as vocal as Father Paolo and possibly even more controversial is Mother Agnes Mariam de La Croix, dubbed 'the detective nun'. The Mother Superior, a Carmelite nun who has been living in Syria since 1994, is based in Qarah, a town 90 kilometres north of Damascus and not far from Mar Musa. Her monastery sits on the foundations of a Roman fort and is called the Monastery of St James the Mutilated. Not only is she an expert on Arab icons – I bought her book *Icones Arabes* from her monastery shop back in 2007 – but she also claims to have some expertise as a chemical weapons analyst. She submitted a 50-page report to the Assad regime after the Ghouta attack claiming to present evidence that the rebels, not the regime, were behind the attack. The basis for her arguments has been systematically dismissed by Human Rights Watch, but Mother Agnes' zeal is undiminished. She seems to seek out the limelight in a most unusual way for a nun, just as she is keen to point the finger of blame in a most un-Christian way. Many, including Father Paolo, see her as regime stooge.

In Aleppo, with its 12 different church denominations – six Catholic, three Orthodox, two Protestant and one Nestorian – the Chaldean Bishop Antoine Audo has avoided expulsion by keeping his statements non-political. In November 2012 he told me his community was nevertheless deeply involved in humanitarian aid, preparing 5,000 meals a day for distribution to the city's poor, and 300–400 food parcels a month to be delivered to the homes of the needy, irrespective of their religion or politics: UN aid on the other hand can only go where the regime permits.

Many of Syria's Christians are to be found in the northeast of the country, in the area known as Al-Jazira, meaning 'the island', because it is a triangle-shaped island delineated by the rivers of the Tigris, the Euphrates and the Khabour. The provincial capital city is Al-Hasakah, where the grandly titled 'Bishop of the Jazira and the Euphrates' has his seat. These days the bishop has fled to Vienna where he lives in some luxury, unloved by his abandoned flock. The Christian community who remain in Al-Hasakah were said to be fine till summer 2013, as were those in Qamishli on the Turkish border with Nusaybin, but those in Ras Al-Ayn have fled into Turkey. Having shared neighbourhoods peacefully with secular Kurds for generations, they found themselves caught up in the fighting that erupted in late 2012 and early 2013 between the PKK militia and extreme Islamist groups like Jabhat Al-Nusra. After three ceasefires had broken down, despite intensive negotiations, some of which were even led by the veteran Christian opposition member Michel Kilo, many decided it was time to leave Syria. After a spell in an uneasy truce, with the town of Ras Al-Ayn split into an Arab-controlled half and a Kurdish-controlled half, the Kurdish groups succeeded by summer 2013 in driving out the extremists.

In a trip to southeastern Turkey in summer 2013 I saw a refugee camp set up exclusively for Syriac Christians near Midyat, some of them from Ras Al-Ayn. A Syriac Orthodox monk called Father Joaqim explained to me how the land had been donated by a Syriac businessman in the hope that many Syriac Christians would come with their families and settle there. Father Joaqim is a young man with a sense of destiny, who has returned from 11 years in Holland to revive the dying Syriac Christian community in eastern Turkey. From the terrace of Mor Augen, his newly restored monastery high on a remote escarpment near Nusaybin, we could look south across the border into Syria.

'Thank God our community is alive again,' he told me, his face radiating out from the distinctive black cap of his Syriac Orthodox habit. 'On Sundays our church is full with worshippers from the village.'

I marvelled at how he had transformed the place from the ruin it had been back in the 1980s when I had first seen it. 'There was no path,' I told him, 'and it took an hour to climb up. This terrace was a vegetable patch and a local family was living in the church shell.'

'Yes,' he replied serenely, 'They were Yazidis. They moved in after the last monk died. They looked after everything very well,' he added.

The thought of a Syriac Orthodox monk being grateful to Yazidis, often reviled as devil-worshippers by Muslims and Christians alike, was a novel one. A small Kurdish community of less than a million worldwide, their 12th century religion with its complex fusion of Zoroastrian and Sufi elements was often misunderstood because their 'Peacock Angel' was wrongly identified with the Devil.

As for the Syriac Christians, this had always been their homeland, the region known as Tur Abdin, Syriac and Arabic for 'Mountain of the Servants of God', and like those at Ma'loula, they still spoke Aramaic, a dialect of Syriac, using it as their liturgical language.

Father Joaqim told me how there were once 80 thriving monasteries on the Tur Abdin. 'This was the first,' he said, 'founded by Mor Augen – St Eugene. He was a 4th century pearl diver in the Red Sea, who taught us the Egyptian monastic tradition.'

He explained – without any trace of rancour – how successive persecutions from fellow Christians, Mongols and Turks had decimated their numbers, leaving just a handful of monks struggling to keep the main monasteries alive.

'When I returned two years ago,' he continued, gently sipping his tea, 'I asked the government for permission to re-open the monastery, and they agreed. They paid for the new tarmac road to reach the foot of the mountain, and they paid to bring the electricity. We paid for the road to continue up here and for the restoration works.'

'That can't have been easy,' I exclaimed, 'getting permission from the government!'

'It was very easy. We were invited back officially.' He explained how EU pressure had gradually forced a change in Turkish policy: 'The politicians now realise it is good to have us here. Rich members of our community are returning from Europe and investing their life savings'.

He paused. 'What is more difficult,' he elaborated, 'is the land disputes with our Kurdish neighbours. In some places they use our churches as stables. We are only a minority of course, but now our local MP is a Christian from our community. He represents the Kurdish Party, so we hope we can resolve our differences.'

I gestured down to the plain below and asked about the war in Syria just across the border, within sight of the monastery: 'Are you afraid it will spill over here?'

'Not at all,' he replied. 'We want our brothers to come back from Syria. Most of them fled there during the First World War. They have always shared our ancient Syriac language and culture. Several of their families are living in our village. They help our church – and our football team,' he flashed a smile.

Across the Tur Abdin some of the long-abandoned villages are slowly coming back to life, not just with émigré families of the Syriac disapora returning from Europe, but also with co-religionists from Syria, separated by an artificial border, returning to the bosom of their community in Turkey. From a low-point of just 80 families, there are now around 150 families. A slick Syriac-staffed factory even harvests the produce of Syriac vineyards, making Syriac wines which are sold in the restaurants of the new boutique hotels in Mardin and Midyat.

Who could have imagined that in a remote corner of eastern Turkey, the war in Syria would be reuniting an ancient community? Only Father Joaqim perhaps. His willingness to forgive and his refusal to cast blame will be sorely needed in the future Syria.

South of Damascus, before the revolution, I had made a number of day trips with Ramzi to the villages of the Hawran, rarely visited places, the very places I had longed to explore when, short of time, I had bypassed them on my first research trip years earlier. Well off the beaten track, life there seemed to go on much as it had done for centuries, simple settlements built of black basalt, the villagers living a rural life with their sheep and chickens. What surprised us was that the inhabitants turned out to be mixed: Muslims and Christians living side by side, each village with its church and its mosque. There were no segregated Muslim or Christian quarters within the villages. They seemed to be genuinely integrated with each other.

The villages fall within the province of Deraa, and there are whole clusters of them – Al-Mismiyeh, Sha'ara, At'taf, Bassim – all on small roads, all bounded by the triangle of main roads that run between Damascus, Deraa and As-Suwayda. They are not on the way to any-where, so only local residents ever have a reason to go there. Yet far from being xenophobic, people welcomed us into their homes; every-one was curious to meet us, everyone interested to know why we had come, what we were looking for. When we explained, they eagerly took us to see the ruins of churches and monasteries, sometimes located outside the village, sometimes incorporated into their own houses and courtyards. They no longer noticed them – the usual way when something forms part of your own landscape – but they were clearly very pleased by our interest.

These villagers were among the first to protest against the regime in the uprising. The 13-year-old Hamza al-Khatib, who later became a symbol of the revolution, was one of the protesters, tragically sepa-rated from his family when the protest was fired upon, then detained and tortured to death, before being returned to them in a body bag as a warning. Still today Muslims and Christians are fighting side by side in these villages of the Hawran, while north of Damascus in the town of Saydnaya the mix of Orthodox, Catholics and Sunni Muslim families share thirteen churches and two mosques whilst sheltering refugees from Homs, Hama, Tell and Derayya. Nine Popes have come from the Hawran, 'Too many,' as the Patriarch of the Melkite Church, in full communion with Rome, joked.

There are even a handful of mixed marriages among the inhabit-ants. The Maronite Patriarch Bechara Al-Rahi, having at the start of the revolution implied that Christians supported the regime because it protected them as minorities, is now starting to distance himself from Bashar. Originally he had sympathised: 'The poor man cannot work miracles.' But now he has changed his stance: 'The Christians are not concerned with the regime, they are concerned with the stability of Syria.' People are starting to see through the regime's policy of dividing Syrians against each other on sectarian lines, the old 'divide and rule' policy so favoured under the French Mandate. 'We will not fall into that trap,' said the Bishop of Aleppo.

I am not a regular church-goer, but in Damascus, whenever possible, I had enjoyed going to one of the well-attended services, to savour how different the atmosphere, let alone the communion with its wine-soaked brioche, was when compared to an English church. The Greek Melkite Cathedral was my favourite, just south of the Street Called Straight, a five-minute walk from Bait Baroudi through the backstreets. I loved the way everyone arrived whenever they felt like it, how the children felt no inhibitions about the place, the way they even climbed up into the pulpit to take photos of the priests processing. It was the same natural way that Muslim children behaved in the mosques – it was clearly a cultural not a religious difference. Its Patriarch Gregorius III said in November 2012: 'We Melkites are Arab but not Muslim, Catholic but not Orthodox, Eastern but not Latin. I am a church of Arabs. I am a church of Muslims. All are welcome. Ours is a church without borders. This is not a religious war. Reconciliation is the only solution. We do not want weapons, no Christians are to be armed.' Interviewed by the BBC in September 2013 just before the Americans were about to launch their reprisal attack for the regime's use of chemical weapons in the Ghouta, Patriarch Gregorius' message was the same: 'No fighting, no war! We are against these strikes.'

On one Epiphany Sunday when I was attending a service at his cathedral, he had processed round the packed congregation, liberally soaking everyone in holy water from his swaying silver bucket. It was a spectacle to behold. There was no set routine or ritual. People seemed to get up, sit down or kneel whenever the mood grabbed them, and no one minded how others acted. As long as everyone arrived in time for the taking of communion, that was all that mattered. Immediately after that, you could leave whenever you felt like it. Everyone present, including the children, had brought plastic water bottles to be blessed, so they could take holy water back to their homes. The congregation contained a wide range of ages and was equally balanced between men and women. Young children sat with their grandparents, and teenage girls in tight jeans sat with their headscarved mothers.

After the start of the revolution the atmosphere during these church services became noticeably tense. Prayers made many references to protecting the Syrian nation and its people, and in the visitors' book of the St Ananias Chapel, where the future St Paul was cured of his blindness, I started to read entries such as these:

I'm begging you my Lord and Hanania Saint to save my country, family and my friends. Bring to them all happiness and love. 15/2/2012.

Jesus save us in Homs 17/2/2012.

The spectre of Iraq loomed large. When Saddam was removed the Christian population had fallen by a million, many leaving for economic reasons as their businesses could not survive the turmoil. Before that Christians had lived in relative stability, for all the imperfections of that regime. In Syria there was also an ongoing Christian exodus under Bashar and his father Hafez, again due to economic factors rather than persecution. Elsewhere in the region, Turkey stands out as a country that has successfully accommodated several religions, judging from what I have seen on my many visits over the last 30 years. I have stayed overnight in monasteries such as Deyrulzaferan and Mar Gabriel in Eastern Turkey's Tur Abdin – where Syrian refugees were later offered hospitality by men like Father Joaqim – attended church services from Istanbul to Trabzon and visited mosques from Edirne to Urfa without ever encountering hassle or prejudice.

෧෮

Pre-revolution, Bashar himself was quoted as saying 'Turkey is the model [for religious toleration in a secular state] because we have the same society and similar traditions.' Bashar and Erdoğan even used to go on holiday together. However, in an October 2013 interview on

Turkish TV Bashar said: 'Before the crisis Erdoğan never mentioned reforms or democracy [for Syria], he was never interested in these issues. Erdoğan only wanted the Muslim Brotherhood to return to Syria, that was his main and core aim.' But many Syrian protesters did not agree, and named their next Friday demonstration: 'Thank you Turkey!'

Over the last ten years under Erdoğan, Turkey has opened up much faster than Syria under Bashar, liberalising its economy, embracing privatisation and free enterprise. As a result its economy has been booming, with growth peaking at about 12 per cent in 2010–11, though that figure has since slackened off considerably. It declared a 'zero problems with neighbours' foreign policy, trading with them all, and in 2009 opened its borders to Lebanese, Jordanians, Iraqis and Syrians, dropping all visa requirements. More and more Syrians started going to Turkey for their holidays, Bassim included. It was his favourite destination, the reason for his choice of Istanbul when he left Syria permanently in July 2012.

But though Bashar's and Erdoğan's spells in power have run side by side, Syria's economy has lagged behind, as if stuck in a time warp. A Swedish government agency produced a report in 2009 explaining why the global economic crisis had not had much of an effect on Syria, claiming it was because Syria did not really have an economy. Sanctions can be imposed but their effect will be limited, the report explained, because Syria's exposure to world markets was minimal – it is used to being isolated. Banning oil exports to the United States and to the EU sounds serious, but the reality is that Syria barely has enough oil for its own needs, let alone enough for export to anyone else, and that will remain the case until a period of prolonged stability allows the exploitation of its extensive new reserves in the eastern Mediterranean. As long as Russia and Iran continue to supply the Assad regime with oil and gas Syria will get by, albeit with shortages, and the high rainfall of 2012 meant good harvests to help with food supplies, albeit with higher prices.

The murky inner workings of Syria's government were briefly illuminated when, in 2009, a Wikileaks cable showed how the Syrian Foreign Ministry saw every encounter with the US as a market transaction – just like in the souk. The US had wanted a new embassy compound in Damascus, but agreement on the actual land deal would not be forthcoming until the Syrians got something in return, namely, the announcement of a new US ambassador to Damascus. Nothing new there – in any negotiation, squeezing concessions out of your adversary is the name of the game. But the US administration held back, considering the Syrian approach unreasonable. Understanding other people's cultures has never been an American forte.

Bashar, on the other hand, did understand these differences, all too well. He spoke often about the gulf of misunderstanding between 'us Syrians' as opposed to 'you in the West'. He even put it in computing terms, self-confessed computer nerd that he is. Before becoming president of the country, he was president of Syria's Computer Society, responsible for introducing the country to the age of the internet – another irony, given that the recent uprising has been dubbed the 'Facebook Revolution'. Facebook was banned for a while in Syria, as were both Yahoo and Hotmail until 2004, when Bashar relented. He explained that the difference between the leadership of Syria and a Western country was like the difference between a PC and an Apple Mac. 'Both do the same job,' he said, 'but they don't understand each other. You need to translate. If you want to analyse me as the East, you cannot analyse me through the western operating system, or culture. You have to translate according to my operating system, or culture.' He had a point.

People who know him say power has changed him, corrupted him, that vanity is a big weakness of his. He sees himself as 'a sort of philosopher king, the Pericles of Damascus' said the Wikileaks cable. He lacks his father's staying power; no ten-hour meetings without a break (the type his father specialised in) – 'bladder diplomacy', as it was called. But he shares his father's preference for abstraction in speeches, something that can make his opinions very tricky to pin down. Whenever I have watched his speeches live on TV, I have always felt the translators and interpreters failed to capture the full force of his Arabic, often making it sound trite, while to a Syrian audience the subject matter would strike much more of a chord. National identity, for example, was always an issue he stressed in his speeches, as well as solidarity with the Palestinians, both highly emotive subjects for his domestic listeners, but dismissed by western audiences as no more than vague ramblings. He displays a clever use of metaphors: one of his best was to describe his position, vis-à-vis the myriad opposition groups, as like that of a man who is ready for marriage but cannot find the right partner. In his relatively rare interviews in English his tone conveys an arrogance that suggests complete denial of what has been happening inside his country. Certainly his ability to lie is impressive. Even nine months into the revolution, in an interview with veteran US journalist Barbara Walters, he insisted: 'We don't kill our own people. No government in the world kills its people, unless it's led by a crazy person.'

Sometimes I wonder if Bashar is trying to be a visionary like his father. One of his foreign policy vanities in 2010 was to see himself at the centre of the so-called 'Five-Seas' project, where Syria sat at the heart of a network of countries all of whom were linked by water: the Mediterranean, the Black Sea, the Caspian, the Red Sea and the Persian Gulf. In the past, when Europe and the US have hardened their rhetoric against Syria, the government has simply turned east, away from them. Russia, China and Iran remain on Syria's side, as powerful allies. Much of Syria's weaponry is Russian-made, senior members of its armed forces were largely trained in Russia and much of the country's infrastructure, like the huge dam on the Euphrates which created Lake Assad, is Russian-built. Most significant of all, on Christmas Day 2013 Russia's state-controlled oil company Soyuzneft-gaz, run by a former Russian energy minister, secured its long-term interests in Syria by signing a 25-year highly significant and contro-versially-timed deal with the Assad regime. The deal awards Russia offshore oil and gas exploration, drilling, development and produc-tion rights in the coastal area between Baniyas and Tartous. Syria's oil refineries are already in Baniyas (and the contested Homs area), while its existing oil fields are all concentrated round Deir Ez-Zour in the east under the control of rebel and Kurdish groups. How real-istic it will be for Russia to implement the deal remains to be seen, but it raises the spectre of an economically viable Alawi state on the Mediterranean coast, free from dependence on the rebel-controlled eastern oil and gas fields, which are in any case predicted to run out in 2015. Maybe it is for this reason that the area round the medieval

Crusader port of Tartous, home to Russia's only Mediterranean naval base, has remained an unusual haven of calm during the revolution, with no communal violence, despite the Sunni majority. Syrian Christians and Alawis, I started to hear, were increasingly heading there from Lebanon as well as Syria. Food and apartments were cheaper than in expensive Beirut, and its other advantages were geographical: closeness to the Lebanese border if fleeing became necessary, and proximity to the perceived safety of the Christian villages of the Wadi Al-Nasara and the Alawi mountains.

These same hilltop villages had in pre-revolution summers been full with Gulf Arabs escaping the heat of their own countries, amusing themselves by taking brides from local families in *mut'a* (Arabic 'pleasure') temporary marriages, a kind of licensed prostitution permitted under Islam. At the end of the summer many girls would be pregnant, their honour lost and their young lives ruined, their Gulf 'husbands' free to leave without responsibility, having paid the girls' fathers the agreed sums. As Syria's personal status law is based on Islamic *Shar'ia*, such temporary marriages cannot be registered in court. The children of such unions are then stateless, since under Syrian law only the father, not the mother can pass nationality to a child, forcing the mother to give up her parental rights and register the child as abandoned. The whole business was a form of sex trafficking under another name. Would such practices return to Syria if extremist rebel groups like ISIS eventually came to dominate the country, with their bans on smoking and their enforced veiling of women? Financed, as such groups are, by wealthy individuals from the Gulf, I could not help wondering if there were some strange parallels between the exploitation of the young girls and the exploitation of Syria's moderate rebel groups, who, desperate for funding and weapons, were prepared to get into bed with such exploiters whose morals they did not share. It was the same for Syrian refugee girls, some as young as 12. Forced to flee into neighbouring countries, they were increasingly being sold to much older men by their desperate families just to pay the rent and survive. Poor Syria, forced into prostitution by impoverished circumstances.

As a young foreign girl I had been blissfully ignorant of such practices when, back in 1978, I had entered Syria en route to MECAS for the first time, via the port of Tartous, inching my Citroen down the rickety ramp of a car ferry where it had been squashed between trucks and Mercedes heading for Iran. Misjudging the distances and ignorant of the curfew in force after nightfall in Lebanon, I had pressed on towards Shemlan in the dark, and crunched into a giant pothole. Still some 40 minutes' drive from the school, I was stuck. Before I even had time to think about what to do next, a middle-aged man stepped out from behind a tree. I was vulnerable but thankfully he was not a sex trafficker.

'Weak legs,' he said, in Arabic, 'Your car has weak front legs.'

We squatted down on the ground and peered under the car, looking at where the wheel was stuck in the deep hole. The front axle was broken.

'No problem,' he said matter-of-factly, 'Tomorrow I will take it down to Beirut on my lorry and get it fixed.' And with that, he gave me a lift in his own beaten-up car, and told me he would bring the car back tomorrow after it had been fixed.

At the school, there was some commotion on my arrival and the director was angry with me for breaking the curfew. I told everyone about the car and how it would be fixed and brought back tomorrow. They laughed at my naivety. 'Don't be ridiculous. You'll never see that car again,' they scoffed. 'What an innocent abroad you are.'

The next morning, during the coffee break, we were sitting out on the school terrace that overlooked Beirut and the coastline. The unmistakeable whine of a 2CV engine labouring uphill, distant at first, grew louder, and I ran to the railing in time to see my car bracing itself for the final assault on the steep driveway up into the school. It became a legendary story. The driver, the man who had helped me the night before, refused all payment, and I never saw him again.

That was Lebanon after three years of civil war, testimony if ever it were needed, to the innate decency of most people of the region. In Syria, after three years of civil war, would the same thing happen now? From stories I still hear from Ramzi the Philosopher, from Rashid the lawyer, from Marwan the shopkeeper, from Maryam the bank manager and from Abu Ashraf the caretaker, I believe it would. But such stories of kindness and human decency never make the headlines. The world prefers to read about 'heart-eating cannibals', skewing perceptions of the conflict. The overwhelming majority of ordinary Syrians have a strong sense of solidarity and sympathy with their fellow victims and sufferers. How else could they have survived four decades of the Assad regime and the Ba'ath Party as remarkably as they have?

'I think it is about desperation,' Bashar had said in his Wall Street Journal interview in January 2011, giving his own take on the matter, when talking about the uprisings in other Arab countries, before his own had started. 'Whenever you have an uprising it is self-evident to say that you have anger, but this anger feeds on desperation. Desperation has two factors: internal and external,' he went on. 'The internal one is that we are to blame, as states and as officials, and the external one is that you are to blame, as great powers or what you call in the West "the international community".'

It was his usual vague and abstract way of speaking, but obvious to all was his blindness to the desperation of his own people.

Asked in early 2011 what he thought about the events of the Arab Spring, he said: 'if you have stagnant water, you will have pollution and microbes; and because you have had the stagnation for decades, let us say, especially the last decade … because we had this stagnation we were plagued with microbes … we need flowing water, but how fast is the flow? If it is very fast, it can be destructive or you can have flood. Therefore it should be flowing smoothly.'

It was one of his clearer metaphors, cautioning against making changes too quickly, but appearing to acknowledge the need for change and reform. Western audiences were impressed with his apparent understanding of the problems. Most Syrians who heard the interview saw straight through him.

Protesters parodied his use of the word 'microbes' or 'germs' in a Facebook Page called 'We are all germs!' showing Bashar as Dr Dettol trying to kill them.

With impeccable timing, again in early 2011, the American edition of Vogue Magazine published a special feature on his wife Asma al-Assad, entitled 'Rose of the Desert.' She was described as utterly charming, irresistible even, talking about her hopes and aspirations for Syria's future, always elegantly dressed 'with cunning understatement' as they put it. She spoke about her involvement in charities, and how she toured the country speaking to disadvantaged groups, listening to their problems and needs, then sending them computers or whatever equipment they needed. She spoke of her life with her husband and their three children, all of whom went to a Montessori school, how they lived in a flat in the city, with real neighbours, just like normal people, not in some fancy palace. Their home was run on 'wildly democratic principles', where they all had a vote. The chandelier made from cut-up comic books that hung over the dining table was, she laughingly explained, something she had been outvoted on by the children. It was superb publicity for the Assads and Asma had the world fawning at her feet. When the article had gone to press the Arab Spring had not begun. Vogue ended up withdrawing the piece from their website. Once again the Western audience had fallen for the PR image, while the Syrian audience knew the truth behind it.

Since then, Asma has gone quiet, just appearing in public a handful of times at Bashar's side, or in specially posed photos with refugees, or once by herself on a visit to the Damascus headquarters of the Syrian Arab Red Crescent, Syria's humanitarian organisation affiliated since 1946 to the International Committee of the Red Cross, but in practice a semi-regime set-up. The visit was at her request, as she had heard about the difficulties they encountered at the *mukhabarat* checkpoints, and how SARC's vehicles were sometimes misused by 'parties without control, creating a situation of fear among the citizens.' They said she expressed her 'deep admiration for their efforts' and 'promised to convey some of their demands to the authorities.' Afterwards, SARC reported, there was indeed an improvement in the behaviour of the *mukhabarat* checkpoints. Who could believe them, given what I was later to discover?

Yes, she did a lot of 'good works'. She was apparently the driving force behind many of the cultural events staged as part of Damascus' year as Arab Capital of Culture, when the Street Called Straight was repaved in black basalt stones a year behind schedule. Her proudest projects, she said, were FIRDOS, the Fund for Integrated Rural Development of Syria, an NGO which focused on micro-finance for small businesses, scholarships for clever pupils and teaching young people IT skills, and Masaar, a child development charity. But Ramzi told me her 5-star NGOs where money was no object were staffed by relations and friends, disconnected from reality, driving round in large 4-wheel-drives on fat salaries. 'They do not touch the bottom,' he said, 'the rings on their fingers alone would fund real projects for years.' It was all show. No modern legal framework exists for NGOs or civil society groups to function independently of the government, despite years of talking about the introduction of new laws. The state even controls the definition of the concept of 'civil society'.

Looking back at some of her pre-revolution speeches in slick international lecture-halls to distinguished global audiences, her words appear to echo Bashar's theoretical understanding of desperation:

Where would a terrorist recruit if poverty did not line up those in despair? ... When people are poor they have no hope, they become desperate and desperation can breed some bad, bad things ...

Wonderful words of sympathy, but both she and Bashar were talking in the abstract, about other people in other countries. Neither seemed capable of acknowledging the desperation of their own people.

On 17 March 2011, just two days after the first tentative demonstrations in Damascus, Asma chaired a conference for Harvard Arab Alumni held at the Four Seasons, Damascus's fanciest hotel. Their website carried the hype about her as a 'thought-provoking, inspiring and tireless leader and advocate.' A mere 30 delegates attended the one day event, most of them scarcely bothering to sit through the day's sessions. And the subject? 'Arab Youth of Today and Tomorrow'. If I were an Arab youth, I would have been tempted to blow them up ... or join the revolution.

15

Thugs and Tamerlane

The world began with war and will end with war.

Arab proverb

When, from April 2011 onwards, reports began to appear in the international news channels about armed gangs, government thugs paid to be the regime's minders, roaming the streets and carrying out hideous acts of brutality, the parallels with earlier centuries were immediately clear.

Armed gangs, paid to do the dirty work of the ruling class, go back a long way in this part of the world; there is historical precedent. As early as the 15th century there are references in the Mamluk chronicles to the *zu'ar* of Damascus, and even before that, there were pre-Mamluk Syrian militia called *ahdath*. The Mamluks ruled Syria and Egypt for nearly three centuries before the Ottoman conquest, and were a meritocratic slave dynasty. Their power was built on their very tough fighting strength, horsemen with bow and arrows, and they were the first power to defeat the Mongols, the most ferocious fighters on earth at that time. The word *zu'ar* in Arabic means young toughs or thugs, and the root has associations with being thin-haired or tail-less. In classical Arabic it is the word used for highwaymen or brigands, who prey on and rob innocent victims, and is still sometimes used. They are the scum that rises to the top in times of war. 'In Syria we have lots of scum,' laughed Marwan bitterly, the last time I saw him.

In Syria today, the gangs are known as *shabiha*, 'spectres' or 'ghosts', as they often act under cover of darkness, coming and going surreptitiously. The word is also used to refer to black Mercedes, the preferred car of the Assad minders. Local people say the *shabiha* are often big men, with beards and wild eyes, sometimes dressed in black, sometimes just in ordinary clothes. They are mostly Alawis, and they first started appearing in the 1970s in the Lattakia area after Hafez al-Assad came to power, probably the result of patronage from some of Hafez's own Alawi clan. Their founder, Muhammad al-Assad, known as 'the Shaikh of the Mountain', was killed 18 months into the revolution by armed opposition militia from the al-Khayer clan. Regarding themselves as above the law, the *shabiha* used to run various smuggling and protection rackets often to do with drugs and weapons. These rackets began to get out of hand in the 1990s, leading, in one of those perverse twists of irony that are everywhere in Syria's history, to Hafez instructing Bashar to rein them in. Bashar did try, even having one of his cousin's bodyguards imprisoned for random violence against a passer-by.

Old habits die hard, and in May 2011 Bashar's cousins Fawwaz and Munir had EU sanctions imposed on them because of their involvement with the *shabiha*. The regime has been using them as enforcers, no doubt handsomely paid for their services. It calls them 'village defenders'. Marwan told me the *shabiha*'s daily rate had shot up to SY2000, making it equivalent to at least six times the average monthly wage. There are thought to be several thousand of them in Syria today. Sometimes they are mixed in with well-practised Iranian Hezbollah militia from Lebanon, both doing the Assad regime's dirty work together. In the battle for the strategic city of Al-Qusayr in May 2013, vital for cutting off the main access route to Homs for Sunni rebel fighters to weapons smuggled in from Lebanon, *shabiha* and Hezbollah operatives were key to the regime's eventual victory over the rebels. It was a turning point in the war.

At Jisr Al-Shughour near the Turkish border, there have been many reports of pro-government *shabiha* thugs carrying out atrocities in the town, randomly attacking defenceless inhabitants. Even worse, at Tell Kalakh, a mainly Sunni village near the Lebanese border surrounded by 12 Alawi villages, early on in the revolution local residents claimed that *shabiha* were carrying out summary executions. It was exactly the type of incident Ramzi the Philosopher was tragically later to be caught up in.

Groups like Human Rights Watch are painstakingly investigating such atrocities, like the May 2013 massacre at Al-Bayda near Tartous. They are fully confident of finding enough evidence to prove war crimes and a deliberate policy of ethnic cleansing. Religion is not stated on the secular Ba'ath ID cards, but the names themselves, together with a birthplace, make it clear to which sect the holder belongs.

Looking back at historical examples, there are interesting clues as to how similar networks of patronage worked. When the Ottomans took control from the Mamluks in the 16th century, the *zu'ar* were not abolished, but cleverly kept on and payrolled, as were the Mamluk armies themselves. The various patronage networks continued to thrive, enabling the Ottoman masters to control popular resistance. Demonstrations against, for example, oppressive taxation would be fiercely crushed using the *zu'ar* gangs. They were the most highly organised groups in the cities, young men who were described as 'wild beasts' who enjoyed terrorising the urban population into submission, in accordance with their masters' instructions. Today the *shabiha* wear colourful wristbands or armbands so that they can recognise each other in crowds, and continue to terrorise.

In Mamluk times the gangs of young men, mainly bachelors, had a distinctive hair style called a *qar'ani*, thought to have been a pigtail at the back with bald top and sides, and were dressed in robes worn over their shoulders as a kind of uniform. Some were known to be shopkeepers, according to the historical sources, and others were carpenters, thread sellers or brokers. The gangs were organised in the quarters outside Damascus' city walls and in the surrounding villages, and were led by *kabir*s or chiefs. From their names it was clear they were commoners, never middle-class notables, and their inspiration was never religious, even though they sometimes included a few minor religious officials in their number.

Just like today, it was in periods of economic decline and political disintegration that the gangs became particularly active, growing in size. When the population of Damascus was seething with resentment and revolt, as it was for much of the late 14th century, for example, during spells of heavy taxation and high unemployment, these semi-criminal gangs would be used to quell popular uprisings. Sometimes they would become impossible for their masters to control and would even turn on the Mamluk soldiers. Historic records show that they would murder tax collectors and kill the police, refuse to attend prayers and barricade the residential quarters of the city. Many rebel groups fall into a similar category in today's civil war, with extremist elements increasingly difficult to control, as they forge unlikely alliances and then turn against former masters. It made me think of the paradoxes of war, such as how, under Syrian law, all Syrians have to give blood on graduating or on receiving their driving licence. As one of the 36 doctors out of the pre-revolution figure of 5,000 still working in Aleppo shrewdly observed in late 2013: 'All share the same blood in some ways. Now when those gangs kill each other, they may be killing someone whose very blood is in their own veins.'

Al-Shaghour, the quarter in the southwest section of the Old City where my own Bait Baroudi stands, had a reputation throughout history for being notoriously rebellious and unruly, with particularly fierce fighters. Battles between the Mamluk troops and the *zu'ar* would sometimes go on for days until the troops finally got the upper hand.

Here again there may be interesting parallels with today. The *zu'ar* from different quarters used to unite if there was a common threat, but they were essentially hostile to each other. There were feuds, assassinations and revenge killings. Like the Assad minority Alawi clan, the Mamluks required military support to quell unrest from the general population of Syria. In the early 1500s the *zu'ar* were recruited for a military expedition against the Hawran south of Damascus, the same province as today's troublesome town of Deraa. Bloodshed and a great deal of pillaging is recorded in the chronicles whenever civil war threatened, as it did in 1503–4. Sometimes, when inter-communal violence became too extreme, the Mamluk governors would try to curb their powers by disarming and disbanding them, but without much success. On one occasion the *zu'ar* themselves organised a massive popular uprising against the government, with records showing that they came to despise the Mamluks and their government. The governors then struggled to disarm them, despite having armed them in the first place. But some of the powerful emirs of Damascus had vested interests in cultivating the gangs, and continued to pay them protection money to act as their custodians. The parallels are almost uncanny, where today's *shabiha* thugs have helped powerful members of the Assad clan with their various smuggling rackets, and where the Assads may well become incapable of controlling and curbing the activities of the paramilitary force they themselves created. Civil war is, after all, total anarchy, with no accountability, no punishment, no curbs.

Back in Mamluk times, when the regime felt strong and no longer needed to buy support, it often had the *zu'ar* arrested and even executed, to stop them becoming too powerful and taking the law into their own hands. If it turned out they could neither crush them nor buy their acquiescence, the safe option was to allow them to prey on the rest of the city, to turn their criminal violence against the civilian population. As a result, all effective opposition to the regime was prevented from organising itself, as the residential quarters of the city were too busy trying to survive the *zu'ar* attacks, and the *zu'ar* themselves had lost their political role and were too busy feeding on the residential quarters. Resistance to taxation was massive – as it still is today, with 45 per cent of the current workforce thought to be in the 'informal sector'. No wonder Bashar had been trying in 2010 to reform employment laws.

In the final years of the Mamluk rule over Syria, with the authority and the power of the state broken by economic hardship and oppression, communal feuds became the order of the day. Vicious disputes broke out between villages, tribes and organised factions of urban quarters. Armed gangs preyed on the rich, extorted money from shopkeepers, pillaged the wealthy quarters, and assaulted people in the streets. In response shopkeepers closed their shops and went on strike, partly to protest against the regime and partly to protect themselves. In today's civil war in Homs, Hama, Aleppo and even Damascus, accounts of precisely such atrocities and worse have leaked out, despite the regime's media blackout.

After two and half centuries of Mamluk rule, internal order

collapsed. When the Ottomans defeated them in 1516, the populations of Syria (and Egypt) welcomed their new Turkish masters with relief. They were ready. Will a similar point be reached eventually in the current revolution, when the weary protagonists fighting a seemingly endless war of attrition against each other have finally had enough and submit to a new rule of law imposed from the outside? Or is there any chance they could find an internal solution – for Syrians by Syrians?

The terminal illness of the Mamluk regime in Syria lasted about 20 years. In today's world of instant global media such a timescale is unthinkable, though Lebanon's recent civil war lasted 15. When I lived in the Christian Maronite village of Shemlan above Beirut during that civil war, I struggled to understand its complexities, its sectarian divisions. The more I read, the more confused I became. Rosa and Munir, the kindly elderly couple in whose home I had lodged, had cheered and danced for joy on the roof of their house as they watched the Israeli bombardment of the Palestinian refugee camps of Sabra and Shatila. Such sectarian vendettas were eventually overcome in Lebanon, though the unresolved issue of Palestine of course remains a running sore in the region, requiring urgent treatment from skilled practitioners. Shemlan is now still Christian, part of the Christian heartland of Mount Lebanon. Today this Christian heartland acts as a buffer, sandwiched between the Shi'ite south, Hezbollah and the Sunni north, with the Druze mainly retreated to their own mountain strongholds. That has been Lebanon's solution, to stop the rival groups killing each other. 'If you can't get what you want,' runs the Lebanese proverb, 'want what you can get.'

Today the former warlords Jumblatt, Geagea, Gemayyal, Franjia and others are not in the dock at the International Criminal Court, but respected members of Lebanon's parliament and society. The death rate was 100,000–150,000 in that civil war, out of a population of three million. In Syria that is the equivalent of 725,000 who would have to die in order to reach the same stalemate. Maher al-Assad has said they are prepared to kill a million, if need be.

Maybe Bashar's strategy has been to create in Syria the same chaos as in Lebanon's civil war, making it ungovernable, playing on its differences and divisions. Why else did he jail and kill peaceful civilian activists yet release many *Salafis* from prison soon after the uprising began, if not to alter the nature of the opposition? Maybe in order to survive with his Alawi militia, he is prepared to retreat to his Alawi heartland round Lattakia. Or maybe Bashar simply has no strategy except a misguided attempt to return to the corrupt old Syria his father created, so that the regime will have to disintegrate internally, dragging the country down with it, and Bashar will end up being slaughtered in the sewer Gadhafi-style, before conditions are right for a total change. No one knows how long any of that will take, while thousands more lose their lives and millions flee as refugees to avoid a similar fate.

The stratification of society in Mamluk times is also reminiscent of today's Syria. The ruling Mamluk class was called *al-khassa* (the special class), and consisted of the sultan and his retinue, along with the highest-ranking Mamluk emirs and senior officials of the commanding elite, a direct parallel with Bashar al-Assad and his ruling Alawi-dominated Ba'athst elite – those that govern today. The lowest level was called *al-'amma* and meant the general public, the masses, commoners, even including low-ranking soldiers and bureaucrats, and just like today, they are the governed, deprived of all advantages of power, with no office, learning or wealth. They are respectable working people who are part of the communal and religious structures but who occupy no distinguished place within them. In the eyes of *al-khassa* they are simply the taxpayers.

In between these two classes, separating them and bridging them at the same time, Muslim writers talk about *al-a'yan*, usually translated as 'the notables'. They were the leaders of the smaller communities, respected pillars of the community who might be religious leaders, scholars, teachers, judges, *shaikhs*, doctors and merchants. They were in proper professions, but they did not govern, just as in today's Syria.

The city's many quarters are basically residential districts with small local markets, separate from the main central city bazaars, with different people grouping together based first and foremost on kinship; no one is truly safe in an unruly world except among his kin. Even today in Damascus people refer to their *hara*, their own small district, and *Bab Al-Hara* (The Gate of the District) is the name of a hugely popular TV soap series, relating the trials and tribulations of the district's inhabitants, a kind of Syrian Dickensian saga.

Beyond that, the next reason for solidarity is religion. Within the walls of the Old City certain areas, like Al-'Amara, were heavily Shi'a-populated, thanks to the Sayyida Ruqayya mosque built by the Iranians in that area, while other groups of Shi'a are concentrated near Al-Amin, or, outside the walls, in Midan, around the Mosque of Sayyida Zaynab.

Al-Shaghour, my district, is mainly Sunni Muslim, and Abu Al-'Izz, the agent who had first told me about Bait Baroudi, said it was known as a district where wealthy Mamluk emirs and officers used to live. Did this explain why, in 1401, Tamerlane had chosen Bab Al-Saghir, the gate leading into Al-Shaghour just yards away from Bait Baroudi, through which to rampage into the Old City of Damascus with his Mongol horsemen, pillaging and razing it to the ground? Aptly named the Gate of Mars in Roman times, Al-Shaghour would once again have been a battleground, taking the full frontal assault of the Mongol warrior's troops as they rode towards the Umayyad Mosque, setting ablaze markets and shops on their way. These scenes of destruction foreshadowed the aftermath of the fires that destroyed Aleppo's souks in the current war, with collapsed stonework and blackened doors.

Afterwards Tamerlane slaughtered most of the population, piling the heads in a field outside the northeast corner of the walls, where a square today still bears the name Burj Al-Ru'us, 'Tower of Heads'. The *waqf* document of the Umayyad Mosque dates from 1413, eleven years after the Mongol assault, and gives a sorry picture of a city in ruins, devastated not only materially, but also by Tamerlane's theft of the city's skilled craftsmen to build his own capital at Samarkand.

In the current troubled times, I have to face the fact that sectarian strife is a real possibility. There are many historical precedents. In 1129 some 6,000 Isma'ili Muslims were killed by Sunni Seljuks, provoked by rumours of an Isma'ili plot to help the Crusaders capture Damascus. In 1860 thousands of Christians (sources range from 7,000 to 11,000) were massacred in Damascus, including the American and Dutch consuls, by Druze and Kurds. The dispute was sparked by a quarrel between two children, one Druze, one Maronite, which then escalated to include their families and their communities, until it got completely out of hand. The French eventually intervened, sending 6,000 troops, who stayed almost a year. It has been described as the first humanitarian intervention by a foreign power.

The Christian quarter in Damascus was burnt during that 1860 uprising, with churches desecrated and missionary schools torched, but in the poorer district of Midan, outside the walls, the Christians were protected by their Muslim neighbours. The Algerian Sunni emir 'Abd Al-Qadir also saved hundreds of Christians, using his army of 500 loyal fighters to escort them from their homes in the Christian quarter to the safety of his own large house on the northern edge of the city walls. His friend Lady Jane Digby, thanks to the fact that her house lay outside the walls in As-Salihiya, escaped unharmed, though the atrocities she witnessed made her become a church-goer. Afterwards, she set up a committee at the British Consulate, then Bait Nizam just yards from Bait Baroudi, to try and rescue the girls carried off by the Kurds, and, as she discreetly put it, 'to discuss the problems that would undoubtedly occur when the raped women and girls gave birth.' Today, elders from the Sunni Muslim community of Homs hold meetings to discuss how to deal with the pregnancies that resulted from the rape of 1,200 girls by Alawi *shabiha* thugs after the district of Baba Amr fell.

My district of Al-Shaghour is also home to many prominent Shi'ite families, and the main street of Al-Amin, where the local fruit market and many shops are, is named after a prominent Shi'ite figure. That explained the mystery of why construction began in 2008 of a new *hawza*, ('a Shi'ite residential teaching school'), on the Street Called Straight, close to the junction with Al-Amin Street. I remember asking Bassim how on earth permission had been given for such a concrete monstrosity to be built in such a prominent location, and he replied that it had all happened very quickly, with none of the usual permissions and bureaucracy, thanks to Bashar's close personal relationship with high-level Iranians. Iranian pilgrims, the women dressed from head to toe in black robes, the men just in normal western clothes, were constant visitors to Damascus' religious shrines and tombs, many of which lie less than 500 metres from Bait Baroudi in the Bab Al-Saghir cemetery. Bassim told me most were not even religious:

'When they are out on the street on view, they pretend,' he said, 'but underneath they do not care. They are just on holiday.'

The same Shi'ite allegiance also explained how the Isma'ili Aga Khan Development Network, heavily involved in historic and cultural restoration work throughout Syria, had obtained permission to convert a whole series of historic buildings in Aleppo and Damascus to luxury hotels. There would be no burden on the municipality to maintain them, as the historic buildings would now be managed as hotels after restoration as well as providing social opportunities for training and tourism. Bashar and the Aga Khan are said to have a 'special relationship', as Alawi beliefs are closely linked to Isma'ili Islam. All the AKDN's employees were granted diplomatic immunity, even Tony the Yorkshire stonemason who lived for two years in my upstairs flat while working on the restoration of the three nearby palaces. 'I am rebuilding Damascus!' he announced proudly.

In the final years of the 14th century Ibn Sasra's *Chronicle of Damascus* tells us of the terror the Damascus residents felt on hearing of Tamerlane's armies advancing towards them. The Mongol chieftain sent a long threatening letter to their sultan, which contained the phrase: 'You are certain that we are unbelievers, and we are certain that you are liars and that this world has seduced you.'

The sultan replied, throwing back in Tamerlane's face all the same threats, and adding: 'If we slay you, how rich is the gain! And if we are killed, then there is but a moment between us and Paradise. Think not of those who are slain in the way of Allah as dead. Nay, they are living.'

Today's propaganda wars are conducted via Facebook, Twitter and bespoke media channels, but how similar they are in rhetoric. It is the time-worn posturing of rival factions, each convinced of the justice of his own cause. Small wonder Al-Ghazali, like St Augustine, viewed any state authority as a necessary evil, to be avoided if at all possible by the genuinely pious. In the same mould, Bashar and his loyal Alawis have been warning that if their regime falls, sectarianism will break out and Syria will descend into the chaos of civil war, just as Iraq did after 2003. The roles have been switched, the players are different, but the overall patterns remain depressingly similar.

Tariq told me that in Homs, his home town, often referred to as 'the heart of the Syrian Revolution', a lot of the fighting had become tribal in nature, with blood feuds erupting, and the core of the central revolutionary message thereby weakened. Alawis dominated the senior jobs in the army, the ministries, the embassies, the universities and the oil and gas companies. Raising sectarian fears in citizens' minds is the regime's only hope of survival, yet even by doing so, Bashar may be sealing his own doom, because Sunnis who were previously happy enough with the regime, now see his Alawi supporters as the main perpetrators of the horrific killings and torture that is taking place across the country. Small wonder the Alawis are clinging together and fighting for all they are worth. They know that if the regime falls, they in turn risk being tortured and massacred.

A number of Syrian friends, including Tariq, had told me that trouble could well erupt in my neighbourhood of Al-Shaghour. It had the right level of poor, disadvantaged residents mixed in with wealthier families, as well as all the requisite pride in its pedigree. It has been a centre of national resistance during the French Mandate, and home to prominent intellectuals and political figures like the Syrian hero and national inspiration, Yusuf Al-Azma. A powerful symbol of courage, sacrifice and dignity, he was Minister of War and Chief of Staff under King Faisal, when, after World War One, the French were handed the mandate over Syria by the victorious Allies. The government surrendered its powers, but Yusuf Al-Azma, even though he knew it was a suicidal gesture, led 4,000 men out of Damascus to fight against the French, to deny their occupation any legitimacy. Aged just 36, he was killed in the battle of Maysaloun in 1920, but his memory lives on in many statues and streets named after him and the battle. His statue stands today in Yusuf Al-Azma Square in the heart of the commercial district, close to the *Muhafaza* Building and the Cham Palace Hotel.

'With the time came the man,' they had said of Al-Ghazali. Maybe Syria's next saviour could even emerge from Al-Shaghour.

16

The Triumph of *Asabiyya*

There's a divinity that shapes our ends,
Rough-hew them how we will.

Shakespeare, *Hamlet* Act V Scene ii

My mother never made it to Damascus. But some of her things did. It was strangely comforting to think of her bedding and towels ending up in Bait Baroudi, now being used by Marwan's mother and by Abu Ashraf and their extended families – a part of her came at least.

Comfort was harder and harder to come by. Once the revolution had entered its fourth month and gradually become an armed uprising by the summer of 2011, the Foreign & Commonwealth Office announced that all Britons should leave Syria immediately while commercial means of travel were still available. That meant no company could now offer travel insurance. Flights began to be cancelled from lack of demand. As explosions became more and more frequent, more and more embassies started to close, including the British Embassy on 1 March 2012, abandoning the country to its fate.

To placate my protesting family in England, and to justify my continuing visits, I set up meetings in advance with my contacts at the Ministry of Tourism. On one occasion I asked for an audience with the new Tourism Minister. It turned my stays into quasi-business trips, so if challenged by the *mukhabarat*, I could produce my guide-books and talk about my pre-arranged meetings.

Each time I wondered what I would find at the other end on arrival. Would they even let me in? So far it had always been simple, no questions at passport control beyond the usual, no challenges. I would phone Abu Ashraf from London a day or two in advance to tell him my landing time, and Bassim would come to the house on the first evening to be sure of my safe arrival. They never once expressed surprise at my coming.

The Syrian Air flights were almost empty. They were spacious Airbus 320s supplied by the French, replacing the old Boeings which had been grounded by US sanctions for lack of spare parts. I always felt strangely reassured by the familiar smells, the clear whiff of ciga-rette smoke coming from the lavatories, the unmistakable liquid soap and the casual absence of the safety demonstration. As we began speeding along the tarmac for take-off from Heathrow, the pilot would announce that, *bi-idhn Allah*, 'with God's permission', we were heading to Damascus. The in-flight staff, always Syrian, began serving everyone with food and drinks with their usual easy charm as soon as the plane was sufficiently airborne. I would look for tension in their expressions and find none.

The route would cross Europe and the Alps, followed by a long spell over the Anatolian Plateau, untamed and uninhabited in vast stretches, yet endowed – and this was particularly clear from the air – with extraordinary quantities of water. Lakes and rivers were every-where. Turkey may not have much oil, making it dependent on both Russia and Iran for supplies, but it has water galore. With the Tigris and Euphrates both having their headwaters in its eastern heart-lands, Turkey enjoys huge power over its neighbours downstream: the broken jigsaws of Syria and Iraq. It can turn the tap off any time it wants.

Erdoğan and Bashar used to be allies and close friends. Turks and Syrians had grown accustomed to popping across each other's borders; Turks for cheap petrol and cigarettes, Syrians for holidays and luxury goods. When the Assad regime took a more violent course, Erdoğan and his government were well placed to mediate, and tried hard in the early months, senior officials shuttling between Ankara and Damascus, to persuade Bashar and his government to behave differently, to listen to the protesters and to introduce reforms.

But their words fell on deaf ears. Erdoğan lost patience, and eventually in August 2011, after repeated warnings to Bashar, gave the green light to the first main opposition grouping, the Syrian National Council, to organise themselves on Turkish soil. Turkey welcomed refugees from the fighting, providing camps for them along the border. At first they were a small trickle, building up to about 10,000 after the first year, then increasing exponentially to hundreds of thousands once the violence in Aleppo flared up. The flow became such that they ran out of camp space, hurriedly building more, while backlogs of desperate refugees piled up on the Syrian side of the border.

Erdoğan's rhetoric against the Assad regime grew increasingly bombastic, with talk of how Turkey's reprisals would lead to Syrian regime collapse. Patriot anti-missile batteries were rushed to Turkey's borders by NATO as air defence. But talk was all it was. No one lined up behind him, and Erdoğan looked more and more isolated, left to manage the refugee crisis alone, puffing himself up periodically by shooting down the occasional Syrian helicopter that had strayed into Turkish airspace.

But the Kurds were the big unknown. Neither Erdoğan nor Bashar knew how best to handle their Kurds. Rashid the lawyer was right. The Kurds had seen in the Syrian revolution a major opportunity to further their aspirations for their own homeland, or autonomy at the very least. The Kurdish street slogan was: 'Democracy for Syria. Federalism for Syrian Kurdistan.'

Bashar finally gave them citizenship in 2012 after 50 years of state deprivation, in an attempt to deter them from joining the revolution, but by then it was not enough. They were already fighting, sometimes against the regime, sometimes against the rebels, not only in the northeast Al-Hasakah and Qamishli areas, but also in Aleppo and north of it, in the Kurdish villages around Cyrrhus, a rarely visited Roman site. The last time I had driven there, crossing two precariously narrow Roman bridges to reach it, I remembered sitting with the local Kurdish village elder beside the tomb of Uriah the Hittite, sampling their excellent olive harvest.

'We were promised our homeland in 1920 but then betrayed, you remember?' he had said, even back then in 2010. Rashid told me that now some Kurds are already talking about eastern Syria as western Kurdistan – 'Rojavo' is their word for it. I knew that under the Assad regime many of them had been stateless and dispossessed, with no ID cards. Rashid explained: 'This means they cannot vote, own property, get a government job, or go to secondary school or university, but they are still forced to do military service. And people forget,' Rashid had added, 'that those PKK troubles already killed 45,000 people back in the 1980s and 1990s.'

No informed observer doubted that the Kurds needed to be courted, by both the Syrian and the Turkish governments. When Syrian regime forces withdrew from the Kurdish border areas in summer 2012, the PKK took control. Many speculated it was even a tacit agreement between the PKK and Bashar; there is a strange link, as the imprisoned PKK leader Abdullah Öcalan is from the rarefied minority of Alawi Kurds. It should have been a dream come true for the Kurds, but it quickly became worse than under Assad, with local Kurds complaining the PKK were mercenaries and criminals.

Although most are nominally Sunni Muslim, the Kurdish identity is based not on religion, but on ethnicity and cultural tradition. In Iraqi Kurdistan, schools do not impose Islam but teach all world religions equally. The last thing Kurds want is to be ruled by an Islamic state. This explains the fighting that broke out around Ar-Raqqah in summer 2013 between Syria's Kurds and the extremist Islamist groups like Jabhat Al-Nusra and ISIS who are seeking to establish precisely such an old-style caliphate. These were the very groups Father Paolo sought to mediate between when he entered the lion's den and was kidnapped by ISIS for his pains. This Kurdish versus Islamist infighting is an unwelcome distraction from the task in hand, namely, to bring down the Syrian regime, but for Syria's Kurds these extremist Islamists represent the greatest menace of all, and they would still choose the hated PKK over the Islamists. The leader of the Kurdish Saladin Brigade declared his position: 'We want a civil democratic government that treats everyone equally.' He may have got his wish, for in January 2014 on the eve of the Geneva II talks where Syria's Kurds were denied a seat of their own, the establishment of Rojavo as a semi-autonomous region was declared, with 22 cabinet ministers based in Qamishli. True to their ideology, the new government is a Christian/Muslim/Kurdish mix.

The international community would not care greatly what the Kurds got up to, except that Iraqi Kurdistan is oil rich, Syria's oilfields lie mainly in its northeast and Turkey's oilfields are in its southeast provinces. A future independent Kurdistan has the potential to control a massive chunk of the Middle East's oil reserves – to say nothing of its water or even its wheat reserves. Rojavo has the 100,000 barrel-a-day Suwayda oilfield which accounts for more than 60 per cent of the country's oil production; the Tigris, the Euphrates and the Khabour rivers; and one of Syria's richest agricultural sectors. What a prize.

≯ᴕ

The Turks and the Arabs, according to the 14th-century Muslim philosopher Ibn Khaldun, have the strongest sense of *Asabiyya* (tribal solidarity) of anyone in the world, but there is no doubt the Kurds have it too. The phenomenon of *Asabiyya* was an expression coined by this 'father of sociology', the first person to write about the philosophy of history. He had himself lived through the exceptionally turbulent years of the Black Death in which over a third of the world's population was wiped out, creating a period of chaos and instability that lasted well over a century. Aged 16, he had witnessed the death of his parents and most of his extended family and teachers from the pandemic. Aged in his 50s, he lost his wife and most of his children in a shipwreck. Wandering from his birthplace in Tunis into Andalusia, then back across North Africa to Cairo, he observed the rise and fall of numerous dynasties and developed his own theories about what accounted for these vicissitudes. He observed how all empires and dynasties arose out of simple tribal beginnings, and noticed how their *Asabiyya,* the intense group affinity that existed within a disorganised collection of tribes, unified by one leader's charisma, religious prophecy or even just circumstance, was the driving force behind history. Despite or perhaps because of his turbulent life, he was a born survivor, serving many masters as a *qadi* (judge). Thinking Tamerlane might be the 'man of the age', as tradition expected, sent at the start of the century as tradition expected, he had even survived a self-engineered encounter with that Mongol leader in 1401 outside the walls of Damascus, where the pair had discussed history late into the night in Tamerlane's tent. Ibn Khaldun died in Cairo at the ripe old age of 75 in 1406.

In modern Syria the *Asabiyya* of the Assad clan, and more broadly, of the Alawis, has always been very strong. But now that it is under threat from an uprising of Sunni Muslims, it has closed ranks and become stronger than ever. TE Lawrence observed this trait well before the Assad era, writing of the Alawis in his *Seven Pillars of Wisdom*: 'The sect, vital in itself, was clannish in feeling and politics. One member would not betray another, and would hardly not betray an unbeliever.' However wayward and despised certain elements of the Assad clan may be, the strength of their *Asabiyya* – the family bonds and loyalties that bind them – will compel them to hold together for the sake of their collective survival. They will meet all threats to their existence with increasing violence. They will do whatever it takes.

Bashar says he has read Ibn Khaldun, not to mention Goethe, which fits with his vision of himself as a sort of philosopher king.

✤

It was always clear when flights from London to Damascus were entering their final stage, as the route turned south to skirt the Turkish coastline in the Mediterranean's extreme northeast corner. This was Hatay, with its capital at Antakya, ancient Antioch, a gift from France to Turkey in 1939, a bribe even, to persuade them to not to enter World War Two on the side of Germany. Syrian maps still show this region, formerly called the Sanjak of Alexandretta, as theirs, taking the view that the French mandated power never had the right to give it away in the first place. Its cession to Turkey was generally considered a breach of the terms of the French Mandate. One of the many reasons my guidebook has been banned in Syria is for not showing this border where the Syrians wanted it. How ironic that Hatay is now where the Free Syrian Army, defectors from the Syrian military, are based while organising themselves to take up arms against the Assad regime's forces. The people in Hatay speak both Arabic and

Turkish, and are predominantly Alevi (the Turkish version of Alawi), another example of how the histories of Syria and Turkey are deeply intertwined. With such artificial and manipulated boundaries, was it any wonder the people affected on the ground were suspicious of the West and its motives?

Moments later the route passed over Syria's Ansariye Mountains, for centuries the refuge of persecuted minorities, including Bashar's own Alawi clan, and headed towards Lebanon's higher snow-covered peaks. As soon as the wheels touched down on the Damascus tarmac the passengers leapt up to retrieve their belongings from the overhead lockers, keeping their balance effortlessly, honed from years of practice. They were coming home after all, and switched effortlessly back into local mode. My own feelings were similar, but each time I returned, now that Syria was in the grip of a violent revolution, I was unsure what I would find.

I need not have worried. It was effortless as ever. Where was the tension, the paranoia? At passport control no one asked me why I was coming, where I was going, just the usual routine questions about my address and job. Perversely, it was the leaving that had now become difficult. Not knowing if each departure might be my last for a long time, I had decided on each trip to take a few specially loved items out with me, back to England, rather than risk losing them forever. The luggage security scan which had previously been a formality where no one even checked the screen, turned into an exercise in harassment. 'Where is the purchase receipt for this carpet?' the stern official questioned me. 'You have too much wine – the limit is only two bottles. I must confiscate these things.'

'But I don't have the receipt,' I said in dismay at the thought of my favourite prayer rug disappearing into the Syrian bureaucracy, 'I bought it years ago.' After satisfying his need to upset me, he took a few things that he clearly liked the look of himself, but let me keep the rug.

On arrival I worried that Abu Ashraf might have been prevented from coming to meet me, that a military checkpoint between his village of Kafr Batna and the airport might have blocked him. But then I spotted his beaming face, the same as ever, peering out from the crowds. He dismissed the taxi touts, who were back now that

Rami Makhlouf's Julia Dumna taxi kiosk had been boarded up, took the trolley from me, and we tried to locate the car – a different one from last time. We would use a different car each time, borrowed from whichever friend didn't happen to need it that day. 'What about the checkpoints?' I would ask. He would toss his head dismissively and tell me he knew the back ways to avoid them.

As he drove me in the long shadows of the late afternoon along the airport road towards the familiar shape of Jabal Qasioun dwarfing the city, I asked cautiously about the situation. Was everything ok in the Old City? How was everyone coping?

Abu Ashraf is one of the most mild-mannered people I have ever known, but now it had become too much, even for him. 'Everyone is lying,' he said bitterly, 'I don't believe anyone anymore, not Al-Jazeera, not the BBC and not the Syrian TV. We are stuck in the middle and we have no voice.'

It was a refrain I had heard regularly from most of my friends and contacts over the course of my many stays once the revolution had broken out. They, the silent majority, felt that a distorted picture of the reality on the ground was being broadcast by the foreign news channels – none of whom were being allowed in to see for themselves – showing hours and hours of repeat footage of bloodied bodies, almost as if eager for news of deaths and massacres. Was the world's media just fanning the flames, they wondered, for the entertainment of their audiences? Was there some outside agenda? Of course they knew the Syrian state-controlled TV and newspapers were giving their own version of events. That was to be expected. They were experts, trained by UK and US PR companies in the run-up to the revolution in how to cultivate their image to their best advantage. The US lobbying company Brown Lloyd had been paid a $5,000 per month retainer to handle the placement of the Vogue 'Rose of the Desert' article for Asma al-Assad.

But from their own sources, the only sources they felt they could trust – friends and relations living in various parts of the country – the reports were quite different, sometimes at odds with both sides. They told me how in the early days of the revolution people on the breadline, who were desperate for cash, had been given SY1,000 a day by opposition activists to go out and demonstrate with their families.

Others told me it had become fashionable among middle-class teen-agers to make gory videos using fake blood and then to upload them on YouTube. They were just playing, showing off to each other.

A highly confused and confusing picture was emerging. What-ever the truth, they told me, the bottom line was that the regime had brought the trouble on itself through its *zulm*, its 'oppression' of the people. Abu Ashraf was eloquent on the subject: *Kul muwatin ya'raf Maher yaksur al-balad, wa Makhlouf yastaghil al-balad*: 'Every citizen knows that Maher is breaking the country, and Makhlouf is exploiting the country.' Bashar needed to exile Maher, he said, as Hafez had done to his brother Rif'at, but he feared Bashar was not strong like Hafez, and could not do it. Bashar was only about number five in the power hierarchy, Ramzi the Philosopher told me, after his brother Maher, his cousin Rami Makhlouf and the two main intelligence chiefs, Assef Shawkat (now dead) and Ali Mamlouk. Things were dire.

Yet as we drove into the Old City everything seemed exactly as usual. The Shi'a Al-Amin fruit market close to Bait Baroudi was busy and the range of things on display was the same as ever: the local produce of tomatoes, oranges, onions, peaches, apricots, even the usual Somali-imported bananas. People appeared to be going about their shopping in the normal way, chatting, friendly and relaxed – no obvious tension. Abu Ashraf performed his usual feat of negotiating the tiny narrow alleys as we approached the house, winding and wig-gling with each dog-leg, missing the walls of the houses by centime-tres. He was a superb driver, with impeccable judgement of the width of his car, even though the car itself changed so often. It was the expe-rience built of years of driving in difficult conditions; he had even been a taxi driver in one of his previous incarnations, it transpired, when I complimented him on his skill.

We squeezed into the space directly in front of the house and I produced my key, just before he produced his. I always wanted this moment to be mine and mine alone. I wanted to enter first. Leaving him to get the suitcases out of the boot, I opened both sets of locks and went in. Passing through the entrance corridor, I stepped into the courtyard with its riot of colour – the wisteria, the bougainvil-lea, the myrtle, the lemon tree, the vine ascending to the roof terrace – it was always magnificent. Abu Ashraf beamed when he saw my face, and I congratulated him on his gardening skills. He opened up all the rooms onto the courtyard using their huge old-fashioned keys. I checked each one and confirmed that all was fine. *Al-hamdu lillah*: 'thank God'. Abu Ashraf showed me the standard supplies he had bought in the fridge, bread, eggs, tomatoes and cucumber, said his goodbyes, and we agreed the time for him to come again in the morning – around ten o'clock, his usual time.

Then I was alone. The Aga Khan tenants upstairs had moved out soon after the embassies had left, so I had the place entirely to myself. I busied myself bringing out the bamboo table and chairs into the *iwan*, unpacked a little, and sat, gazing at the world in front of me, bounded by my own walls. I was at home. A feeling of total peace came over me, the like of which I have only ever known here, in Bait Baroudi. The light gradually changed all around me as the sun dropped. The dusk call to prayer rang out from all the mosques, dominated and outdone in length and beauty as ever by the choir from the Umayyad Mosque. The palm doves flew down to peck at the courtyard and to drink from my Roman birdbaths. I had become part of the scene again.

Those final trips were surreal. I would see my friends and contacts, all of whom were delighted to see me. True, Damascus was virtually empty of foreigners, but in that respect it was the same as I had first known it. Yet it made me sad to see the unemployed guides meeting at the National Museum café, optimistically discussing with the director general ways of improving the museum in the hope that it was just a temporary lull, sad to see the employees at the Azem Palace sitting patiently on duty at their desks, floors washed daily, waiting for visitors who never came.

The aftermath of war has long exerted a morbid fascination. The Iranians would continue to come no matter what, for religious tourism, to visit the Shi'a shrines, but they were not big spenders, staying in low level hostels in the southern suburbs around Sayyida Zaynab, not in the fancy boutique hotels of the Old City. Many of these hotels, my friends told me, were now shut or running on half-staff, desperately hoping for a miracle. The owners, having ploughed their life savings into renovating the hotels, were now helpless bystanders as their livelihoods slipped away before their eyes. I went into one such boutique hotel, Bait Zaman on The Street Called Straight, to see for myself, and the girl at reception could hardly contain her excitement, thinking I was a prospective tour guide leader for a group coming next season. All sorts of deals and bargains were offered, and I assured her I would do my best to find her custom, knowing full well I would not succeed.

As the security situation deteriorated across the country, and refugees fled from places like Homs and Hama to the relative safety of Damascus, most of the boutique hotels opened their doors to wealthier refugees who had the money to rent rooms long-term. The Old City, perceived as the safest place of all, thanks to its narrow tank-proof streets and absence of official government buildings that might be targets for the rebels, became crowded with thousands of extra residents. Not what the hotel-owners had planned, but the more business-minded among them charged hefty rents and made money after all. Unscrupulous landlords kicked out long-standing tenants on peppercorn rents to make way for families who, desperate to come inside the safety of the regime-controlled walls, could be charged inflated sums. War economies evolve in unexpected ways.

❦

After consulting Bassim, I decided to take out the rest of my Syrian pounds from the bank account and change them into foreign currency while it was still possible. There was a strong chance the currency would collapse in the future, and if I did it now, I would still be able to convert it to hard currency to keep its value. Exchange rates for sterling, the dollar and the euro were all still stable, artificially propped up by the regime. After Maryam's sacking I was no longer sure where my account was. Had she really taken it with her to Jisr Al-Abyad, or was it still in my original branch? Marwan had always told me it was best to go to the bank before ten, to avoid the queues, and in any case I had my appointment with the new tourism minister at 11, so needed to be finished well before that.

The Souk Al-Hamadiya was near empty as I walked its full length to exit the Old City, the shop owners and vendors still in the process of opening up. As the only foreigner, I felt a little conspicuous, but no one gave me a second glance.

At the bank the guard checked my bag in the usual way and asked my business. I said I had an appointment with the manager and was waved upstairs. Would any of the staff recognise me? I saw with relief that Maryam's assistant was among the people at a desk outside the manager's office. Was my account still here? I asked her to check, handing her my deposit book, and she confirmed that it was. Could I have a statement so I could then make a withdrawal? She nodded and I sat down with relief to wait.

After she handed me the printed statement I asked if I could make an arrangement for someone else to collect a fixed amount from my account each month. I was thinking of Abu Ashraf and how to pay him his salary after I was gone, in case things got really bad and I could not visit again. It was not possible, she said, unless my lawyer set up a power of attorney to that person. Rashid already had his own power of attorney on the account and had frequently needed to take out funds to pay for court costs and such like. I trusted him totally not to abuse the privilege. Since Abu Ashraf was illiterate and like most Syrians did not have a bank account, I decided the simplest thing was to take all the money out, leaving just enough to keep the account open. It was a big decision, but I felt I had to act to protect myself against the worst conceivable outcome.

After some delay, the new bank manager waved me forward to the cashier's desk. 'Why are you taking your money out?' he said, 'We are giving six per cent interest now on this account.'

'Since when?' I asked.

'Since this morning,' he replied.

'It's a good rate,' I replied, 'but I need the money now.' A few minutes later the cashier handed me several large wads of Syrian bank notes, which I put at the bottom of my large canvas handbag. It was the residue of the rental from the Aga Khan tenants upstairs.

I left, relieved it had all been that straightforward. All I had to do now was to find someone to change it into foreign currency. Hurrying along Al-Nasr Street, mindful that I still had to meet the Minister by 11.00, my eye was caught by a neat black digital camera in a shop window. I decided on impulse to stop and buy it, my first purchase with my newly-withdrawn funds. There, in full view of everyone who might have been interested in my movements, I examined and then

bought a Sony camera – I who had been so cautious that I had pur-
chased the most basic camera-free mobile for my Syria trips, to make
certain it would not be confiscated at the airport, I who never brought
my laptop into the country. The shopkeeper was delighted as I pulled
out my cash to pay, wishing me the very best of luck for my future
plans, whatever they might be. It had full video facilities and I think
he thought I was about to film a demonstration.

He evidently knew more than me, for as I walked on, I suddenly
saw a large group of Syrian women waving banners walking on the
other side of the street. I turned instantly and instinctively away down
a side street, but almost immediately more demonstrators appeared
from another street opposite, then more from another street, then
more again, some men, some women, all with banners or flags and
all looking properly organised. Suddenly they were everywhere; there
was no escape. Desperate, I searched for a way out. A Syrian Air office
loomed up in the street and I scurried inside. The employees were
amused. 'Don't worry,' they said. 'This is a pro-regime demonstration – you will be quite safe, no one will arrest you.' With huge relief
I watched the crowds surge by, sweeping along the streets. 'Since I
am here,' I said. 'Can I check my reservation for my return flight?' 'Of
course,' they said, and set to checking the references on my ticket. 'All
fine,' they said, returning me the confirmation slip.

When the crowds eased, I set off again, trying now to pick up a taxi
to get me to Al-Malki on time for my appointment with the minister. But it was hopeless. The streets were log-jammed because of the
demonstrators – Al-Malki Street was closed, one man told me, when
I stopped him to ask the best way. 'Don't bother going there today,'
he said, 'No one will be in their office anyway.' I sent a text to Amal,
my contact, saying I was on my way, but would be a few minutes late,
expecting to hear nothing back. Moments later I got a reply: 'We are
waiting for you,' it said simply.

I redoubled my pace in the summer heat, asked the way several
times and eventually arrived at the temporary block where the minister's office had now been relocated after an accidental fire had
burnt down the original building beside the Suleymaniye Tekke. I
was escorted immediately to the minister's audience room. In the
moments before the minister came in, Amal, her headscarved face

beaming, urged me to take handfuls of sweets and chocolates from the display dish. 'Take these,' she said, stuffing them into my bag, 'these are the best ones. Have some tea, have some water.' 'Thank you,' I said, wiping the perspiration from my forehead.

The minister, only in her job a few months, awarded her post as part of Bashar's reshuffle in response to demonstrators' demands, was a harassed, exhausted-looking woman with big black rings round her eyes. And who can blame her? What a job. With Syria's image in ruins round the world, how could she ever begin to build it up again? Her position was impossible. She talked about the need for reforms, about the possibility of attracting visitors from China and Russia, Syria's remaining allies. The country desperately needed the foreign currency that tourism brought in, which had accounted for 12 per cent of national revenue before *al-Ahdath*, 'the events'. It was interesting that she used the same euphemism that the Lebanese had used for their civil war. Europe and America were lost causes, she said, there was no point in even having a budget for marketing there this year – it would be scrapped completely, and maybe started again next year … I commiserated with her position and with the country's tragedy and dilemma. Tourism in the country would change now, she said. The Europeans were the only ones interested in the high-level cultural tourism they had been cultivating in recent years. Her predecessor had had a wonderful time, with a big budget to host major international events like the annual Silk Road Festival, where posses of foreign journalists were bussed round the country on full expenses. I had been one of them. Now it would go down market. I felt desperately sorry for her, for the situation, for everyone.

She said she wanted to order 1,000 copies of my guidebook to use as promotional gifts. I told her it had failed to pass the censor, but that if she wanted to go ahead anyway, she needed to contact the publishers directly for such an order. She looked surprised. We agreed to keep in touch and I said I would help her in any way I could. Like all the ministry employees I ever encountered, she was just someone trying her best to do her job, without ever having been given the training. She was an engineer. Syria suffers from a dire lack of experts. Most have left the country.

When I emerged from the building, the streets were still thronging and the sky was thick with balloons – thousands and thousands of them, in the national flag colours of red, green and black. Later I saw it on TV. It had been the largest pro-regime demonstration ever, the reporter said, orchestrated the day after the president had addressed the nation, to show him support – and I had accidentally been part of it. Yet if it was so orchestrated, why were none of the ministry staff attending it? Civil servants were meant to have a three-line whip to attend such things, I had always been told. During the meeting they had even said to me in despair: 'Did you speak to the people on the streets? Ask them, ask them if someone has forced them to take part.' The Syrian Air staff had clearly not been coerced to attend either, I later realised. Maybe there was a rota system, maybe it just wasn't their turn that day.

On the walk back to the Old City and the refuge of the house, I passed a bank with the exchange rates displayed outside. A man at a table in the street whispered to me, asking if I wanted to change money.

'Maybe,' I said, turning to face him. 'Do you change from Syrian?'

'Yes,' he replied. 'You want dollars or euro?'

'Sterling,' I said.

'Follow me,' he said, and led me off down an alley and into a tailor's shop. He shouted upstairs: 'Do we have sterling?'

'No,' a voice came down. 'We have euros and dollars.' The man gestured me to go upstairs and I climbed the rickety steps up into a small room.

'You want dollars?' he stuck his head out from behind a curtain.

'What are the rates?' I asked. He told me, and I asked for a calculator. 'OK,' I said, 'I will have euros.' I produced my wad of Syrian notes from my canvas bag and he began to count them. The transaction was quick and simple. He took the Syrian money and gave me a much smaller wad of euros. Now my only problem would be how to get it out of the country, as I recalled the limit for taking out foreign currency was very low.

Passing an official exchange office on the way back, I stopped off out of curiosity to check the exchange rate and to ask if they would change Syrian cash into euros. 'Of course,' came the answer. The rate was even slightly better than that I had been given in my tailor's shop.

'And the limit to be taken out of the country?' I enquired. 10,000 euros, came the reply, an amount way higher than my sum. How ironic that Bashar's banking reforms were now in action. What timing.

❦

Bassim called round at Bait Baroudi later that afternoon and we sat together in the *iwan* having tea. I told him about my mother, about the light behind her eyes when she was dying. 'This is because you were close to her,' he said simply, with complete understanding, 'and accepted her death. If someone else had been there, they would not have seen it, unless they also were close to her.' It made me think with slight shock of what the Sufi Shaikh Muhammad Al-Ya'qoubi had said at Ibn Arabi's tomb about the light being shrouded for most people by veils.

He asked if I would like to see his new purchase, an old house he had bought some months ago near the Nawfara Cafe. He had now had an offer for it of treble the price he had paid, and was seriously considering taking the money and putting it into a property in Turkey, a flat in Istanbul maybe. 'If things get bad here, I am thinking of leaving the country and moving to Istanbul,' he explained. 'To leave my country is a very big decision,' he said slowly, 'I do not want to become a refugee, but I have to think about these things, I have to think about my family and their future.'

His house by the Nawfara was a total ruin. 'Yes,' he said, 'it fell down in the storm last month, but it does not matter. Most of it would need to be rebuilt anyway.' He showed me round, explaining how he would redesign it, and I marvelled at his vision, and at the fact that anyone was prepared to offer him such a high price for it.

Back at Bait Baroudi we sat again in the *iwan* to discuss things further. 'Have you taken my advice and started to make sure you have lots of stocks of food and water in your flat?' I asked. 'You really should be prepared for whatever might be coming.'

He looked at me. 'I will tell you something,' he said, 'something you will not like, but I will tell you anyway.' He took a deep breath. 'Last week I was arrested.' I looked at him in disbelief. 'I am only now recovering.' He explained how it had happened, how, on a routine visit to his local police station to get a standard administrative permit renewed, a police officer had asked for his name and details and then entered them into his computer.

There was clearly some sort of match, for the policeman then told Bassim he was under arrest. Within minutes he was taken in handcuffs to a police car and driven to a prison on the outskirts of the city. He was able to make one phone call to a friend from his mobile to let him know what was happening, then, at the prison, he was made to hand over his watch, his mobile, his keys, his belt, his shoelaces and his cash. Then he was led, still in handcuffs, into a cell. It was small and crowded with men who looked like real criminals, drug dealers, thugs with heavy tattoos. He was terrified.

For 17 hours he was kept locked up in the cell, from seven o'clock at night until midday the next day. His friend eventually told Bassim's father what had happened, and he in turn told Bassim's mother. They were all in a state of shock. When he was released, suddenly and with no warning the following day, the police officer told him it was a case of mistaken identity. There had been someone else they were looking for with the same name, so the computer had made the match in error. There was no apology, no compensation, nowhere to address a complaint, and he even had to bribe the guard to get his possessions back. 'After this,' Bassim said, 'I felt so humiliated, so angry, I wanted to rush out and join the protesters immediately.'

'Did you tell your wife about it?' I asked.

'Yes,' he said. 'She is still recovering too.' Now I understood why he was thinking about leaving for Istanbul. 'The worst thing,' he said, 'was not knowing how long I would be locked up. If I had known it would be less than a day, less than a week even, it would have been OK, I would have been able to manage it. It was the not knowing that was the worst thing, and of course it could happen again at any time at any roadblock – so I try to avoid all roadblocks.' It was a story I heard repeatedly from other friends over the following months as things continued to deteriorate.

In the morning I went out to buy new locks for the main door to the street. Increased security, Bassim had said, would be necessary. The shopkeepers were friendly and polite, as if it was the most normal thing in the world to buy locks at eight in the morning. My eye was caught by another large poster of a smiling Bashar hung on a billboard, this time its slogan reading: '*Na'am lilltatweer wal-tahdeeth*' ('Yes to development and modernisation'). He was keeping up with the times, but his images were harder to find now in shops and offices, people keen to deflect any kidnapping risk through association with the regime or perceived wealth. Even the price of a Mercedes had dropped by 25 per cent, while the price of ordinary more discreet cars had risen.

Abu Ashraf in his simple wisdom had said to me: 'Destroying something is easy – that is quick. But building something up again – that takes generations.' In one sentence he had managed to sum up the whole young versus old divide of the revolution, where the urgency of youth wanted immediate results, overnight transformation of the type that he knew full well was utterly unrealistic. Idealism is wonderful, and the overwhelming majority of Syrians want to see reforms and an end to corruption and nepotism. But how to get there, that is the question, without destroying the country along the way?

The exiled Syrian poet Adonis wrote an open letter to Bashar three months into the revolution, published in a Lebanese daily: 'It seems it is your destiny to sacrifice yourself for your mistakes and to give back voice to the people and let them decide.'

But Bashar has a different idea of his destiny. 'Bashar and his Alawi clan will never go voluntarily,' Bassim explained, 'or be forced out of power by bankruptcy.' The Alawi *Asabiyya* will never let them give up; they will fight to the last man. Yes, there might be a trickle of defections to join the Free Syrian Army, it might even turn into a proper stream, but would it really ever be enough to dislodge the regime? Not as long as Bashar's army defied the predictions and held together against all the odds. 'Why is it still so strong?' I asked Marwan. 'What you have to understand,' he replied, 'is that, at any one time, 80 per cent of Assad's army is confined to barracks. Without its army, this regime would be finished, and they know it. Most of them – at least 70 per cent – are Sunni conscripts, and they are not allowed out because the regime knows most of them would not return. So their commanding officers – who are mainly Alawis – keep them locked up in their military camps, with no mobile phones, no land lines, no access to anything other than the Syrian state TV channels. So lots of them still believe the regime mantra that they are fighting armed terrorist gangs who threaten the security of the Syrian nation.' He went on, 'The other thing they do, to stop them banding together and potentially hatching any anti-regime plots, is that they move them constantly, to break up any groups. All leave has been cancelled, because otherwise they do not return to duty. Morale inside the army is very low, according to the defectors.'

But the opposition factions, so high-minded in their democratic ideals during the early peaceful stages of the revolution, struggled, but tragically failed, to unite as they gradually took up arms to defend themselves. Without *Asabiyya* they were at a huge disadvantage. 'What do people expect?' said Marwan in exasperation. 'After forty years of oppression how can we simply unite now and be in perfect harmony? We have no experience of opposition. We need a leader to unite behind. He is there, somewhere, but it will take time.' It was true. Most people had simply become politically apathetic in the face of years of dominance by the Assad regime. They realised it was too dangerous and difficult to do anything else, just wanting to get on with their everyday concerns. And who could blame them? Even families are sometimes divided, parents quarrelling with children, husbands with wives, and even sons fighting each other on opposite sides.

I watched the disunity perpetuate itself in the world beyond Syria's borders. The more the foreign powers argued about the best course of action – or inaction – the more the moderate elements among the rebels were being worn down, worrying deeply about their leaders' selectivity in funnelling light weapons and funds from other countries and groups. 'We are fighting to have a democratic country, not so we can install people with American or European or Saudi agendas,' they lamented. 'We want to topple the regime, so whoever offers us help, we will call our units whatever they want, as long as they support us.' Gradually it became clear that many moderate elements felt forced to adopt Islamist names, slogans and imagery in order to get funding, to grow beards if required. If that was what it took to get proper ammunition and equipment to fight the regime, then so be it. Successions of bearded Islamist groups posted videos of themselves on YouTube, sitting rigidly facing the camera while their leaders read out monotonous statements proclaiming their imminent victory over the regime. 'We just want to finish,' they said.

'Yes, everyone wants to finish,' Marwan told me, 'except Bashar. I think he will stay on until May 2014 when his second seven-year term finishes. Maybe he will even get voted in again, God help us.'

Hafez had indeed prepared the country for his son Bashar for 20 years, as he had promised. In those preparations the careful composition of the army had been key. Over his three decades in power Hafez set about ensuring that fellow Alawis, together with a sprinkling of Sunni capitalists, were installed as officers and non-commissioned officers, so that they would have a stake in the regime's survival. Soldiers within the Syrian army have for decades been trained, not to say brainwashed, into a highly nationalistic way of thinking, taught that they exist to fight enemies of the Syrian nation, enemies of unity, freedom and socialism.

Ramzi the Philosopher used to tell me stories about his own military service. The mere thought of Ramzi in military uniform defied my imagination. 'They used to laugh at me,' he recalled, good-naturedly, 'when they heard I had been at university. When they learnt I had studied English literature they laughed even louder. They told me: "None of that will help you here!"'

'What did they do to you?' I asked.

'Nothing much,' he replied, 'just hide my things, destroy my books and that sort of thing. They just teased me really, like a plaything. I was lucky, for some it was much worse.' I knew what he meant, having heard the male-rape stories, but even so, imagining the gentle Ramzi subjected to this sort of humiliation for two and half years was hard to rationalise.

Whatever shade of government eventually replaces Bashar, corruption and incompetence will not miraculously disappear overnight. Such things are too deeply embedded in the psyche, the result of decades of living under authoritarian rule. And as lawlessness and corruption thrive in the struggle for day-to-day survival, the social fabric will be put under huge strain. Syrians will be put to the test.

Tariq's father left Homs in August 2011 with tears in his eyes, knowing he would probably never return, knowing the war was getting closer. At 89, a veteran of many wars, he said it smelt to him like the start of the Lebanese Civil War in 1975. That war lasted 15 years, and even now, over 20 years later, Lebanon is hardly a model of stability. Homs has suffered the heaviest toll in civilian casualties so far, yet is running its own underground social care service for the injured, with covert hospitals in people's houses. There are still signs of hope among the suffering.

The exact course of future events cannot be known, but the lessons of history are there to be learnt from. An earthquake, a plague, an act of God – many things can determine the course of history. Ibn Khaldun looked for the meaning behind history. He instinctively looked below 'the surface of mundane perception', and saw that patterns of human behaviour were circular, that each thing that rose would also fall. He witnessed the 1348 Black Death, experienced traffic jams of coffins in the streets and a crisis in the application of inheritance law because of the wiping-out of whole families. Muslim scholars saw death from the plague as martyrdom for Muslims, and as punishment for non-Muslims. They did not believe in contagion, citing the Prophet Muhammad's question: 'Who infected the first?' Islam has a long tradition of martyrdom, and in the current conflict too, each side refers to their dead as martyrs. Boys as young as 15 have declared: 'I want to be a martyr. My mother is sad, but I want it.' A British Muslim convert from East London, found fighting on the front line in Aleppo, declared: 'I will stay here until I die. I want to die in Syria. We must all taste Paradise and when that happens is decided already.' Such belief can make a huge difference in a war, and I doubt many regime soldiers have such belief in their cause. Most are simply locked into the system.

Whatever course history takes, Damascus might be bombed, Bait Baroudi might be looted, destroyed or sequestrated, I know that. My eyes have been open from the start. But apart from my obvious concerns for the fate of my friends and for the country itself, does it matter to me at this stage what might happen to the house? I am not sure it does any more. In a way I have already learnt and experienced so much, thanks to Bait Baroudi, that I no longer need the physical reality of it. My experiences have been real, and nothing can take away their memory. I have learnt how to perceive things differently, how to be open to a spiritual dimension. I have learnt the importance of trust and faith in individuals, if not in the system. I have learnt the value of patience and going with the flow. I have glimpsed the extraordinary depths of Islamic art. I have enjoyed the shared pleasure of meals eaten off my pomegranate tablecloth in my *'ajami* room uplifted by my Sufi inscriptions, with Zulfikar providing the candlelight during power-cuts. My profound friendships with Bassim, with Ramzi the Philosopher, with Marwan and with Tariq are real and will exist still, whether or not I ever return to Syria, whether or not I ever set foot in Bait Baroudi again. No matter what happens, it will always be deep in my heart, safe, the place where I have learnt the real meaning of Al-Ghazali's *dhawq*. Yes, I decided, I can live with that.

As for the Syrian Revolution, that too is real. It has been 'tasted' by too many people now. For the families directly involved, who have lost loved ones, there is no going back. If only Tariq's father was wrong. If only civil war could be avoided. Civil war, Al-Ghazali wrote in the 11th century, is the most damaging thing of all for a country. 'The tyranny of a sultan for a hundred years causes less damage than one year's tyranny exercised by the subjects against one another ... any kind of order is better than anarchy.'

Abu Ashraf would agree. Yet Syria's tragedy is worse even than civil war, for it is also being waged far beyond Syria's borders between foreign players: the Russian and Iranian governments have their own agendas in backing the Assad regime, as do the American, Turkish and Saudi governments in backing the opposition groups. With such a line-up of heavyweights, fighting may go on indefinitely, embroiling Syria in years of pointless conflict as a pawn in proxy wars. Early NATO-backed intervention, of the type the Syrians witnessed in Libya, might have set the revolution on a straighter course by supporting the rebel Free Syrian Army. Instead, western inertia created a power vacuum which Al-Qaeda-affiliated groups were quick to fill, escalating unchecked. Getting rid of them now will be a gargantuan task, beyond the capability of any single foreign power, however heavyweight. Imaginative formulas must be found either at peace conferences or better still on the ground, enabling all key players to claim victory, especially the rebel activists. 'Give us the excuse to accept a deal,' said one 29 year-old dissident, 'Something so we can look in the mirror.' The foreign players must be united by what they now see as the overriding shared objective, namely, to eradicate Al-Qaeda terrorism before it spills over into arenas uncomfortably close to home. They must come together to kill the Frankenstein monster that they themselves created. Only then may Syria still be saved from the destruction of its identity.

17

Future Imperfect and Perfect

Grieve for the living, not for the dead.

Turkish proverb

So Bait Baroudi has become a refuge, fulfilling the function for which it was always intended: to shield people from the dangers outside. Only now there are dangers inside as well – the *zahir* and the *batin* have become entangled. Syria's struggle continues and I live it every day through the house. I can no longer enter the country legally: the Syrian ambassador in London had always advised me to put 'housewife' on my visa applications. 'We know who you are,' he had said, smiling. But once the Syrian embassy in London closed, all my contacts for getting visas had become irrelevant.

The house plays its role for me as a sanctuary for those displaced from their own homes. No longer is it the archetypal womb that it was in Ottoman times when it protected one extended family, with all generations sharing the space together in harmony. It has become instead a microcosm of the discord that is mirrored in every shared house across Syria, where different families are forced together by the circumstances of war.

The first of my friends to suffer the awful fate of displacement was Ramzi the Philosopher who had the misfortune to live in Douma.

Very early on in the revolution, the inhabitants of Douma, a poor town on the northwest edges of Damascus, planned to march to Umayyad Square – the equivalent to Cairo's Tahrir Square – a huge roundabout complete with fountain at the confluence of seven main roads. The authorities were determined to stop them, and many marches were intercepted and violently dispersed, resulting in several deaths. Douma smouldered resentfully, organising night-time demonstrations, and was sorely punished. It all got too much for Ramzi when there were ten checkpoints in his street alone.

'It is ridiculous,' he said, the last time I met him in the Old City, 'It takes me one hour now just to get out of Douma.' We met in the tea gardens of the National Museum, where many of the guides now met regularly, all unemployed, all wondering what the future held for them. Ramzi himself looked strained and tired, but tried to put a brave face on it. He had lost weight and his hair had greyed at the temples. All his work as a tourist guide had dried up and he said he had decided to move up to the family's simple house in the Sunni village of Al-Haffeh, near Saladin's Castle above Lattakia. He would take his mother and two of his sisters who had lost their jobs when their schools closed in Douma, while the other two sisters who were also teachers but still employed in Damascus would stay in Douma. The family would split. I could see the sadness in his eyes but it was as nothing compared to what came later.

He stayed in the village house, tending his olive trees, mending the roof, looking after his family. I was in touch with him regularly and did my best to see the bright side: 'Think at least with this new found leisure of all the books you can read, all the things you can study,' I said, trying to make my voice cheerful.

'Yes, of course, now I have the time … but not the mood. It is difficult to concentrate … and all I can do is watch the satellite channels to see the news, hoping for a miracle.'

Bassim had said the same thing. Every time I asked him to prepare me the accounts, knowing I owed him money for various repairs and equipment at Bait Baroudi, he promised he would do them, and each time he did not.

'I go to my office,' he said, 'and I try to start, but I cannot. Maybe next week … '

Once Ramzi had transferred to Al-Haffeh, it was too dangerous, he said, to travel from there to Damascus, too many checkpoints, too many unknowns; and he was afraid to leave his family and house unguarded. I spoke to him at length from the landline at Bait Baroudi, which was more secure; mobile communication networks were by then erratic and subject to interception. His deep voice was the same as ever:

'I long for my old life,' he said, 'meeting so many people, showing them the beauty of my country.' I told him how I had visited the Maristan Nur Ad-Din in the Old City the day before and found it full of young students training to be guides, taking it in turns to pose as tour-leaders holding forth in broken English to the others. Their training school is just behind Bait Baroudi and I marvelled how they could still pretend that everything was normal. Some of the young women were in *hijabs*, some in tight jeans and tops, mixing with the young men freely and laughing together at each other's efforts. 'They know nothing,' Ramzi said simply. 'They just do as they are told.'

It was with horror a few weeks later that I read of the regime's attack on Al-Haffeh, with many massacres committed. I texted him immediately, offering him and his family refuge in my house, and waited anxiously for a reply. The next day it came:

'Dear Diana, We are well & lucky, left before the attack! It is hard times to live in war atmosphere & our heart crying for this tragedy. Nowadays living in Lattakia, my second half of family moved from Douma to Dummar, staying with their sister there. The way of life is stressful! In urgent case, I will let you know. Many thanks for your kind care & attention. Ramzi.

A few weeks later he replied to another text:

Many thanks, we are all well in Lattakia but our mood with a deep sigh is low: at the village the house was robbed which makes me sad. Property at such terrbilent time is not the most important. We are safe thank goodness. B regds, Ramzi.

I knew his position was hugely understated. The village house had been his only consolation, and tending his olive trees a form of occupational therapy. How could he keep his sanity now, deprived even of the dignity of tending his olive trees? He would know the chances of returning to Al-Haffeh were very small, as reports continued to come in of heavy fighting in the area. The regime army was using Alawi villages to launch their attacks on nearby Sunni villages, so the Free Syrian Army in turn attacked those Alawi villages. Even Qardaha, the Assad village itself, was being attacked. In retaliation the Alawis were forming their own armed groups to attack the Sunni villages, and their Facebook pages even showed that the Turkish Alawis were now becoming active, starting to join in to help their Syrian co-religionists. Things were becoming more dangerous and difficult by the week, and could so easily escalate and spiral out of control. Was this a deliberate tactic of the regime, setting village against village, making the area ungovernable? Bashar has been gambling that his enemies will continue to fight each other, incapable of uniting against him. Maybe it was the beginning of Alawi mobilisation, to create their own enclave here as under the French? After all, the same thing had happened in Lebanon, with the Lebanese warlords fighting each other, finally retreating into their respective strongholds: the Druze to Deir Al-Qamar and Beiteddin, the Maronites to the villages above Beirut like Shemlan. When all parties, worn out by fighting, finally recognised no single faction could win, the surviving community leaders had come together in Taif and a power-sharing peace deal was brokered with the help of Saudi Arabia and, to a lesser extent, America, behind the scenes. The Lebanese warlords who might once have risked being tried for war crimes were rewarded with seats in parliament instead. It is not inconceivable as an outcome in Syria.

Meanwhile, there was no one I would rather have had living in my house than Ramzi – especially given later developments in Bait Baroudi – dear Ramzi, with his sensitive soul. Lattakia was overflowing with refugees, packed into the sports stadium, staying with friends or renting apartments, according to their means. Ramzi is one of thousands. He is Sunni, though not an active mosque-goer – something his mother used to chide him for. He told me a long time ago that he believed in God, but felt no need to go to pray in a public place. After months in crowded Lattakia things settled enough for him to return to the village, which was by now back under regime control. The family cleaned up and repaired the house and started to tend the olive groves again.

Life took on a form of normality, until his village once again got caught in the crossfire. In October 2013 a 105-page report was issued by Human Rights Watch forensically analysing the evidence for a massacre of over 190 unarmed civilians, including women and children, in 11 Alawi villages around Al-Haffeh, which took place on 4 August 2013. A further 200 were held hostage. It was the first time in two and a half years of civil war that these villages had been attacked. Loyal to the regime, they had considered themselves safe up in the Alawi heartlands. The report relied for its sources of information not just on interviews with witnesses and survivors, but also on hospital records which confirmed death by multiple gunshot wounds, decapitation, stab wounds and burning. The attack was planned and coordinated, the HRW report concluded, carried out by 20 extremist Islamist opposition groups acting in concert, led by the black-flagged brigades of ISIS, Jabhat Al-Nusra, Jaysh Al-Muhajireen wal-Ansar ('Army of the Emigrants and Helpers'), Ahrar Ash-Sham ('Free Men of Syria') and Suqour Al-Izz ('Falcons of Glory'). None of them had links to the Free Syrian Army.

The following day, the regime launched a counter-offensive which raged for 13 days, until they gradually succeeded in regaining control of the area. After the HRW report was issued, the whole episode hit the world's media with headlines about rebels committing massacres of innocent civilians and there was talk of referrals to the International Criminal Court for war crimes. Before that, the regime had been remarkably quiet about it, with Syrian state TV simply mentioning that control had been reasserted over the area, no pictures of mutilated bodies, no mention of massacres. Why was that, when the natural expectation would be that the regime would maximise the bad publicity for the rebels, flaunting graphic pictures of carnage to show the world what they were trying to save Syria from?

I realised immediately that this was the same incident that Ramzi had been caught up in, used as a human shield. He had texted me to say he had been detained with all the men of his village, told it was for their safety. After being released he and all the other men had left the village, so their houses had been looted completely, even down to the doors and windows.

When I texted back to ask by whom he had been detained, he replied saying he was worried about going into details and was still scared to go back, even to harvest the olives.

Once again, armed Alawi groups under the umbrella of the regime's army had evidently retaliated against Sunni villages after the attack by extremist rebels on Alawi villages. The precursor to the initial attack on the Alawi villages, it emerged, had been the defection of a Sunni officer from the regime army, who had taken 30 men with him. That same officer was then part of the 4 August operation against the Alawi villages. It had been a revenge attack, only this time it had been worse than the first time:

> We wish we could live again in our village house but it needs a lot of money for repairing and generally the situation has not settled yet.

His mother, he explained, had been dispatched from the village to Lattakia along with the other women and children, while he and the other men were kept back. The poor woman was in despair and nearly died of relief when, some days later, he reappeared:

> it was hard time for her indeed and when I come back, for her was a reward from heaven; there is nothing like mother heart !

Meanwhile, back in Damascus things were also getting worse, and bombardments of the suburbs began to intensify over the course of summer 2012, forcing more and more people to leave their homes and crowd into the Old City. By autumn 2013 Damascus's population had trebled to 12 million or more, swollen with refugees bulging out of the areas that were perceived as safe. The pattern was always the same: punishment of areas where the Free Syrian Army or other rebels had their strongholds: Jobar, Derayya, Qadam, Yarmouk, Zamalka, Barzeh, Moadhamiya and other villages of the Ghouta, where the chemical attack was the final manifestation of the regime's frustration at being unable to rid itself of the troublesome rebels who were refusing to give up. The regime would first cut off water and electricity to the area, forcing residents to evacuate and shops to shut. Then the aerial bombardment would begin, using either fighter jets or helicopter gunships or fixed artillery mounted on Jabal Qasioun above the city.

Finally, after days, weeks or even months of shelling from a safe distance – with no risk to pilots given the rebels' lack of anti-aircraft guns – *shabiha* and regime soldiers would go in and search house to house, flat to flat, looking for weapons, slitting throats or raping anyone who was left behind. They had licence to do anything, with no accountability. This was when the massacres happened, when unarmed civilian residents were left behind in a bombed area. The open flats were then prey to looters. On the fringes of the Old City second-hand shops started springing up, selling not antiques, but armchairs, sofas and flat-screen TVs. Stallholders insisted they were from families selling up before leaving the country, but Marwan told me it was the contents of flats looted in the suburbs by regime soldiers. The high-value stuff, he said, was kept in warehouses in Mezzeh 86, the regime's Alawi district. Booty, *ghanima* in Arabic, is permitted in Islam, legitimate spoils to the victor.

Marwan's mother endured this when her suburb of Zamalka was targeted. First, when the water and electricity cut out, she left to go and live with another son in a different suburb. When, after three weeks, she returned, she found her flat burnt and looted. Her sons tried to repair it, but each time they did so, the doors were kicked down again. They gave up trying. 'My family is angry with the rebels,' Marwan told me, 'if they didn't use these residential areas, this wouldn't happen.'

The Free Syrian Army commanders were aware that their policy was turning residents against them, but felt they had little choice. 'We try to hide our positions, but we are plagued with informers. Of course we don't want to bring trouble. We target only military and security buildings, but they take their revenge on civilians. They do this on purpose, to make people turn away from us. We understand, but in the end, once we succeed, the people will thank us.'

It was difficult to imagine Marwan's mother's flat, where I had enjoyed such happy family occasions, now just a charred shell. A few weeks later her other son's flat in the western suburb of Kafr Sousseh also became unsafe and Marwan asked if his mother and her other son could move, with his wife and children, to Bait Baroudi. I agreed, glad that the house would be occupied and of use, since I had by then left for London. I told them they could live in the upstairs flat rent-free.

With the regular regime bombardments of Kafr Batna, Abu Ashraf's village, I knew that he and his family would almost certainly also have taken refuge in Bait Baroudi, as I had told him he should, if ever he needed to. On my last visit he had insisted he could still collect me from the airport at 3.30 in the morning. Sure enough, on arrival, there he was. When I marvelled at how he had managed it in the middle of the night, he explained he had stayed at the house. In Kafr Batna it was now too difficult, he said, to move around after dark, so he had come early to the house, still using the back ways to avoid the checkpoints. But his face was tense and worn, tired round the eyes in a way that was new, and on the drive into the city he told me about various doctors who had gone missing from his village just for tending the injured. On the narrow approach to the house, he misjudged the width of the car and scraped the wall for the first time ever. His son, who had planned to marry and live in Syria, had returned to Qatar, to his job as a furniture maker. The extra floor Abu Ashraf had added onto his own house for his son and new wife was no use now that all of Kafr Batna had become uninhabitable.

I had no idea how many of Abu Ashraf's family might at any one time now be staying downstairs at Bait Baroudi, but knew that his daughter, son-in-law and grandchildren had become permanent residents after their own home in Kafr Batna had been totally destroyed by shelling. The numbers downstairs would wax and wane according to the conditions in the Ghouta, ranging between five and thirty. Mattresses were laid out to accommodate them all, sometimes even in the courtyard and the *iwan*. As numbers swelled, and as various families were sharing the same space, privacy became an issue and curtains were erected to divide the courtyard, reminiscent of the dividing wall that had been in place when I first bought the house. Frictions began to develop between the families, especially between the wives, who could not be seen unveiled in front of men from different families. Such traditions run deep in conservative households.

I found myself trying to visualise how the house was coping with the extra demands on its infrastructure, whether the two water tanks on the roof would suffice, how long the power cuts might be, how the families would be managing. With *mazout* 'heating oil' now in short supply it would be far too expensive to run the house's central heating or the generator. I wished I had followed my instinct and installed solar heating panels. During the renovation years Bassim had found me a Swiss boiler and a German pump to power the system, with old-style radiators from the salvage yards, persuading me that *mazout* was so cheap – it was heavily subsidised – that it was the only sensible option. Back then in 2005 it had been SYP8 per litre, so cheap there had been a thriving smuggling trade selling it illegally to Turkey and Lebanon. In an attempt to curb this, the government raised the price to SYP25 in 2010, and three years into the war the official price is SYP100 – if you can get it at all. Rebel groups like ISIS now control the oil fields in the eastern provinces. They have broken the pipelines, creating environmental disasters, then welded on crude taps from which they fill queues of tankers. The valuable cargo is then trundled mainly into Turkey and sometimes even into regime-held areas of Syria, where prices rocket. It is a money-making exercise, free of overheads, that has turned the bearded chiefs into millionaires. Thousands of amateur refineries have sprung up, converting the crude oil to petrol, diesel and *mazout* heating oil, sold in smaller canisters to anyone who has the money. None of them will give that up without a fight. How could *mazout* ever be subsidised in the future, whatever complexion of government the country might have?

More problems began to surface in Bait Baroudi. Perverse things happen when the authorities are distracted. Illegal construction is mushrooming all over the country, with imports of timber and cement soaring. Abu Ashraf saw it as the perfect opportunity to swindle the system. War corrupts and erodes morality. His son-in-law was an electrician so with Abu Ashraf's connivance and approval he fiddled both the electricity and the water meters so that bills would be almost non-existent. Since the whole house was on one meter system, both upstairs and downstairs would benefit, but Marwan's mother was very upset. 'Don't you understand that this is stealing?' she said to Abu Ashraf and his son-in-law. 'How can any government function if nobody pays for the services it provides?' They were also worried it would somehow be found out and they might be arrested as a result. They wanted to pay and stay on the right side of the law.

They referred the problem to me to adjudicate back in England and I had to make one of my rare calls to Abu Ashraf by mobile. It was best, on the whole, I felt, to let the families sort things out themselves, but on this occasion, to placate Marwan's mother, I embarked on what I knew would be a fruitless attempt to make Abu Ashraf change his attitude. He told me he had heard that in areas under rebel control, 'liberated' areas as the rebels called them, people no longer paid their bills, so why should he? When I pointed out that in rebel areas they no longer had electricity because they did not pay their bills, he did not want to hear what I was saying. His mind was made up. As far as he and his family were concerned, it was simply a chance to save themselves some money. Bait Baroudi's situation was far from unique, so Marwan told me. In houses all across the city, the attitude was similar. Rebuilding trust in the state will be one of Syria's biggest post-revolution problems and challenges.

Mindful of the need to have proper paperwork to show for when the *mukhabarat* called round to check the houses for rebels and for weapons, Marwan had asked Rashid the lawyer to draw up a lease agreement for his mother and family. No money passed hands, and the figures entered on the paperwork were fictitious as ever, but the documents were duly registered at the *Muhafaza* building in accordance with the law. Rashid had my power of attorney for everything to do with the house, so he was the named landlord in the lease. It was a situation based on trust, which he could so easily have taken advantage of, but never did.

Downstairs the situation was more troublesome, with Abu Ashraf's family, especially the son-in-law who was now in permanent residence, starting to behave as if they owned the house. Rows broke out each time the doorbell rang and someone from upstairs went down to see who it was. Over the Eid it was especially difficult with lots of people paying visits to each other, as was the usual practice at holiday times. But with one communal doorbell and a shared entrance there was no way of knowing in advance whether the caller was for upstairs or downstairs. Much shouting went on. The boiler and generator were

upstairs on the roof terrace, so when they needed repair or maintenance, access had to be via the upstairs flat. Conversely, the electrical
controls for the hot water and boiler were downstairs in the entrance
corridor, so if someone from upstairs wanted the boiler switched on,
they had to come downstairs to flick the switch.

Tensions ran high. The fabric of society was breaking down. My
own worry, hearing about all these quarrels from so far away, was
that Abu Ashraf's son-in-law was planning to make life so unpleas-
ant for Marwan's family upstairs that they would feel forced to move
out, leaving him in total control. Maybe he even wanted then to rent
it out himself and pocket the money. I had never met him, or any
other member of Abu Ashraf's family for that matter, so how could
I know his motives? Even if I did, how could I prevent him from
taking over? He had no tenancy agreement because he pretended to
be the owner, and the longer I allowed that situation to continue, the
harder it would be to evict him at the eventual end of the war. Dis-
entangling the son-in-law's intentions from the father's had become
impossible.

Life went on like this for months in Damascus. To make sure the
rebels did not come inside the Old City, the regime appointed *lijan
sha'biyya,* so-called 'people's committees', to guard the neighbourhoods. Checkpoints began to appear, manned by predominantly young
people, sometimes even teenagers, who were appointed from families the regime knew to be loyal, and paid a good salary of SYP15,000
a month, the same as any middle manager might reasonably expect.
They would sit at little tables on street corners, smoking and playing
backgammon, guns casually tossed over their shoulders. Some had
been sent to Iran or Russia for training in how to use them, Marwan
later told me, others probably had no idea. They were a deliberate mix
of Christian, Sunni, Alawi and others, and often included women.

Abu Ashraf said it did not feel as though they were there to protect
the citizens against the rebels, but rather to control the citizens themselves. 'They are all armed and with permission to shoot. Sometimes
we are more frightened of them than of the regime or the rebels!'
he told me when I met him in summer 2013 in Lebanon's resort of
Byblos. Dressed in his best shirt and trousers for the occasion, he had
come out for the day specially to meet me.

'How on earth did you manage it?' I asked him, noting how much more gaunt and strained his face had become even since last time.

'It was easy,' he said, almost proudly, 'easier than coming from my village to Damascus!' He has no passport, and he told me it was his first ever trip outside of Syria. At dawn, armed with no more than his ID card and some small change, he had got into a shared taxi in Damascus and braved the regime checkpoints along the main road to the Lebanese border, then on to Beirut and Byblos.

'From my village', he said, 'I have to come through four regime checkpoints and two Free Army checkpoints. To come to Lebanon, it is only four regime ones.' The Beirut-Damascus highway, the essential official conduit to the capital, remains firmly in regime hands, and apart from the checkpoints, the regime has dug in deeper with one of its favourite roadside planting campaigns 'to activate the relation between the citizen and the trees.' They were too small for Abu Ashraf to notice.

The incentive for him to come was clear, since I had brought with me six months' salary in US dollars to protect against the collapsing Syrian pound. It was a paltry sum by western standards, but enough to feed his family until December. I could have passed the cash via Syrian friends who still went in and out, as I had done before. He did not need to come in person, but I sensed he wanted more than money. He wanted to talk.

He had never seen the sea before, let alone the sexes mixing so freely in public, and was mesmerised by the frolickers on the beach below, Lebanese of all ages, in shorts and bikinis, running in and out of the wave. He made no comment, and I wondered what he was thinking.

We talked about the house, about life in the Old City. I told him how Byblos had declared itself a 'War Free World Heritage Listed City', trying to save itself from future dangers. Too late for Aleppo, but what chance did Damascus have of being spared?

'Don't worry,' he said, 'The Free Army will not come inside the walls. The price is too high. They know that we have thousands of civilian refugees sheltering in the houses. If the rebels come in, the regime will bomb us, and thousands will die.'

He told me how tightly the regime now controls the Old City.

'The regime is very strong, they know exactly who lives where,' he explained, 'and still come round regularly to search the houses for weapons, but now it is the *lijan sha'biyya* who come, not the *mukhabarat*. They are rude to us, bullying us to do deals with them, so now they take our bribes instead. It is much worse than before. They come round all the time, checking on us.'

'What do you reckon,' I asked, 'how many people are like you, stuck in the middle? Around 60 per cent?'

'More,' he replied without a moment's hesitation, 'in Damascus maybe 75 per cent, maybe even 80 per cent. The armies fighting are only about 10 per cent on each side.'

It was a sobering thought. Millions of people deprived of a voice, silenced by fear, fear of the consequences of speaking out, fear of the system that was supposed to be protecting them.

Tears welled up when the sun began to set and it was time for him to go back to that world. It is one of Syria's many paradoxes that he can come out but I can no longer go in.

'Next time in Damascus, *in sha Allah*', we said, struggling to smile.

What a mess. But if I were Abu Ashraf and living through what he is living through, I would probably do the same: put my family first and be silent. His overriding duty, as he sees it, is to protect his children and grandchildren as best he can. He is too old to change his ways and too poor to leave.

Those who do have enough money to leave head across the border to Lebanon to stay with friends or extended family. Over a million Syrians are now in Lebanon, destabilising its population of four million and straining its infrastructure, just as Syria's own infrastructure had been strained by the influx of millions of Iraqi refugees post 2003, and thousands of Lebanese refugees in summer 2006. Many wealthier Syrians have flats in Lebanon anyway. Maya, the hotel owner in whose Damascus boutique hotel I had spent that morning whilst deciding if I wished to go into the hotelier business, had closed down her tour-operator company and was now in Beirut, which she said looked like a small Damascus. She was keeping busy by refurbishing her apartment, hoping to go back and pick up where she left off.

Palestinians are less fortunate, only allowed to stay in Lebanon for 15 days. Some refugees, like Bassim, then catch flights from Beirut, as Damascus airport is barely functioning. Amman, Cairo and Istanbul are the commonest destinations, where refugees try to find jobs. Most succeed eventually, but in Istanbul poor Bassim, despite all his qualifications and experience, is struggling because of the language barrier. He had to start all over again. It was tough. He had failed to find a buyer for his ruined house in the Old City. Even so, he is one of the lucky ones. He knows that and has never once complained about his lot.

Tariq left in summer 2011 with his wife and baby daughter, fearful for their safety. He continues his involvement on the humanitarian front, becoming increasingly emotional. Like many wealthy expatriate Sunni businessmen, he began to channel funds to help friends and relations who could not afford to leave. His father's house, where I had stayed, is now a haven for refugees.

'It's all media hype,' he said, 'this talk of Saudi and Qatar channelling in humanitarian aid. Or if it *is* coming, it's not hitting the ground. So far the charities have received nothing, not one penny from outside. The only money our guys have is from us, and they are desperate.' He made several trips to the Turkish border to see for himself, and returned deeply shocked by what he had seen. 'How do you talk to a twelve year old girl,' he said, 'who has been gang raped and is now pregnant? We have lost a generation here – no schooling, no clean water, no vaccinations – there will be terrible disease.' I thought of Ibn Khaldoun and the Black Death. 'I don't know what will happen,' said Marwan, 'or where it will go next. Now we hear that Rami Makhlouf is paying Alawis and all sorts to join a special militia based in Lattakia, training them and giving them weapons.' I thought of Ramzi being detained in his village. 'The clan cannot survive economically if they run away to their Alawi enclave,' he continued, 'unless Iran funds them, like it does Hezbollah – maybe Iran will fund them too, God save us ...' Pigs might fly, but if Iran were to abandon the Assad regime, lured by the incentive of a US rapprochement, the dynamic on the ground might change very fast.

Maryam, my Christian bank manager, could not or would not leave. She says she suffers from terrible headaches most days, but her family has lived in Damascus for generations. 'I cannot leave,' she says, 'I CANNOT.' However hard it gets, she will stay and accept whatever fate brings her. *Qadar wa- Qada.* She wrote that little Ruby, now aged 10, had been shot in the stomach by a sniper while being driven to school by her father. They had no idea why or which side the sniper was on. She had been in hospital for five days, but was now slowly beginning to recover. 'Death is all around,' she wrote, 'every day we have one or two explosions added to the bombing, and whenever you go out, you know you may not be back. Ruby, like most young people in Syria, if they survive, I wonder what will be inside them.' It is a question too awful to contemplate, how children resolve inner turmoil with no treatment, no access to counselling. Ruby at least had her family's support. Many orphans are not so lucky.

As for Marwan, he is finding himself pulled more and more into humanitarian involvement. When I last met him he was with an angry doctor who had thrown in his well-paid job to run a clinic treating the injured. Despite his heavy beard, strong voice and commanding manner, the doctor spoke rationally about the inclusiveness that would follow the downfall of Assad regime: 'They, this regime, they are the sectarians. The Ba'ath Party has always been sectarian this last forty years, by excluding everyone else. You are with them or against them – that is all. We will end this system and become truly free. It will not matter whether you are Sunni, Alawi, Christian or Druze.'

He himself is a moderate Sunni, Marwan told me when I asked him later, as are 70 per cent of the population. Patriarch Gregorios in Damascus had expressed a similar sentiment: 'In Syria we have a long tradition of religious tolerance. It is nothing to do with Assad, it was here for centuries before him. This desecration of churches is something new, coming from the outside.'

On Fridays Marwan is unavailable, helping with the field hospitals and treating injured demonstrators. Friday is their busy day, with the protests that always follow the Friday noonday prayers, the one time in the week when people can legitimately gather in large numbers. Even the regime cannot ban people from going to pray.

Marwan told me how he no longer carries a medical kit with bandages in his car. 'If they stop you at a checkpoint and find medical kit and bandages in your car,' he said, 'they will accuse you of helping demonstrators and arrest you. We have to be very careful.' Most shocking of all was what he went on to tell me about the Syrian Arab Red Crescent (SARC). He had applied for and got a job with them as a project manager, after many stages of testing and interviews. When he started work, he was horrified to discover his work colleagues were useless, all of them at their desks purely on the strength of their connections – *wasta* again. He was even more horrified when he was then put in charge of a project that turned out to be selling blood and organs to unnamed third parties. He complained to his boss, saying he could not sign papers agreeing to this. 'But you must,' said his boss, 'You are the only one here who knows how to run these projects. None of the others know anything.' Marwan refused, and quit, though his boss continued to phone him for weeks after, offering him more money and bribes. There may be some good people in SARC, but many of them are contaminated. It made me think of the gory poster of Bashar that had been prevalent in public places back in 2007, well before the revolution and before the US and British PR firms had advised the Assads on the importance of developing a more benevolent, smiling image. Beneath the stern face of Bashar the caption read: *'Nuba'eek bid-damm ila al-abad'*, 'We pledge allegiance to you in blood to the end.' The words *bid-damm*, 'in blood', were coloured red, with blood dripping from them like an advert for a vampire movie.

As for the faithful Abu Ashraf, he will never leave; I am sure of it. His duty is to his family, to Bait Baroudi. Where else can he play such a role? He knows that to become a refugee and live in a tent on the Turkish or Jordanian border like hundreds of thousands of others – a hundred thousand had sometimes crossed in one month alone – is to become like an animal, a dependent, something that exists just to be fed and watered. Where is the dignity in that? 'In Syria you die once. In a Jordanian camp you die a hundred times.' No, Abu Ashraf will not leave. He will stay in Bait Baroudi, waiting for an outcome. He will perform his ablutions in my Mamluk fountain, go to the mosque on the corner for his prayers five times a day like the devout Muslim that he is. He will live his life as best he can, not paying his bills, but accepting the dangers and whatever comes his way, following the flow in total faith. *Qadar wa qada'*.

※

The problems of the future are immense. Syria is sinking deeper and deeper into the quagmire. The longer war drags on, the more likely it is that the militias will inevitably fracture into mafia-style groupings. There are already reckoned to be over a thousand separate armed rebel groups; sometimes they unite again as in groupings like the Islamic Front or the Syrian Revolutionaries Front; sometimes their commanders turn to crime as their main occupation rather than fighting. Waves of random kidnappings have become commonplace, often under the guise of arrests, sometimes by regime *mukhabarat,* sometimes by rebel groups. A ransom demand follows, which even when paid, can result in the return of a corpse rather than a loved one. The daughter of a wealthy businessman, ransomed for $395,000, was returned sexually abused, tortured, traumatised. No one even knows by whom or what side they are on. Dress has ceased to be a clue, as groups dress like each other in order to blame each other and further confuse the picture. It is a new and gruesome development. In the past, even in kidnappings, there have been norms of behaviour, recognised patterns that have evolved over 40 years of Ba'athist rule.

'At least before,' said Bassim, 'everyone knew what the system of corruption was, how it worked. Now even that has changed and all the old rules of corruption have gone. No one knows who to bribe for what anymore.' Some get rich on the misfortunes of others. Lawlessness is everywhere, encouraged by Bashar's deliberate release of non-political criminals from prisons; many of these ex-prisoners then join the *shabiha.* Ideals of any sort, let alone revolutionary ideals, become impossible to uphold in such a primordial soup.

'None of the fundamental problems of 1914 were resolved by the war,' reads 'Aftermath of War', the final plaque in the last room of France's *Historial de la Grande Guerre* in Péronne. The ten million lives lost in that war were lost for nothing, not 'sacrificed' but wasted: the war achieved none of things it set out to achieve. Quite the reverse: extreme nationalist movements grew up rapidly in Italy and Germany; imperial tensions multiplied in India and Ireland; irreconcilable promises were made to Arabs and Jews about their national aspirations, creating the framework for decades of conflict. Inflation rose higher than before and the value of money was reduced by two thirds. The real victors were outside powers, who profited from reconstruction contracts. The theme is uncomfortably familiar.

Whether or not Bashar and his gang ever flee to Lattakia, whether or not the opposition rebels ever unify, whether or not the Islamists succeed in imposing their ideology, the country is slowly disintegrating. Many state institutions are no longer functioning. Extremist rebel groups or Kurdish rebel groups control the oilfields. Order has broken down in many parts of the country, and all over the countryside new authorities have been springing up to replace the old ones. Sometimes they function well, sometimes they don't.

North of Aleppo, for example, in Azaz near the Turkish border, an enthusiastic economist created and led a 30-member political council elected by consensus. The Turks began dealings with him, allowing cargo trucks over the border to bring rice, flour and petrol. Shops reopened for the first time in months. A young imam at the mosque took charge of the civil courts, conducting marriages and divorces and settling civil disputes. There was even a nascent criminal court system run by local Muslim clerics, using Islamic law as the basis for decisions. The council's highest priority was declared to be the prevention of revenge attacks on Alawi villages. The public swimming pool was reopened and abandoned regime tanks morphed into exciting adventure playgrounds. Delivering supplies to the front line in Aleppo now only took 90 minutes, whereas before it had been a dangerous two-week smuggling operation by mule.

The tender green shoots of a model democracy were beginning to sprout – until the Al-Qaeda-affiliated rebel group ISIS muscled in to take control. Rebels began fighting rebels, and chaos ensued again: same scenario, different players. By the end of the 15-year Lebanese Civil War, nearly every party had allied with and subsequently betrayed every other party at least once. The age-old pattern is the same: when groups like ISIS begin by ingratiating themselves with the local population, providing them with food and medical services, they seem at first to be a godsend, then, the reality reveals itself and their hard-line Islamist agenda comes to the fore, with compulsory Quranic schools, summary public executions and enforced veiling of women. But this is not the real Syria: women pull their headscarves out of their handbags and put them on at black-bannered check-points, then stuff them back again.

Sometimes there are flickers of hope. Where the interests of con-flicting parties happen to coincide, deals can be struck very quickly, as the September 2013 unanimously binding UN Resolution on destroy-ing Syria's chemical weapons showed. In Aleppo, in late 2013, media reports leaked out about elements of the regime and elements of the Free Syrian Army reaching agreements to cooperate. Schools in some neighbourhoods were permitted to reopen and government employ-ees were allowed to return to work and be paid for the first time in over a year. A brief and tiny miracle.

For most it is too late. A generation has been lost, traumatized, decimated, abandoned to its fate. There are no specialists, no NGOs to give training on how to deal with trauma. The young are suffering most and the old will have to help them come to terms with their past and future, while teaching them to accept their present. Formal edu-cation across the country has deteriorated, even from the huge pre-revolution drop-out rates in schools and universities. Iraq provides a terrible example: before the 2003 US-led invasion it was hailed as the most educated country in the Middle East, and now a quarter of its population is illiterate. Syria's education system requires a complete overhaul, to rid itself of Ba'athist brainwashing, and to move forward towards new visionary ideals.

'No revolution is pure,' said Ali Ferzat patiently, after his hands had healed and he could draw his cartoons once more. 'There will be victims and violence and it will take a long time. But after fifty years of injustice, a tsunami of public discontent has been unleashed, and it won't stop until the sun shines on Syria again.'

'O God, spare us from change,' says the Arab proverb. Nostalgia for the past is a powerful thing, pulling many an unhappy refugee in Lebanon back to their home in Syria, in spite of the dangers: 'It was like Paradise before,' said one young Syrian woman who had been earning well as an English interpreter for foreign film crews in Beirut. 'Every-thing was better than here, even the traffic. Our houses, our schools. Hospitals in Syria are free or very cheap. Here they're very expensive. I don't want to be hated. I'll go home to war in Damascus.' Refugee after refugee is quoted as saying: 'I just want to go back to my old life.'

But that can never be. Just as after an acrimonious divorce, things can never return to how they were. All thoughts of blame and retribution must be laid to rest, and that will be the hardest part for many. Revenge runs deep in Arab culture. One glance at the proverbs is enough to confirm it. Looking for Arab proverbs on forgiveness, I found just one.

But on the theme of retaliation, a Turkish one rang true: If you dig a grave for your neighbour, first measure it for yourself.

Endless cycles of retribution must be stopped – everyone knows that the UN Chemical Weapons deal only happened because there was a rare consensus and no blame was attributable. Maybe such a consensus can be found again, this time to rid the country of the growing extremist groups like ISIS. Maybe moderate elements from the rebels can find a common cause and unite against this greater Al-Qaeda-affiliated menace whose terrorist jihadi agenda threatens not just Syria's future but the future of the entire international community. Maybe it will be Syria's second revolution, a revolution to find Al-Ghazali's middle-ground carrot, in which even the 'silent majority' may find its voice.

For such a second revolution to succeed, everyone must forget that the first began with peaceful protests, everyone must forgive regime troops for gunning down unarmed protestors. The diversity of Syria's identity must be its strength, not its weakness.

Then the professional well-qualified Syrians in exile will return, working to create the new education system and vision so needed for the country's children. The social and cultural renaissance will be driven by individuals and organisations operating at grass-roots level. Ramzi's teacher sisters will do their best. Tariq will try again with his new school in Homs, and I may be its headmistress. Independent media outlets like the internet-based *SouriaLi,* a non-profit radio station, will help mend social rifts created by violent conflict, encourage youth activism and women's empowerment. Its clever name has a double meaning, 'Syria is for me' and 'surreally'. Khalid will return to his mission to create environmental awareness in the young. Hundreds of exiled wealthy Syrian businessmen have already pledged their fortunes. On his defection, Firas Tlass, the regime's richest opponent, his wealth second only to Bashar's cousin Rami Makhlouf, publicly promised to fund an organisation to deal with post-revolution chaos. 'But this is nothing,' he declared, 'If I give all my money, it is not worth one gram of the blood spilt by the Syrian people.' When Firas' younger brother Manaf defected to Paris, the banners of Kafr Nabl declared: 'The Charles de Gaulle Brigade led by Brigadier General Manaf Tlass has seized control of the Champs-Elysee!'

Health will have regressed, with poor diet and no vaccinations for thousands of displaced children. Diseases will have spread. Maryam's pharmacist sister will do her best. She will not run away to Dubai like Bashar's pharmacist sister Bushra. The young entrepreneurs from Bosra will make their medicines and herbal remedies for the local market, not for export. Bassim's violinist former girlfriend will rejoin the national orchestra and play sweet music to soothe the troubled minds of the audience. But what will happen to the armed forces and the security services? In Tunisia, after the fall of Ben Ali's government, a civil servant told me that a quarter of the *mukhabarat*, 'the ones who were too evil to be accepted', fled the country, mainly for Italy. 'Let us hope at least half of them leave Syria,' Marwan spat.

Amal and her colleagues in the Ministry of Tourism will strive to rebuild Syria's image. So will I and so will Ramzi the Philosopher, waiting patiently to receive the first visitors. When he greets them, he will add a new chapter to Syria's history, explaining carefully, leaving nothing out. People will marvel at his words and weep.

It will be slow. It will be painful. The uniform Ba'athist cladding shrouding the national identity must be stripped off, just as Bait Baroudi's grubby, neglected outer-cladding was stripped off. Like Bait Baroudi, its faulty infrastructure, its failing plumbing, wiring and drains will have to be torn out and discarded. Then will come the years of agonising reconstruction, moving from tentative beginnings towards full national reconciliation. Those years will be the hardest, when it will seem that everything is going backwards, when unforeseen setbacks will spring up like a plague of *mukhalafa*s.

In my dreams I imagine the day when, like Bait Baroudi emerging from its wreckage, Syria will reveal itself in all its multi-coloured splendour. The quest for the perfect environment, for the space in which to belong and feel at peace is ongoing and will not die. I visualise long-forgotten secret ceilings emerging from dark cobwebbed corners, delicate patterns of stonework and intricate woodwork released from oppressive cold cement. On the strong foundations of its new infrastructure, I see the black and white *ablaq* walls boldly confronting the future. Even with my eyes closed I can see the magenta leaves of the bougainvillea swirling in the breeze; I can hear the water playing gently in the fountain; I can smell the intoxicating jasmine; I can feel the warmth of the sunlight embracing me in my kaleidoscope courtyard. Thanks to the lessons of Al-Ghazali I can 'taste' it all – Syria as it should be.

Maybe I am a hopeless dreamer.

Someone has to be.

Acknowledgements

The first draft of this book was begun on New Year's Day 2010 in the tranquil surroundings of the Scottish borders and submitted to publishers in February 2011. The timing could not have been worse. With the start of the Syrian Revolution in March 2011, it could no longer be a peaceful book. Each subsequent year I attempted a redraft. But with the conflict escalating into civil war, casualty figures soaring and refugee numbers reaching incomprehensible levels, finding the right balance became harder and harder. Serial rejections followed. It was thanks to the astute comments and constructive criticisms of my brother, Mark Taylor, that I was spurred into the final reworking required for the manuscript to catch the imaginative eye of Ellie Shillito at Haus, the publishers with whom the book has found its home.

※

My fullest practical acknowledgement must be to family friend John Bourne without whom my purchase of Bait Baroudi would never have been possible. A fellow Arabist, he was open to persuasion to share the costs, since he also shared an interest in preserving national heritage that was clear from his desire to build traditional boats during postings in both Cairo and Kuwait before the old craft methods died out. I knew the idea of buying and restoring Bait Baroudi would appeal to him as a way of keeping alive a link to the Arab world. He remains part owner, though he has only ever visited the house twice briefly, both times before restoration began. I will be forever grateful not only for his financial support, but also for the total trust he placed in me from the start.

My inspirational debt must be to Axel Munthe, whose *The Story of San Michele* I first read as a teenager. Its quest for a spiritual home in a distant location must have struck a deep chord, though I did not recognise it till later in life. Before the revolution the first draft of this book was called *The Story of Bait Baroudi*.

For giving me an unusual degree of freedom as a child, I increasingly appreciate my late parents, who never sought to curb my dreams. Had they been stricter or more conventional, things might have been very different.

To friends who read earlier drafts – Tita Shakeshaft and Paul Chevedden – I am indebted for their support and encouragement when I had all but given up. Both had Damascus links: Tita through spending part of her early childhood in a courtyard house in the Old City, Paul through doing his PhD on the Damascus Citadel.

My husband John McHugo and my children Chloë Darke and Max Darke, by virtue of being so close to me throughout, shared the emotional roller-coaster of writing this book. I realise it was not always easy. They know how much emotional energy I have invested, and how much I have wanted this story to reach a wider audience. Their support and understanding has been crucial. My daughter Chloë's editorial skills on early chapters gave me pointers on how to craft the rest of the book, my son Max's suggestion that Zulfikar, the nomadic tortoise, be included in the cast of characters was quickly taken up, and my husband John's encyclopaedic knowledge served as a constant reference for factual accuracy. I make no claims as a historian or political analyst. My concerns have been social, cultural and philosophical, to be a different voice for Syria.

My Syrian friends, versions of whom appear in this book, know who they are. Their names have been changed and I will not list them here. But they also know how much they have given me, how much they have taught me. Their warmth and wisdom will remain with me always. It is my deepest wish that they will one day be able to resume their lives, free in a new Syria. They deserve it more than words can say.

Glossary

Ablaq	patterned stonework of alternate black basalt and white limestone
Adoubi	traditional building material made from clay, sand, water and straw, formed into bricks and baked in the sun; used in the construction of Ottoman houses
Aga Khan	hereditary title of the Ismaʻili sect within Shiʻa Islam; he claims descent from Isma'il, the seventh imam, who died in 760. The current Aga Khan is a renowned philanthropist for development projects in the Islamic world; his wealth derives from receiving over a tenth of the revenues of his followers
Ahdath	pre-Mamluk Syrian militia
'Ajami	painted lacquer wooden panelling, usually 18th century, influenced by Persian styles
Ahrar Ash-Sham	Free Men of the Levant, a highly conservative (*Salafi*) Islamist armed rebel group, with mainly Syrian fighters, now part of the Islamic Front
Alawis	Syria's largest religious minority and the sect of the Assad clan that has ruled Syria since 1970; it is a Muslim sect with strong elements of Neo-Platonism, Christianity and Zoroastrianism
Al-Kuhoul	alcohol (derived from the Arabic)
Asabiyya	intense tribal solidarity

237

Ash'arites	adherents of the Al-Ash'ari school of a 9–10th century Muslim speculative theology founded by Abu Al-Hasan Ali Al-Ash'ari (d.936). His doctrine is now known in the West as *Occasionalism*.
Ayyubid	dynasty founded by Saladin (a Kurd) that ruled from 1169–1258. Ayyubid rule was marked by economic prosperity and a period of Sunni revival, with Damascus turned into a city of fine schools and *hammams* many of which are still extant.
Ba'ath	Arabic for 'renaissance', the name of the Arab socialist movement founded with Arab nationalist, anti-imperialist ideology; its slogan was 'unity, liberty, socialism'. Ruling party of Syria since 1963.
Batin	the inner, hidden aspect that can only be sensed, not seen
Badia	Syrian desert steppeland
Bab	door, gate
Bahra	little sea or pond, the word used for the octagonal fountain pool in the centre of a house courtyard
Bait	Arabic for house; in Syria all houses, irrespective of their size or grandeur, are named after the family that inhabits them
Baraka	religious blessing
Bustan	orchard, garden
Caliph	from the Arabic *khalifa* meaning successor, used as the title for Muslim leaders who succeeded the Prophet Muhammad
Cardo maximus	main thoroughfare running north–south in a Roman city
Chador	Iranian all-black enveloping robe for women
DAESH	Arabic acronym for the Al-Qaeda-affiliated rebel group ISIS (ISIL), ad-Dawlat al-Islamiyya fil-Iraq wa-sh-Sham
Decumanus	main street running east-west across a Roman city
Deir	monastery

Dhawq	Arabic word for 'taste', used by Al-Ghazali to express the concept of real experience
Dhikr	Sufi ceremony aimed at achieving mystical union with God
Druze	distinct religious community whose origins were in Shi'a Islam. There are about one million worldwide mainly in the mountains of Lebanon and Syria
Eid	religious festival, always a public holiday
Eid Al-Adha	Feast of the Sacrifice, the biggest Muslim festival of the year
Emir	commander, prince
Fana'	annihilation of the self
Fatwa	religious opinion issued by an Islamic jurist
Free Syrian Army (FSA)	the first rebel fighting group, composed of defectors from the regime army and volunteers, which sprang up spontaneously in late July 2011 to defend peaceful protestors. Its aim is the removal of the Assad regime, rather than political power
Ghanima	booty, spoils from looting permitted under Islam when fighting *jihad* (Holy War)
Hammam	public bathhouse with steam room, adapted from the Roman baths but with no pool
Hanafi	belonging to the Hanafi Sunni School of Islamic Law, named after Abu Hanifa (d.767), son of a Persian slave. It is the oldest and largest by far of the four Sunni Islamic Law schools, (accounting for about half the total number of Muslims in the world) and the most liberal and tolerant. It insists on the right of judicial speculation, including analogical deduction and the role of reason. It permits female judges. Hanafi law applies in Syria's *Shar'ia* courts. Most Ottomans were Hanafis (as are Turks to this day) and they believe that ablutions need to be conducted under running water, not stagnant water in a basin like the Shafi'is. Hence *hanafia* is Arabic for 'tap'.

Hanbali	belonging to the Hanbali Sunni School of Islamic Law, the strictest and most conservative of the four, adhered to by most *Salafis* in Saudi Arabia, Qatar and small pockets of Syria. It was founded by Ahmad Ibn Hanbal (d. 855 in Baghdad), the last and smallest of the four schools, and rejected the principle of 'consensus', insisting on uncompromising adherence to the letter of the Quran and the Hadith (sayings of the Prophet Muhammad).
Hara	small neighbourhood within a quarter of a city
Haram	forbidden under Islamic law
Haramlik	private family/female quarters within a large Ottoman house
Hawza	Shi'ite residential teaching school
Hezbollah	Lebanese Shi'ite militia and political party, led by Hassan Nasrallah, supported financially and militarily by Iran. Currently represented in the Lebanese Parliament and considered more effective than the Lebanese Army.
Hijab	woman's headscarf covering the hair but not the face
Ibn Sasra	Syrian historian under Mamluk rule who wrote a 14th century chronicle of Damascus
Imam	spiritual and general leader
Al-insan Al-Kamil	the Perfect Person, a Sufi concept, the final stage in man's evolution
ISIS (ISIL)	Islamic State of Iraq and Sham (the Levant), an Al-Qaeda-affiliated Islamist extremist armed rebel group, known as DAESH in Arabic, with mainly non-Syrian fighters
Islamic Front	Group formed in late November 2013 of seven rebel brigades, thought to number 45,000. Bankrolled mainly by Saudi Arabia; supports an Islamic state and welcomes foreign fighters, but is not as extreme as ISIS

Isma'ili	sect within Shi'a Islam; Isma'ilism has many offshoots including the Alawis and the Assassins, whose titular head is the Aga Khan
Iwan	roofed but open reception area, often north-facing and thus the coolest place in summer, with an arch giving directly onto the courtyard
Iz'aj	annoyance, trouble, irritation
Jabal	mountain
Jabhat Al-Nusra (li-ahl Ash-Sham)	Support Front (for the People of the Levant), an Al-Qaeda-affiliated Islamist extremist armed rebel group, with some foreign but mainly Syrian fighters
Jalsa	meeting where everyone sits together round a room
Jaysh Al-Muhajireen wal-Ansar	Army of the Emigrants and Helpers, Islamist extremist rebel group affiliated with ISIS, with many foreign non-Syrian fighters
Jihadi	from the Arabic root meaning 'to strive, make great efforts', but now commonly used for Muslims waging Holy War against those they consider non-Muslims (*takfiris*)
Juhaal	the 'ignorant', uninitiated members of the Druze sect
Karama	'dignity', watchword of the Syrian Revolution, often demanded in banners and chants during peaceful demonstrations
Khadamlik	servants' quarters of a large Ottoman house
Khamr	wine
Lijan sha'abiyya	Peoples' Committees, sometimes also called 'National Defence Force', made up of civilian armed groups appointed by the regime to guard neighbourhoods
Maktab Anbar	headquarters of the Damascus Old City Council
Maktoub	what is written, i.e. fate

Malaki	one of the smallest and earliest of the four Sunni Islamic Law schools, founded in Medina by Malik Ibn Anas (d.795), dominant in Egypt and North Africa, and leaning to the conservative side, though not as extreme as the later Hanbalis.
Mamluk	slave soldier trained to be part of a military elite. The Mamluks founded an empire in Cairo that ruled Egypt and Syria from 1250 till the Ottoman conquest in 1516
Mamnou	forbidden, punishable under the civil law
Maristan	hospital and school of medicine in the Arab world
Maronite	the dominant sect of Christianity in Lebanon, named after a 5th century saint called Maron. Some claim descent from the Phoenicians
Maysir	game of chance involving gambling, mentioned in the Quran
Mazout	diesel heating oil
MECAS	Middle East Centre for Arabic Studies, the British Foreign Office school for Arabic language training in the village of Shemlan, above Beirut, closed in 1978
Melkite	also called the Greek Catholics. Today they are in full communion with Rome and belong to the Patriarchate of Antioch
Merlon	step-sided triangle used as an ancient Mesopotamian architectural decoration, found throughout modern Syria (including crowning the walls of the Damascus Umayyad Mosque), and even in Petra
Mi'raj	the Prophet Muhammad's ascent to Heaven
Muhafaza	municipality building, like the town hall
Mukhtar	local mayor or head of an area within a city
Muqarnas	'stalactite' decoration in wood or stone, effecting a transition to a dome
Muqatilat	female snipers

Mukhabarat	the intelligence or security services
Mukhalafa	'violation', contravention of a rule
Musalsalat	'soap' series on Arab TV
Naranj	bitter orange tree
Nargile	traditional water pipe
Nawfara	public fountain
Pasha	Ottoman honorific often given to the governor of a province
PKK	Kurdistan Workers' Party which fought against the Turkish state for an autonomous Kurdistan from 1984–2013
Occasionalism	philosophical theory about causation formulated by Al-Ash'ari, a theologian in 9–10th century Basra, Iraq, in which the belief is that God is constantly recreating the world according to his own will
Ottoman	Turkish dynasty with its capital in Istanbul which ruled Syria through appointed governors from 1516–1918
Qa'a	enclosed reception room off the courtyard of an Ottoman house
Qadar	fate
Qadar wa qada'	God's decree and judgement
Qadi	Muslim judge
Quran	(also Qur'an) meaning 'Recitation', the collected revelations made to the Prophet Muhammad orally by God over a 23-year period, written down after his death to form the Muslim holy text, the main source for *Shar'ia* or Islamic Law. Considered 'the word of God', so only ever recited in Arabic, the language in which it was 'revealed.'
Salafi	rigid adherent to traditional early Muslim ways, highly conservative
Salamlik	reception area for male guests in an Ottoman house
Sarraf	money-changer

Shabiha	'ghosts', Assad militia, usually of the Alawi sect
Shafi'i	one of the four schools of Sunni Islamic Law, dominant in southern Syria and Damascus, named after the Imam Al-Shafi'i, born in Gaza (d. 820 in Cairo). It is the second most numerous and considers itself 'the golden mean' between the more liberal Hanafis and the more conservative Hanbalis and Malakis who dominate in the Arabian peninsula.
Shaikh	elder or head of a tribe
Sham	Arabic for both 'Syria' and 'Damascus', according to context; originally meaning 'the north' or 'the left' (as seen from the Arabian heartlands of Mecca and Medina); also written *Cham* in the French transliteration style
Shar'ia	Islamic Law
Shi'ite	follower of Shi'a Islam, the second largest Muslim sect; the sect split off from the Sunni orthodoxy, believing that Ali was the Prophet Muhammad's rightful successor
Souk	market of stalls, bazaar
Sufi	Muslim mystic
Sultan	Muslim ruler
Sunni	follower of Sunni Islam, the largest Muslim sect; the orthodox Islam that follows the '*sunna*', the 'tradition'
Syrian Revolutionaries Front (SRC)	Grouping of moderate opposition forces, formed in December 2013, thought to number about 15,000
Syrian Arab Red Crescent (SARC)	Set up in 1942 as a humanitarian not-for-profit organisation, admitted to the International Committee of the Red Cross (ICRC) in 1946, but subsequently contaminated with corruption and regime affiliation. Headquartered in Damascus, with 14 branches round the country

Syrian National Coalition	formed November 2012 to be a broader and more representative political opposition than the SNC, based in Istanbul and Cairo. Supported by the Free Syrian Army but not by the extremist rebel *jihadi* groups. Aims to be a transitional government with Muslims, Kurds and Christians as members
Syrian National Council (SNC)	first main political opposition to the Assad regime in exile, based in Istanbul. Formed August 2011, supported by the Free Syrian Army. Now the largest bloc within the Syrian National Coalition, but criticised for consisting largely of Syrian expatriates
Tabou	Ottoman title deed
Tasallsul mulkia	list of previous owners, a register begun under the French Mandate
Tahwil	bank transfer
Takbir	to say 'Allahu Akbar', God is the Greatest (sign of a devout Muslim)
Taqiyya	dissimulation, concealing of identity
Tawakkul (ala Allah)	total trust in God
Tawhid	doctrine of the unity and oneness of God, literally 'making into one' in Arabic
Tekke	Sufi monastery
Ulema	learned Muslim scholars, religious elite
'Uzla	isolation, withdrawal from society
Wahhish	wild beast (nickname and surname of Hafez al-Assad's father)
Wali	holy man or saint in the popular religion of Islam
Wasta	a kind of patronage system, having connections in the right places, necessary to get favours done in bureaucratic governments
Waqf	system of Islamic trusts needed to maintain a religious building
Ya Rabb!	O Lord! Exclamation to invoke God's protection

Yazidis	Kurdish community of less than a million found mainly in Iraq, Turkey, Armenia and Georgia. Their 12th century religion is a complex fusion of Zoroastrian and Sufi elements. Wrongly labelled 'Devil Worshippers' and historically persecuted by Muslims and Christians alike.
Zahir	the exterior surface, the visible appearance
Zakat	alms tax for the poor, one of the Five Pillars of Islam
Zu'ar	Mamluk term for 'young thugs', 'robbers'
Zuhd	renunciation of worldly concerns and goods

Cast of Characters

Abu Ashraf   my elderly illiterate Sunni caretaker at Bait Baroudi, whose home is in the rebellious village of Kafr Batna in the Ghouta, bombed in the August 2013 chemical attack. He now lives in Bait Baroudi with his extended family

Adonis   pen name of exiled Syrian poet (born 1930), now based in France and Lebanon

Amal   headscarved manager at Syrian Ministry of Tourism

Asma al-Assad   British-born and British-educated Syrian Sunni wife (born 1975) of Bashar al-Assad, married in 2000 becoming First Lady of Syria, former investment banker working for JP Morgan, still in Syria with her three children

Bashar al-Assad   Alawi President of Syria 2000–2014, General Secretary of the Ba'ath Party, second son of former president Hafez, studied Medicine at Damascus University, Ophthalmology in Tehran and London. Studies interrupted and groomed for presidency in Homs Military Academy after older brother's death in 1994. Married 2000 to Asma by whom he has three children. Born 1965. Still in Syria.

Basil al-Assad — Alawi eldest son of former president Hafez, older brother of current president Bashar, studied Mechanical Engineering at Damascus University, PhD in Military Sciences, groomed for Syrian presidency but killed in car crash (1962–94)

Bushra al-Assad — Alawi first-born child and only daughter to former president Hafez, studied Pharmacy at Damascus University, married to Assef Shawkat, former Syrian Head of Military Intelligence (born 1960), now in Dubai

Hafez al-Assad — Alawi former president, ruler of Syria from 1970–2000. Rose to prominence in Syrian Air Force and Ba'ath Party, becoming Defence Minister. Married Anisa Makhlouf (born 1934, now in Dubai) by whom he had five children of whom three are still alive. (1930–2000)

Maher al-Assad — Alawi youngest brother of Bashar, known as 'Butcher of Deraa', studied Business Administration at Damascus University, now a General, commander of the Republican Guard and the army's elite 4th Armoured Division (born 1967), married to a Sunni Syrian, reported to have lost a leg in the July 2012 bomb in Damascus, never seen in public since

Majd al-Assad — Alawi younger brother of Bashar (1966–2009), studied Electrical Engineering at Damascus University, died in London and had mental health problems

Rif'at al-Assad — Alawi exiled brother of former president Hafez (born 1937), responsible for the 1982 Hama massacre, now living in London

Ribal al-Assad — Alawi son of Rif'at, cousin of Bashar, now living in the USA

Bait Baroudi	my Ottoman courtyard house inside the walls of the Old City of Damascus, in the Muslim quarter of Shaghour. The name means 'House of the Gunpowder Seller')
Bassim the architect	Sunni Muslim architect in charge of restoring Bait Baroudi; now in Istanbul
Ali Ferzat	Syria's most famous cartoonist, now in exile
Ali	son-in-law of the Prophet Muhammad, husband of the Prophet's daughter Aisha, revered by Shi'ites as the first imam and rightful successor to the Prophet Muhammad, and by Sunnis as the fourth caliph (601–661)
Al-Ghazali	one of Sunni Islam's greatest philosophers, of Persian descent, born (c. 1056) and died (1111) in Tus, Iran. He spent two key years in Damascus
Hussein	grandson of the Prophet Muhammad, son of Ali (626–680)
Ibn Arabi, (Muhiyiddin)	one of Islam's greatest Sufi mystics, also known as Muhyiddin ('reviver of religion'), born 1165 in Murcia, Spain, died 1240 in Damascus
Ibn Khaldun	14th century Muslim philosopher, widely considered the father of modern sociology, the first person to write about the philosophy of history. Born in Tunis, died in Cairo. Met Tamerlane in 1401 in Damascus. (1332–1406)
Father Joaqim	Syriac Orthodox monk who has revived Mor Augen Monastery near Nusaybin in southeast Turkey, and is now living there, reviving the community
Khalid	young Syrian environmentalist, now working in Amman
Hamza al-Khatib	13-year-old boy tortured, mutilated and killed by Assad regime soldiers near Deraa during a peaceful protest in 2011. Widely seen as the icon of the Syrian Revolution

Walid Maqta	PR Director at Syrian Ministry of Tourism
Marwan the shop-owner	Sunni businessman in Nawfara district of the Old City, nephew to Rashid the lawyer, still in Damascus
Maryam the bank manageress	Christian manageress at Commercial Bank of Syria where my bank account is held; still in Damascus
Maya Mamarbachi	Syrian Christian businesswoman and hotelier, now Beirut-based
Caliph Mu'awiya	originally the Prophet Muhammad's scribe, founder of the Umayyad dynasty with Damascus as its capital, married a Christian for political reasons, supreme military leader, established the first Muslim navy. Buried in Damascus, died 680.
Muaz al-Khatib	elected head of the main opposition group, the Syrian National Coalition. Highly respected former imam at the Umayyad Mosque. Resigned March 2013, but still issues occasional statements.
Prophet Muhammad	founder of Islam, not considered 'divine' (like Jesus) but as the 'Messenger of God', the last of the prophets of whom Jesus was one. Born Mecca c. 570, aged 25 married Khadija, a businesswoman many years his senior, who remained his sole wife till her death in 619. Illiterate, worked as a shepherd and merchant, even once visiting Damascus. Had his first 'revelation' from God aged 40. Fled to Medina to avoid persecution in 622, date from which the Islamic calendar begins. Died 632 in Medina.
Nazir	eldest brother of the Baroudi family, previous owners of my house, still in Damascus

Nizar Qabbani	Syrian love poet, publisher and diplomat (1923–1998), born into a middle class merchant family living in the courtyard house adjoining Bait Baroudi in the walled Old City of Damascus. One of the most revered Arab poets of the 20th century.
Father Paolo dall'Oglio	Italian Jesuit priest who revived Mar Musa Monastery during the 1980s in the desert between Homs and Damascus. Born 1954 in Rome. Fierce advocate for Muslim/Christian reconciliation. Captured by rebel ISIS fighters in Ar-Raqqah in summer 2013. Subsequent fate unknown.
Rami Makhouf	maternal cousin to President Bashar al-Assad, Syria's richest businessman thanks to his connections, controlling up to 60 per cent of Syria's economy. Owner of Syriatel mobile phone company. Born 1969. Location unknown.
Ramzi the philosopher	highly cultured Sunni tour guide, displaced twice from his home, now in the Lattakia region
Rashid the lawyer	Kurdish lawyer for my house, uncle to Marwan, still in Damascus
Sayyida Ruqayya	daughter of the Shi'ite martyr Hussein
Ibn Sasra	14th century chronicler of Damascus
General Assef Shawkat	former Head of Syrian Military Intelligence, killed in the 18 July 2012 explosion inside the Damascus National Security Headquarters. Bashar's brother-in-law, married to Bushra Al-Assad, Hafez's eldest child and daughter, who helped get him promoted through the ranks to General (1950–2012).
Tariq	wealthy young Syrian Sunni businessman whose family is from Homs, now London-based
Umar	youngest of the Baroudi brothers, previous owners of my house, still in Damascus

Shaikh Muhammad Al-Ya'qoubi	highly respected Syrian Sufi shaikh, former imam at the Umayyad Mosque, exiled to Morocco in 2012. Born 1963 in Damascus.
Yusuf al-Azma	Minister of War and Chief of Staff before the French Mandate. Killed by the French at the Battle of Maysaloun in 1920. Born 1883.
Sayyida Zaynab	granddaughter of the Prophet Muhammad and sister of Hussein
Zulfikar	tortoise of Bait Baroudi, named after twin-bladed sword of Ali. Good luck symbol. Last seen living in the Ghouta. Current status unknown

A Note on the Choice of Charity

Higher education as the charity of choice for Syria perhaps requires some explanation, at a time when it is the youngest children, destitute and parentless, who catch the imagination and the headlines in Syria's tragic war. But this 'lost generation' of the very young, if they are to have any chance of a better future in a better Syria, will desperately need a pool of talented Syrians who can help rebuild their country. Some 60 per cent of Syria's population is under 25, and at least half of its university students have had their studies interrupted.

When a country goes through the kind of terrible physical and psychosocial destruction that Syria has suffered for the last three years, the political transition phase will inevitably be fragile. Skilled leadership with well-educated support will be essential to help steer the country through this critical post-conflict period, yet, research shows that higher education is one of the slowest areas to recover, making relapses more likely. Graduates in law must, therefore, be one of the top priorities, to set up a fair and depoliticised legislative system which will gradually rebuild trust in the state, so absent for so long. Economics and management will also be priorities, to start regenerating the businesses and industries that will create future employment and prosperity for the country.

Just before the Syrian revolution broke out, the Saïd Foundation had planned a 10-year programme to modernise the out-dated Syrian curriculum and to improve the quality of teaching at Damascus University. Once conditions permit, work on this will resume and in the meantime students who have fallen out of higher education because of the crisis are being helped to access it elsewhere in the region.

The Saïd Foundation also supports Syria Relief, a UK-based charity set up by Syrians in summer 2011 to bring humanitarian and medical relief into the parts of Syria where UN and other international agencies have not been permitted to operate.

The sheer scale of the challenge is immense, but that makes it all the more important to help in all ways possible. The most important message of this book, despite the horrors, is one of hope, hope for what must ultimately emerge as a better and stronger Syria: higher education is all about giving knowledge, confidence and hope.

www.saidfoundation.org
www.syriarelief.org.uk

The author will donate 15% of her royalties and the publishers will donate £1.50 per copy sold of this book to a higher education fund for Syrians administered by the Saïd Foundation.